THE EFFECTIVE ECHO

A Dictionary
of
Advertising Slogans

Valerie Noble

SPECIAL LIBRARIES ASSOCIATION
New York
1970

Standard Book Number 87111–196–9
Library of Congress Catalog Card Number 71–110487
© 1970 by Special Libraries Association
235 Park Avenue South, New York 10003

Printed in the United States of America

Contents

The American consumer of the 1840's could identify few products by either specific brand or name. He was still buying his crackers out of an unmarked bin and his fabrics from anonymous bolts of cloth. The end of the Civil War, however, produced a resurgence in the country's business and commerce. Railroads carried the interrupted migration further and further west. Factories were running at full capacity. At the same time, much of the population was moving away from traditionally home made goods and furnishings. Manufacturing, though, was still highly localized and there was no such thing as national distribution. It was a seller's market. Goods were bought as fast as they could be produced.

From this welter of post-Civil War merchandise, the buyer began to distinguish between manufacturers' products and to ask for them specifically. He, then, and not the manufacturer, was instrumental in bringing about branded merchandise by his stated preferences.

The battle of the brands was on!

In modern commerce, advertising is charged with the task of building a favorable image for each of a myriad products and services. Every trick of the art is applied in the battle for the eye and the wallet of the buying public. In this continuing contest, hundreds of companies and countless advertising agencies utilize an old advertising tool—the slogan. This device has moved along a route from simplicity to, in many cases, rambling and meaningless generalities. For instance, many contemporary slogans may be applied to almost any product or service, rather than functioning as an integral part of the specific case and often serve no other use than flattering a company president. In a profession which prides itself in many areas on increasingly sophisticated techniques, vacuous statements are still created for numerous national advertisements because a penchant for banal rhyming and fatuous phrasing lingers on.

Effective advertising sloganeering has been at a low ebb during the past decade due, perhaps, to the profession's heavy emphasis on scientific research methods including post-testing, pre-testing, and, increasingly, automation. Even though the slogan, because of its unpredictable appeal, has fallen a victim of these new advertising methods, the current situation can not deny its basic salesmanship—the appeal to man's elusive memory; and, once again, products are being infused with that subtle emotional snare: the brief and personal phrase. The contemporary, revised use of this traditional device reverts to the basic reason for sloganeering—the importance of linking an easily remembered phrase to the product or service. Many phrases, as in earlier times, live on as separate entities even though they once originated as campaign themes. They have become, in themselves, priceless identification assets.

What is the reason for the slogan's staying power in advertising? Should it be equated with Tyrannosaurus rex—long dead but fondly remembered—or with women's hemlines which change with the times? Is it something which is the mark of the older advertising man and should be disdained by the dynamic world of contemporary advertising? Is it merely symptomatic of a mind which is enamored with words, hang the public and the client? Is its appeal limited to the poorly educated? The sustained appeal of the advertising slogan is strong enough to warrant periodic discussion and investigation by business publications. Even though a few attempts have been made to analyze the power and popularity of these tenacious taglines, the "Why" has never really been adequately investigated and may never be since the area doesn't lend itself to experimental study. What is surprising, however, is the lack of any preliminary analysis of the use of slogans.

This fact became readily evident when the writer was requested to find the author of the quotation, "There is nothing stronger than an idea whose time has come," and to determine if the phrase had ever been used in an advertising context.

The answer to the first part of the question was relatively easy, thanks to Stevenson's *Quotations*.* The second part, however, produced nothing. Searching revealed that the only recent published source of slogans was Sunners' *American Slogans*.† Not only was it out of print but out of date with a publication date of 1949. *Printers' Ink* (now *Marketing/ Communications*) had, at one time, maintained a collection of slogans but the service was no longer readily available (see Appendix A).

The resulting frustration led, first, to collecting slogans from print media for staff use. As the file cards began to accumulate, two questions began to form,

Why do so many advertisers utilize slogans? Is there a logical reason for their use which is either taken for granted or unrecognized by most of the people who formulate them? Out of these questions came the following pages with a three-fold purpose.

Out of these questions came the following pages with a three-fold purpose:

1) It is an attempt to furnish a ready reference source which classifies and identifies over 2,000 slogans in current use;
2) It provides a brief, documented recapitulation of the slogan as an integral facet of the history of advertising; and
3) It postulates a theory about the psychology of slogans.

The scope of the collection is comprised of phrases from both print consumer-oriented and business publications. Phrases from broadcast media, match covers, the mouths of politicians, warriors and religious leaders are excluded. Nor is there an attempt to analyze what constitutes the good or bad slogan or why institutions seem to willfully abandon excellent phrases. The writer believes that such areas have had ample coverage elsewhere.

A slogan, as selected for this study, was defined as "any short statement which stands apart from the text of an advertisement and is linked closely with the logotype, thus constituting the total presentation's final statement." The length was not a consideration; some slogans are stated in two or three words, some ramble to ten or twelve. In most instances, the phrases have appeared several times between early 1965 and the beginning of 1969. This is *not* a *How To* compendium, nor will it attempt to establish the final answer for the basis of a successful phrase.

The November 1866 issue of *Harper's New Monthly Magazine* reported the following item in a general survey of British and American advertising:

"Advertising stratagems are sufficiently numerous to merit almost a sheet of examples. One of the most curious, "whereby hangs a tale," belongs to England, and deserves a place in *Harper's Monthly*, the receptacle of all things literary worth preserving. The story is that, some few years ago, a hatter in London speculated in the purchase of the entire stock of a bankrupt brother tradesman; but, soon after his purchase, he found that he had overstocked himself. He was on the point of reluctantly dismissing some of his "hands" when a sharp-witted friend came to the rescue. By his advice a hand-bill, announcing the cheapness of the hatter's wares, was prepared and distributed exactly as had been already done for some time, except in one particular item. The bill was headed, "Who's your Atter?" and throughout its contents the goods were invariably mentioned as "ats"; "Youth's Silk Ats"–"Best Beaver Ats"–"Ladies Riding Ats"–and so forth. The remainder of the advertisement was in unexceptionable English. The result perfectly justified the inventor's applications. These bills were sought after as typographical curiosities. Men shouted with laughter at the ludicrous effect of what many considered ignorance on the part of the printer or of the writer. They carried these bills in their pockets and merrily showed them to their friends. One or two elderly gentlemen, previously perfect strangers, came to the shop, bought "ats" and expostulated gravely with the "atter" upon the solecism.

---

*Stevenson, Burton. *The Home Book of Quotations*. 9th ed. N. Y., Dodd, Mead, 1964.
†Sunners, William. *American Slogans*. N. Y., Praebar, 1949.

Young fellows purchased gossamers for the fun of the thing, begged for hand-bills, and held jocular conversations with the shopkeeper. The shop became known, and the proprietor frequently smiles as he hears the street-boys calling out *the established phrase* [italics the author's] of "Who's your Atter?" the origin of which, but for the publication of this little episode in advertising, might possibly in a few short years have been lost forever to the antiquarian. To this day the pronunciation of the now popular inquiry is that of the original hand-bill."

Acknowledgements

The practitioner of non-fiction can not escape indebtedness to outside sources for materials and to other people for help. This endeavor is no exception. Thanks, then, to David Bascom, former Senior Vice-President of the San Francisco advertising agency, Dancer, Fitzgerald, Sample, Inc., and to Dr. Laurel Grotzinger, professor in Western Michigan University's Department of Librarianship. Although he isn't yet aware of it, Mr. Bascom was instrumental in kicking the fledgling out of the nest. Dr. Grotzinger *is* aware that she helped the bird fly, as she patiently survived innumerable questions and was of inestimable help in smoothing the original rather rough draft of the introductory essay, "The Effective Echo."

VALERIE NOBLE

Kalamazoo, Michigan
December 1969

Today's world of convoluted words used in unusual ways would possibly define the ideal slogan as "a miniaturization or capsulization of the desired total awareness concept," and therein completely lose the reader. Fortunately, Graham offers another definition which is more comprehensible (1):

> *Slogan:* A relatively pithy phrase or sentence used repeatedly in advertisements by manufacturers and service organizations for the purpose of influencing the buying behavior of consumers.

To create a good slogan deliberately is one of the most difficult tasks of creative advertising writing.* This is, essentially, because an outstanding slogan must discharge, with a modicum of words, a number of responsibilities and, as Whittier notes (2):

> It should be a statement of such merit about a product or service that it is worthy of continuous repetition in advertising, is worthwhile for the public to remember, and is phrased in such a way that the public is likely to remember it.

The use of the slogan might also be interpreted as fixing a stamp of quality upon an article, much as did its medieval ancestor, the craft guild's mark. Advertising slogans and characters are an extension of the trademark and, in many cases, have actually become the trademark. The device may or may not be an extension of advertising copy. In numerous instances, the appropriate headline has become the best slogan of all, as, for example, *Look at All Three.* The effective advertising slogan is product and province of the educated ear. Hopefully, it is tuned to at least one of the following: the client, the times, the product or service, and the audience.

HISTORY—WHERE DID IT ALL START?

There is no evidence documenting the use of slogans as an advertising device prior to the mid-19th century. As late as the 1870's advertising was a mixture of no-nonsense selling, rhyming couplets and advertising cards. Finally, in 1868, heralding the brassy era of patent medicine, the marketer of a hair preparation coined the phrase that it was *scientific, rational, safe* and a dental cement manufacturer made *everyone his own dentist.* After this slow beginning, the momentum picked up and by the 1880's, there was a widespread fondness for slogans. Usage developed to the extent that, for many advertisers, slogans were the only advertising copy used. Royal Baking Powder's *Absolutely Pure* and Ivory Soap's *It Floats* and *99-44/100% Pure* were among the earliest subjected to national dissemination.

---

1. Graham, Irvin. *Encyclopedia of Advertising.* N.Y., Fairchild, 1952. p. 478.
2. Whittier, Charles L. *Creative Advertising.* N.Y., Holt, 1955. p. 403.
*Protection for these difficult-to-create phrases came late in their history with the 1946 Lanham Act. They are not protected to the extent that the U.S. Patent Office accepts on the principal register only those which integrate the product name. Those which identify or distinguish the products to which they refer are carried on the supplemental register.

By 1890, the first copywriters and artists appeared in the larger advertising agencies. Along with them came heavy usage of slogans and, in fact, slogans had become the rage. No advertised product was respectable without its slogan. They had moved from simple phrases to apt and sometimes memorable aphorisms. The expression did not stand alone, but was often coupled with an illustration. Many were correlated with characters, but even more carried the message in solitary splendor. This was the era of Pears Soap, the Gold Dust Twins and Fletcher's Castoria. The great bicycle craze hit Americans in the last ten years of the 19th century and this fiercely competitive industry proclaimed a product that *Leads the World* and was the *Apex of Bicycle Perfection*. The two-wheeler's popularity bloomed quickly and waned by 1900 in the face of a newly emerging four-wheeler. George Eastman's new product was merchandised to Americans with the promise, *You Press the Button—We Do the Rest,* and customers were further warned, *If It Isn't Eastman, It Isn't a Kodak.* Eastman, in fact, was forced to revise *You Press the Button . . .* in the mid-1890's because it had so caught the public's fancy that, not only was the name *Kodak* in danger of becoming a generic term, but people had interpreted *We Do the Rest* as meaning that film was developed only at the factory *(3).*

Slogans also grew directly from doggerel—that brief and catchy poetry which was on the country's lips toward the end of the 1800's. There was a fondness for rhyming the praises of the product. One of the earliest and best known expressions was *The Ham That Am.* Perhaps the slogan even borrowed a bit from the miraculous guarantees of the thriving patent medicine business—although no "respectable" firm would admit that!

Right on the heels of the slogan avalanche, which ran merrily over the turn of the century and into the early part of the 20th, came the advertising jingle which can be termed a "singing slogan." This form, too, saturated the public. Often these were cutely coy and sometimes trite, but the jingle, nevertheless, resulted in sales increases of staggering proportions. It reached fad dimensions and was often memorized by fans across the country. It even cropped up in popular music and on the stage. It was hummed, sung, strummed and parodied. Indeed, modern radio and television singing commercials can trace their lineage back to these ancestors of the early 1900's.

The early years of this century saw an abundance of slogans as well as jingles:

> *When It Rains, It Pours.*
> *Say It with Flowers.*
> *Milk from Contented Cows.*
> *The Schoolgirl Complexion.*
> *The Instrument of the Immortals.*

They were a substantial part of advertising and some, which could apply to almost any product, innundated the public's eyes and ears. In innumerable cases, the slogan still *was* advertising. Some have shown a remarkable longevity. *His Master's Voice,* for instance, which was developed as both a trademark and slogan, was first used in London in the 1890's, immigrated to the United States in 1901 with the founding of the Victor Talking Machine Company, and is still in occasional use.

With the advent of the automobile, advertising began to experiment with several selling techniques . . . from coldly analytical, mechanical copy to unadulterated, romantic praise. As early as 1903, Ford was the *Boss of the Road* and Packard was confidently advising people to *Ask the Man Who Owns One.* We started *Watching the Fords Go By* in 1907. The pre-war Cadillac of 1912 was already the *Standard of the World.* By 1916, Maxwell came out with an advertising campaign based on the slogan, *Pay as You Ride!*

Gathering impetus and strength, the advertising industry rolled on through the decade. In addition to the slogan and jingle, the first concentrated effort by an advertising agency to move into the area of long copy occurred with John E. Kennedy and his

---

3. Wood, James Playsted. *The Story of Advertising.* N.Y., Ronald, 1958. p. 265.

Salesmanship in Print. This was the heyday of mail-ordering and, by the 1920's, techniques were being developed to measure advertising effectiveness. Kennedy was the forerunner of such advertising leaders as James Orr Young whose *You May Offend without Knowing It* sold Odorono; Raymond Rubicam's *The Priceless Ingredient of Every Product is the Honor and Integrity of Its Maker* emphasized the merits of Squibb products; Sterling Getchell's *Look at All Three* advantageously compared Plymouth to other automobiles. Some of the outstanding slogans of the earlier part of this century originated with advertising's greatest names.

Slogans continued to be a prime advertising technique. World War I capitalized on patriotic product sloganizing. Campbell Tires were devoted to *Being a Real Service to the Nation,* and rubber heels were cushioning American's marching feet while they were *Stepping on to Victory.*

The mighty cigarette company clashes of the period produced *Be Nonchalant—Light a Murad.* Following the war, Lucky Strike's *Nature in the Raw is Seldom Mild* and *Reach for a Lucky Instead of a Sweet* exemplified good sloganizing. *So Round, So Firm, So Fully Packed . . . .* spelled a $10,000 bonus for the copywriter.

By the 1920's, the first flights into fashion prose hit the press and such a flattering implication as *You Just Know She Wears Them* and, more pragmatically, *Longer Wear with Every Pair* were coaxing the female consumer. All areas of industry continued to use the slogan approach. Once Ford had shown the way, Buick promised in 1925, *When Better Automobiles Are Built, Buick Will Build Them.*

The hue and cry raised against the advertising industry in the 1930's included several best selling anti-advertising books and the Federal Trade Commission deeply involved in advertising claims.* Ipana users could still expect the *Smile of Beauty,* but the *Pink Toothbrush* fell before the government agency's cease-and-desist orders. For two decades, external and internal restrictions limited the use of and enthusiasm for the slogan. Even in the early 1950's Lucky Strike was allowed to continue *It's Toasted,* but was enjoined to stop both *Preferred 2 to 1 by Tobacco Experts* and *Less Irritating to the Nose and Throat.* The depression brought trouble to advertising, and it fought back with a strident voice. Listerine's *Even Your Best Friends Won't Tell You,* which survived many more abrasive campaigns, was symptomatic of a rash of advertising intimately concerned with the human body *(4).* The end of this turbulent decade gave rise to Coca-Cola's *The Pause That Refreshes.*

The 1940's brought World War II and the extension of sloganology to patriotic uses. America's War Advertising Council, private enterprise and communication media joined in concerted efforts. We were admonished that *Loose Talk Costs Lives,* and urged to *Help US Keep Prices Down.* The best known and still remembered recruitment campaign was, of course, *Uncle Sam Wants You.* Occasionally war effort phrases as for example, *Use It Up . . . Wear It Out . . . Make It Do . . . Or Go Without* found their way into selling copy. As Frey commented *(5):*

> Appropriately enough, the slogan . . . was used during World War II years more than it had been for some time previously. Slogans afforded an apt way of conveying ideas intended to stir patriotic action. The government as well as private advertisers used them extensively.

From the peace treaties of 1944 and 1945 to the present day, the slogan has

---

*Sloganmen were not indigenous to America. Before World War II, Hitler's Third Reich, under Goebbels, utilized slogans as part of the propaganda war. Germans were spurred to dreams of glory by "A New Germany Rises from the Ashes of the Past." In England, Britons were warned that "Careless Talk Costs Lives." Ref. (3), p. 450-51.

4. Rowsome, Frank. *They Laughed When I Sat Down.* N.Y., McGraw-Hill, 1959. p. 172.
5. Frey, Albert W. *Advertising.* N.Y., Ronald, 1947. p. 262.

continued its peripatetic growth. The numerous examples found in the major portion of this tool show its heavy usage. Many advertising agencies decry it as unsophisticated and scientifically uncontrollable. Others have used it creatively and with good effect. Needless to say, it still has its uses and can be as influential as its history has indicated. If this brief look at its history has shown anything, it has demonstrated the slogan's unique staying power.

Within the matrix of an ad, the meaningful, pungent slogan can help the consumer resolve his conflicts because it can accomplish many things: imply status, build trust in a company, promise romance, project integrity, create assurance, justify purchases. The good slogan will wear well over the years. As corporations grow, and products spawn, the on-going slogan acts as a stabilizer.

People are enmeshed in great changes, many beyond their comprehension. Although they may be honestly fascinated with this vortex, many are doggedly resistant to progress as it threatens them and their security. The really good advertising phrase does not change every year and, therefore, acts as a small but comfortable stabilizer. Even modified, it is a continuing, humanizing element.

The advertising slogan may catch on immediately, or take many months to click—about the time the ad manager is ready to abandon it. The successful phrase may be remembered literally years later when it comes to a final buying decision. Thus, it is an invaluable selling tool. Many campaigns and products have long since disappeared from the scene, yet their watchword lingers on, more often than not, welded to the product name. Discerning use of an effective slogan should be evident in all phases of an advertising campaign as continuity creates a greater impact and heightened consumer awareness.

THE PSYCHOLOGY OF THE SLOGAN

Slogans and Memory

In the continuing mental process of sorting, storing and discarding, there is a tendency to reduce conceptual thought to its simplest form. Unless trained early in abstract thinking, the human mind works best in patterns. It continually searches for likenesses and relationships. No matter how long an impression or thought lies buried, patterned association will often trigger memory to full recall of long-stored items. Or, to put it another way, ideas and images do not start independently in the mind but, as links in a chain, there is one before and one following after. This partially explains the magical power of a metaphor and simile in joining like to unlike, familiar to unfamiliar. Strange combinations and associations are more likely to be remembered than the ordinary. The imagination never stops working. The constant process of reflection, association, rationalization and analyzation generalizes and abstracts, plans and predicts, accepts and rejects, wanders and burrows. As a result of this unique mental process, valid psychological use of language and writing is strongly related to that same organized phenomena. Or, stated in a slightly different framework (6),

> People respond no less to the stimulus that revives a concrete picture or memory than to
> words that rouse the emotions; no less to novelty than to repetition, rhyme, rhythm or
> old associations.

Thus, within the functions of memory, the slogan acts as a handle. It is a mnemonically structured device which is a conscious or unconscious effort to hook into the reader's subconscious. Used effectively, it can succeed as no other single element in advertising

---

6. Robbins, Phyllis. *An Approach to Composition through Psychology*. Cambridge, Mass., Harvard University Press, 1929. p. 15.

can. Committed to memory, that phrase can be an effective spur to brand loyalty. It is the only aspect of an advertisement which has the chance of becoming a contemporary figure of speech or part of everyday speech patterns. Its success, and the resultant realized dream of becoming a household word, is usually accomplished by repetition, regardless of correct grammar or even of questionable benefits or common sense. Beyond casual conversation, it will likely follow further trails into cartoons, editorial matter and, not infrequently, into parody. Lucas and Britt have noted *(7)*:

> People sometimes pick up slogans or catch phrases from advertising purely for use in conversation. Later, they find themselves making important market choices on the basis of these same compelling words. Here, the slogan has done its job in merchandising the product as part of the overall plan.

Slogans, Poetry, and Music

In addition to the appeal of the slogan to associative memory, when the phrase rhymes or has a cadence, it takes on the power of poetry. In such instances, the slogan is a strong reinforcer of mind and imagination. The poetic phrase or slogan has the quality and power to haunt, to tease and, above all, to remain fixed in the memory of the consuming public. An effective slogan, then, can be linked to the basics of poetry as it contains the same raw materials—alliteration, rhyme, allegory and simile—as does verse. An effective slogan, as an effective poem, may be a mnemonic device, a memory jogger which says, essentially, "remember me, remember what I represent" and act. Thus, a small string of alliterative or lyrical words may become an easily recalled abbreviation for a great corporation and its products.

Besides simple mnemonic devices, poetry has been linked to music and music, in turn, has been linked to pleasure. The power of both music and poetry historically stem from the physiological rhythm inherent in every human being. Both music and poetry are capable of kindling our emotions and our emotions are inseparable from our sensations. Man's basic nature is keyed to orderly rhythm: breathing, heart and pulse beat. It is, in fact, nearly impossible for the human organism to deny a rhythmic pattern of an external force as, for example, dancing or keeping time with a musical beat. Poetry, with its rhyming and alliteration, appeals to this innate nature of man. There is a basic liking of rhythm and a high sensitivity to repetition. And, again, through repetition, comes association. The rhythmic aspect of writing and speech has a staying quality, the power of living on in the mind. Mario Pei has written that *(8)*:

> The language of poetry frequently reflects a syntactical freedom which the colloquial tongue has relinuished. Poetic license . . . may also be viewed as a modern extension of archaic conditions, when the abundance of lexional endings permitted a greater range in word-order.

In the pre-analytical days of the late 19th century, those poets laureate of early advertising somehow capitalized on the knowledge that through rhymes they could create a solid product awareness. The advertising sloganman took advantage of the fact that poetry is easily remembered and related to other subjects—in this instance, products to be sold. He profited from the appeal of imagery which readily kindled the imagination. The effective slogan with its musical structure was used and is used to build or create an image in the mind. To this day, advertising writers are encouraged to follow the long-standing tradition of utilizing a rhyming scheme. Sloganeers are still advised to create a phrase which will rhyme with the brand or company name—an idea which might be termed corporate poetry.

---

7. Lucas, Darrel B. and Britt, Steuart H. *Advertising Psychology and Research.* N.Y., McGraw-Hill, 1950. p. 73-74.

8. Pei, Mario. *The Story of Language.* Philadelphia, Lippincott, 1949. p. 134.

The following phrases illustrate its association and the debt of advertising slogans to memory association, rhythm, poetry and music.

ALLITERATION. Two or more syllable sounds, sound groups or letters at the beginnings of words in a phrase, as:

>*Portable Power for Progress*
>*Sell Simpson and Be Sure*
>*Everything Hinges on Hager*

METAPHOR. To suggest a resemblance, a term is applied to something to which it is not literally applicable, as:

>*A Rainbow of Distinctive Flavors*
>*The Money Truck*

SIMILE. To express a resemblance of one thing to another, using "like" or "as if," as:

>*Sleeping on a Seely Is Like Sleeping on a Cloud*

ALLUSION. Link to a literary character or situation or to a proverb or topical saying, as:

>*The Fourth Necessity*
>*The Strength of Gibraltar*
>*Don't Be a Pale Face*
>*All Is Vanity – All Is Vanity Fair*

HYPERBOLE. Extravagant statement not intended to be understood literally, as:

>*The One Man Gang*

CHIASMUS. Inversion in the second of two parallel clauses or phrases of the structure of the first, as:

>*Sells Hard Wherever Hardware Sells*
>*At Last a Perfume That Lasts*

ANALOGY. Comparison of similarities in two things, as:

>*Where Beauty Is Material*
>*Our Work Is Child's Play*
>*A Diamond Is Forever*

PERSONIFICATION. Abstract ideas of lifeless objects named as person, as:

>*The Grass People*
>*Clark Is Material Handling*
>*Garrett Is Experience*

TRANSFERRED EPHITHET. Abnormal use of adjective with noun, as:

>*Sail a Happy Ship*
>*Fly the Friendly Skies of United*

PUN. Play on words, as:

>*It's a Snap with Dot (fasteners)*
>*It's Matchless (heating system)*
>*The Sound Approach to Quality (high fidelity components)*
>*When It Rains, It Pours (salt)*
>*Best Glue in the Joint*

The remembered slogan will have a cadence to it—a lilt, if judiciously handled, which borders on the poetic. It can generate a rhythmic echo which is much harder to forget than the ordinary statement. A brief string of words can, through repetition, be the magic linking of words to emotion. These little phrases which wheedle, cajole, brag, promise, guarantee, gild or stultify are all a direct appeal to the emotions and, ideally, to action.

The history of advertising is, briefly, a movement from slogans to jingles to copy. Advertising jingles went slogans one better and selling text replaced the poetry in the evolution from simplicity to complexity. Do slogans change with the times? Do they reflect a buyer's or a seller's market? Are they symptomatic of hard sell and soft sell? They may well reflect the times—the more affluence, the less rigorous but more sophisticated the selling effort. Although their effective use has declined in recent years, we may well be witnessing a resurgence of slogan usage. A good phrase, used as a primary advertising tool, can create both success and profit. Such a resurgence would mirror the continuing need to identify the particular product or service above all other competitors. In a time of increasing impersonalization, the brief and human phrase is still able to creep into the mind and stay. It is, indeed, *The Effective Echo*.

Slogans in this section are arranged in alphabetical order with one exception: where the product, service, or company name precedes the phrase, that name is placed at the end of the phrases. For example:

> Builds photographic instruments a little better than they really have to be, Bell and Howell

> Makes good eating sense, Mazola.

In most instances, the searcher's interest is in the primary *theme* of the slogan. By placing the product or company name at the phrase end, the main theme falls more readily into alphabetical order.

If the phrase is too general to identify easily, specific product or service is placed in parentheses. For example:

> America's No. 1 low-calorie cola (Diet Rite)

> Built better because it's hand crafted (television)

Sogans which are legally protected are indicated as follows:

> Copyrighted (C)

> Registered (R)

> Trademark (TM)

Titles of periodicals are indicated by italics.

A

À votre service
  Air France
"Accent is on you, Southern's"
  Southern Railway Co.
The accepted name for value (office
    furniture)
  Haskell, Inc.
Accustomed to the finest. . .you'll find it in a
    Beechcraft
  Beech Aircraft Corp.
The action line (building materials)
  Evans Products Co.
Action-People (The Yellow Pages)
  American Telephone and Telegraph Co.
Add a fiber from Celanese and good things
    get better
  Celanese Corp.

Adds science to fisherman's luck (fishing
    tackle)
  True Temper Corp.
Advertise for action (The Yellow Pages)
  American Telephone and Telegraph Co.
African business is our business
  Farrell Lines, Inc.
Aged for 8 (Bell's Blended scotch whiskey)
  Heublein, Inc.
Agent in your community is a good man to
    know, the New York Life
  New York Life Insurance Co.
Air-freight specialists
  Flying Tiger Line, Inc.
The air valve people
  Numatics, Inc.
Airline of the professionals
  American Airlines, Inc.

The airline that knows the South Pacific best
    Air New Zealand
The airline that measures the midwest in
    minutes
    Ozark Air Lines, Inc.
The airline that treats you like a maharajah
    Air-India
The airline with the big jets
    Delta Air Lines, Inc.
The Alaska flag line
    Pacific Northern Airlines
All around the world
    Western Union International, Inc.
All fresh-fruit good (jellies, preserves)
    Kraft Foods Division, Kraftco Corp.
All is vanity. . .all is Vanity Fair (lingerie)
    Vanity Fair Mills, Inc.
All over the world BOAC takes good care of
    you
    British Overseas Airway Corp.
All the bank you'll ever need in Texas
    Texas National Bank of Commerce of
        Houston
All ways look to Linton for leadership
    (musical instruments)
    Linton Mfg. Co.
Always a step ahead in style
    Connolly Shoe Co.
"Always an adventure in good eating"
    (Duncan Hines packaged foods)
    Procter and Gamble Co.
Always first quality (retail store)
    J. C. Penney and Co.
Always first with the best (Poly-flex
    housewares)
    Republic Molding Corp.
Always right on the job (mining machinery)
    The Bowdil Co.
Always smoother because it's slow-distilled
    (Early Times bourbon)
    Brown-Foreman Distillers Corp.
Always virgin wool
    Pendleton Woolen Mills
America lives in Dacron
    E. I. duPont de Nemours and Co.
America lives in R and K Originals (women's
    apparel)
    R and K Originals, Inc.
America's best fleet buy (Rambler)
    American Motors Corp.
America's best-liked cereal assortment
    Kellogg Co.

America's best-tasting little cigar (Between
    the Acts)
    Lorillard Corp.
America's biggest selling weekly magazine
    T. V. Guide
America's cities are Bergstrom's forests
    Bergstrom Paper Co.
America's fastest growing fuel
    Thermogas, Inc.
America's fastest-growing tire company
    Cooper Tire and Rubber Co.
America's favorite fun car (Mustang)
    Ford Motor Co.
America's favorite mayonnaise (Best Foods)
    Best Foods Div., CPC International, Inc.
America's favorite mayonnaise (Hellman's)
    Best Foods Div., CPC International, Inc.
America's finest basement door
    Bilco Co.
America's finest campers
    Highway Cruisers, Inc.
America's finest camping tents (Hoosier)
    Hoosier Tarpaulin and Canvas Good Co.
America's finest cooking centers
    Jenn-Air Corp.
America's finest fishing rods
    Browning Arms Co.
America's finest power-loomed rug
    Karastan Rug Mills, Div. Field Crest
    Mills, Inc.
America's finest writing instruments since
    1846
    A. T. Cross Co.
America's first, finest and favorite pork and
    beans
    Stokely-Van Camp, Inc.
America's first name in lighting
    Lightolier, Inc.
America's foremost leg specialists
    Plastic Industries, Inc.
America's foremost manufacturer of
    decorative accessories since 1890
    Syroco Div., Dart Industries, Inc.
America's foremost producer of custom
    steels
    Sharon Steel Corp.
America's greatest luggage value
    Baltimore Luggage Co.
America's largest builder of camping trailers
    Nimrod Ward Mfg. Co.
America's largest leasing system (automobile)
    Ford Authorized Leasing System

America's largest manufacturer of custom
        day beds and sofa beds
    M. Mittman Co.
America's largest manufacturer of lighting
        reproductions
    Ruby Lighting Corp.
America's largest selling camping trailer
    Nimrod Ward Mfg. Co.
America's largest selling corn oil margarines
        (Fleischmann's)
    Standard Brands, Inc.
America's largest selling residential locksets
    Kwikset Div., Emhart Corp.
America's leading airline
    American Airlines, Inc.
America's leading bearing specialists since
        1925
    Detroit Aluminum and Brass Co.
America's leading energy company
    Enco Div., Humble Oil and Refining Co.
"America's leading producer of quality
        canvas products"
    Fulton Cotton Mills Div., Allied Products
        Corp.
America's leading silversmiths since 1831
    Gorham Div., Textron, Inc.
America's most customer-minded oil
        company
    Sunray DX Oil Co.
America's most distinguished motorcar
        (Lincoln Continental)
    Ford Motor Co.
America's most distinguished source for fine
        English furniture
    Wood and Hogan
America's most interesting state
    Tennessee Department of Conservation
America's most modern cola (Diet-Rite)
    Royal Crown Cola Co.
America's most popular boats
    Starcraft Co.
America's most recommended mover
        (Mayflower)
    Aero Mayflower Transit Co., Inc.
America's most used products away from
        home
    Fort Howard Paper Co.
America's no. 1 low-calorie cola (Diet Rite)
    Royal Crown Cola Co.
America's oldest and largest showroom
        distributor of fine decorative furniture
    Knapp and Tubbs, Inc.

America's number 1 mover
    Allied Van Lines, Inc.
America's original sparkling malt liquor
        (Champale)
    Metropolis Brewery of New Jersey, Inc.
America's pioneer manufacturer of pre-
        finished metals
    American Nickeloid Co.
America's premium quality beer
    Falstaff Brewing Corp.
America's resourceful railroad
    Milwaukee Road
America's standard of fine shoe value
    The Florsheim Shoe Co.
America's "wake-up" voice
    Westclox Div., General Time Corp.
An American leader in advanced systems of
        photo-optics for information
        processing
    Itek Corp.
An extra measure of quality (electronic
        instruments)
    Hewlett-Packard Co.
An idea whose time has come!
    Harlan Insurance Co.
"An inch of Pinch, please." (scotch
        whiskey)
    Renfield Importers, Ltd.
And away go troubles down the drain
        (machinery)
    Roto-Rooter Corp.
And who makes great skis? Head, of course.
    Head Ski Co.
"Angels of the highest order" (Seraphim)
    Capitol Records, Inc.
Ankle-fashioned shoes
    Nunn-Bush Shoe Co.
Another carefree Johnson
    Johnson Motors Div., Outboard Marine
        Co.
Another clinical-strength medication from
        Warner-Lambert
    Warner-Lambert Pharmaceutical Co.
Another example of how Monsanto moves on
        many fronts to serve you (chemicals)
    Monsanto Co.
Another fine creation by Krueger (furniture)
    Krueger Metal Products Co.
The answer is wool. . .it costs less in the
        long run
    Wool Carpets of America
Anticipating tomorrow's needs today
    Enjay Chemical Co. Div., Humble Oil and
        Refining Co.

Any Palizzio is better than no Palizzio
(shoes)
Palizzio, Inc.
Anything can happen when you wear Fame
Parfums Corday, Inc.
Anywhere in the wide world (automobile
leasing)
Hertz Corp.
Applying advanced technology to bring you
exciting new products
Eaton, Yale and Towne, Inc.
Approved by professional hair colorists
(Nestle Color Tint)
Nestle-LeMur Co.
Are not just for dancing, Danskins (women's
apparel)
Danskin, Inc.
Aren't you glad you use Dial. Don't you
wish everybody did?
Armour and Co.
The aristocrat of fine corsetry
Cordé de Parie, Inc.
The aristocrat of liqueurs (Cherristock)
Schenley Import Co.
The aristocrat of polyester neckwear
Wembley Ties, Inc.
Artistry in carpets
Painter Carpet Mills, Inc., Div. Collins and
Aikman
As long as you're up get me a Grant's (R)
(Scotch whiskey)
Austin, Nichols and Co., Inc.
As you travel ask us (R)
Standard Oil Div., American Oil Co.
Ask Allied Chemical
Allied Chemical Corp.
Ask anyone who knows (high fidelity sound
equipment)
Ampex Corp.
Ask for K-V. . .it's a known value (hardware)
Knape and Vogt Mfg. Co.
Ask the man from Northern Plains
Northern Natural Gas Co.
Assurance of quality
National Automotive Parts Association
Assurance of quality, dependability since
1917
Moorhead Machine and Boiler Co.
At home with your young ideas
Bassett Furniture Industries, Inc.
At last a perfume that lasts (Taji)
Shulton, Inc.
Australia's round-the-world jet airline
QANTAS

Authentically ski (R)
Ski Industries America
The authority in the exciting world of
beauty (cosmetics)
Max Factor and Co.
The authority on fastening
The Apex Machine and Tool Co.
The automated answer to the paper
explosion
Remington Office Systems Div., Sperry
Rand Corp.
Automatically better (cigarette lighters)
Ronson Corp.
Automation is economical (electronic data
processing
Fusion, Inc.

B

Babies are our business. . .our only business
(R)
Gerber Products Co.
Backed by a century-old tradition of fine
craftsmanship
Amana Refrigeration, Inc.
"Bait of champions"
Fred Arbogast Co., Inc.
The bank for bankers and businessmen
Irving Trust Co.
The bank that means business in California
Crocker-Citizens National Bank
The bank that works hardest for you
Chemical Bank New York Trust Co.
The bank with the international point of
view
Bank of the Southwest
The bankers who do a little more for you
United Bank of California
Basic chemicals and cost-cutting ideas
Chemical Div., PPG Industries, Inc.
Basic for better beer
Froedtert Malt Co.
Basic in catalyst chemistry
American Cyanamid Co.
Basic producers from mine to finished
product
Industrial Chemicals Marketing Div.,
Tennessee Corp.
Basic products and engineering for industry's
basic work
Link-Belt Co.
Basic provider of chemicals in volume
Abbott Laboratories

Basic to America's progress
  Allied Chemical Corp.
The bat with the most on the ball
  Adirondack Bats, Inc.
Be profit wise. . .sell only Buss (fuses)
  Bussman Mfg. Div., McGraw Edison Co.
Be seated by. . .Bemis (bathroom fixtures)
  Bemis Mfg. Co.
Be specific, route Union Pacific
  Union Pacific Railroad
Be specific. . .say "Union Pacific"
  Union Pacific Railroad
Be sure, insure with INA
  Insurance Company of North America
Be sure to get a quote (lift trucks)
  Allis-Chalmers Mfg. Co.
Be sure with Pure
  The Pure Oil Co.
Be suspicious! (Sanforized)
  Cluett, Peabody Co., Inc.
Beautiful hair (shampoo)
  John H. Breck, Inc.
Beautiful on the table. Carefree in the
    kitchen. (Weavewood-Ware)
  Weavewood, Inc.
Beauty designers (Dermetics cosmetics)
  Turner Hall Corp.
Beauty mark of fine lighting
  Champion Mfg. Co., Inc.
Because . . . (Modess)
  Personal Products Co.
Because it might rain (raincoats)
  Harbor Master Ltd., Div. Jonathan Logan
"Because there is a difference"
  The Northwestern Mutual Life Insurance
  Co.
Because you love nice things (lingerie)
  Van Raalte Co., Inc.
The beer that made Milwaukee famous
    (Schlitz)
  Jos. Schlitz Brewing Co.
Beginning a second century of leadership
    (Chase and Sanborn coffee)
  Standard Brands, Inc.
The beginning of taste
  Syracuse China Corp.
Behind every Olga there really is an Olga
    (foundation garments)
  Olga Co.
The best aid is first aid
  Johnson and Johnson
The best anti-freeze since mink (Zerex)
  E. I. duPont de Nemours and Co.

The best birch line
  Kitchen Kompact, Inc.
Best buy Boling
  Boling Chair Co.
Best cooks know foods fried in Crisco don't
    taste greasy!
  Procter and Gamble Co.
Best for all engines, Champion
  Champion Spark Plug Co.
Best for your money (wallets)
  Buxton, Inc.
The best friend your willpower ever had
    (Slim-Mint gum)
  Thompson Medical Co., Inc.
Best glue in the joint (Elmer's)
  Borden Chemical Div., Borden, Inc.
The best in tapes has "Able" on the label
  Arno Adhesive Tapes, Inc.
"The best in the house" (R) in 87 lands
    (Canadian Club whiskey)
  Hiram Walker, Inc.
The best known and most respected name in
    reclining chairs (Barcalounger)
  Barcolo Mfg. Co.
The best name in all-weather coats and
    rainwear
  The Alligator Co.
The best pump—the best buy
  Reda Pump Co.
Best pumps in the oil patch
  Harbison-Fischer Mfg. Co.
The best seat in the house (bathroom
    fixtures)
  C. F. Church Div., American Standard,
  Inc.
Best-selling aerosols are powered with Freon
    propellents
  Freon Products Div., E. I. duPont de
  Nemours and Co.
The best to you each morning (breakfast
    cereals)
  Kellogg Co.
The best tobacco makes the best smoke
    (Camel cigarettes)
  R. J. Reynolds Tobacco Co.
The best way to better yarns (R)
  Whitten Machine Works
Best way to close an opening (fire doors)
  Cookson Co.
Best year yet to go Ford!
  Ford Motor Co.
Better air is our business
  American Air Filter Co., Inc.

Better because it's gas. . .best because it's
    Caloric (domestic appliances)
  Caloric Corp.
Better buy Birds Eye
  Birds Eye Div., General Foods Corp.
Better by design
  Mesta Machine Co.
Better castings through advanced foundry
    technology
  Meehanite Metal Corp.
Better ideas from UOP
  Universal Oil Products
Better medicines for a better world
  Parke, Davis and Co.
Better pans for better baking
  Chicago Metallic Mfg. Co.
Better products at lower cost through better
    methods
  Standard Tool and Mfg. Co.
Better products for man's best friend
    (Sergeant's)
  Polk Miller Products Co.
"Better than money" (R) (traveler's checks)
  First National City Bank
Better things for better living. . .through
    chemistry
  E. I. duPont de Nemours and Co.
Betters continuous production through
    continuous research! (institutional
    food equipment)
  J. W. Greer Co.
Big enough to serve you—small enough to
    know you (meat packer)
  E. Kahn's Sons Co.
The big job matched line (tractors)
  Massey-Ferguson Inc.
Big name in batteries
  Ray-O-Vac Div., ESB, Inc.
The big name in little wheels (materials
    handling)
  Cushman Motors Div., Outboard Marine
  Corp.
The big sky country
  Montana Highway Commission
Biggest name in fleet cars and trucks
  Chevrolet Motor Div., General Motors
  Corp.
The biggest should do more. It's only right. . .
    (automobile leasing)
  Hertz Corp.
Birthplace and centre of modern optics
  Carl Zeiss, Jena

Birthplace of the nation
  Virginia Department of Conservation and
  Economic Development
The Blue Chip company
  Connecticut Mutual Life Insurance Co.
The body cosmetic (Cashmere Bouquet
    talcum)
  Colgate-Palmolive Co.
The bold engineering comes from Ford
  Ford Motor Co.
Bonded for life. . .because they're built that
    way (power tools)
  Ingersoll-Rand Co.
Boost profits with the competitive edge
    (agricultural chemicals, machinery)
  Tyler Corp.
Border to border...coast to coast!
  Trailer Train Co.
Born 1820, still going strong! (Johnnie
    Walker Red Label scotch)
  Canada Dry Corp.
Born in America. Worn round the world
    (hats)
  John B. Stetson Co.
Bowl where you see the Magic Triangle
  American Machine and Foundry Co.
Brainpower builds profits, Minnesota
  Minnesota Department of Business
  Development
The brand with loyalty to quality (Billy the
    Kid slacks)
  Hortex Mfg. Co.
The Brandy of Napoleon (Courvoisier
    cognac)
  W. A. Taylor and Co.
Breakfast of champions (Wheaties)
  General Mills, Inc.
Breathin' brushed pigskin (R) (Hush Puppies
    shoes)
  Wolverine World Wide, Inc.
Brewed only in Milwaukee (Miller High Life
    beer)
  Miller Brewing Co.
The bright new silicates for industry
  Allegheny Industrial Chemical Co.
A bright new world of electric housewares
    (Norelco)
  North American Philips Corp.
Brighten up with Instant Tender Leaf Tea
  Standard Brands, Inc.
The brighter tasting tea (Instant Tender
    Leaf)
  Standard Brands, Inc.

The brightest name in aluminum
    Nichols Aluminum Co.
The brightest star in golf (Burke-
        Worthington)
    Victor Golf Co.
Brings out the expert in you (automati-
        cally!), Bell and Howell (cameras)
    Bell and Howell Co.
The brisk tea
    Thos. J. Lipton, Inc.
"Build a truck to do a job—change it only to
        do better"
    Motor Truck Div., International Harvester
    Co.
Builders in and of the South
    Daniel Construction Co., Inc.
Builders of better refrigerator bodies
        (refrigeration transportation)
    Hackney Bros. Body Co.
Builders of the tools of automation
    Reliance Electric and Engineering Co.
Builders of tomorrow's feeds. . .today!
    Allied Mills, Corp.
Build-in satisfaction. . .build-in Frigidaire
        (domestic appliances)
    Frigidaire Div., General Motors Corp.
Building business is our business
    Tenneco, Inc.
Building with Chicago and the nation since
        1863
    First National Bank of Chicago
Builds better bodies, Batavia (refrigeration
        transportation)
    Batavia Body Co.
Builds for the future, Mannesmann
    Mannesman-Export Corp.
Builds photographic instruments a little
        better than they really have to be, Bell
        and Howell
    Bell and Howell Co.
Builds tough trucks, Dodge
    Dodge Div., Chrysler Corp.
Builds walls for keeps, Smitty
    Edwin G. Smith and Co., Inc.
Builds what it promises
    General Development Corp.
Built better because it's handcrafted
        (television)
    Zenith Radio Corp.
Built like a sky scraper (R) (files, desks)
    Shaw-Walker Co.
—built means better built, Ford
    Ford Motor Co.

Built stronger to last longer
    Powell Muffler Co.
Built to last longer (Econoline van trucks)
    Ford Motor Co.
Built to take it. . .beautifully
    Daystrom Furniture Div., Daystrom, Inc.
"Built tough for you" (automobiles)
    Toyota Motor Distributors Inc.
Built with integrity, backed by service
        (household products)
    Sunbeam Corp.
Business case that knows its way around the
        world
    Samsonite Corp.
The business jet that's backed by an airline
        (Fan Jet Falcon)
    Business Jets Div., Pan American World
    Airways, Inc.
The business management magazine
    Dun's Review and Modern Industry
A business paper for the farm chemical
        industry
    Croplife
Buy today's best truck. Own tomorrow's
        best trade.
    Hyster Co.
Buy us like advertising. . .use us like salesmen
    Home State Farm Publications
By design. . .furniture distinguished for value
        since 1904
    Thomasville Furniture Industries, Inc.
By the world's largest maker of dishwasher
        detergents (Electrasol)
    Economics Laboratories, Inc.

C

California's premier wines
    Almaden Vineyards, Inc.
Call the man from Cozzoli
    Cozzoli Machine Co.
Call the man who puts the farmer first—your
        Standard Oil Farm Man
    Standard Oil Div., American Oil Co.
Call your Investors man—today! (insurance)
    Investors Diversified Services, Inc.
The calm beauty of Japan at almost the
        speed of sound
    Japan Air Lines
The camera you never leave at home
    Minox Corp.
Can do, Kelly (temporary employees)
    Kelly Services, Inc.

The can opener people
  Dazey Products Co.
The canned dog food without the can,
    Gaines-burgers
  General Foods Corp.
Capability has many faces at Boeing
  Boeing Co.
Capitalist tool
  Forbes
Car plan management and leasing specialists
  Peterson, Howell and Heather
Carefree furniture
  Vĭko Furniture Corp.
Cares for more complexions than any other
    soap in the world, Palmolive-
  Colgate-Palmolive Co.
Carpets of distinction
  Patcraft Mills, Inc.
The catsup with the big tomato taste
  Hunt Wesson Foods, Inc.
Centaur. . .your symbol of quality, the (Remy-
    Martin cognac)
  Renfield Importers, Ltd.
Certifies the most in dry cleaning (One Hour
    Martinizing)
  Martin Equipment Sales, American
  Laundry Machine Industries
The chair that stands by itself
  Stakmore Co., Inc.
Chairs for all businesses
  Boling Chair Co.
The champagne of bottle beer (Miller High
    Life)
  Miller Brewing Co.
The "Champagne Touch"
  Moore-McCormack Lines, Inc.
Change for the better with Alcoa Aluminum
  Aluminum Co. of America
Charcoal mellowed drop by drop
  Jack Daniels Distillery
Check with Koppers
  Koppers Co., Inc.
The cheese with the paper between the slices
  N. Dorman and Co.
Cherished as one of the world's seven great
    fragrances (Intimate)
  Revlon, Inc.
The chevron—the sign of excellence
  Standard Oil Co. of California
Chief of the mouldings
  Ponderosa Moulding, Inc.
Choice of better mechanics
  Snap-On Tools Corp

The choice of businessmen lets you choose
    with confidence
  Aetna Insurance Co.
The choice when you want quality, too
    (office furniture)
  All-Steel Equipment, Inc.
The cigar that never lasts long enough
    (Antonio y Cleopatra)
  American Brands, Inc.
The classic name in the building field
  Bird and Son, Inc.
Classics of optical precision (Schneider
    camera lenses)
  Burleigh Brooks, Inc.
Cleans like a white tornado (TM) (Ajax)
  Colgate-Palmolive Co.
The close electric shave (Norelco)
  North American Philips Corp.
Clothes that enhance your public appearance
  The House of Worsted-Tex
Coast to coast to coast
  National Airlines, Inc.
The coat rack people
  Vogel-Peterson Co.
Coatings, colors and chemicals for industry
  Sherwin-Williams Co.
The coffee served at the Waldorf-Astoria
    (Savarin)
  S. A. Schonbrunn and Co., Inc.
The coffee-er coffee (Savarin)
  S. A. Schonbrunn and Co., Inc.
College is America's best friend
  Council for Financial Aid to Education
The "color Guide" (TM)
  Wembley Ties, Inc.
Color is nature's way of saying flavor.
    Stokely is your way of getting it.
    (vegetables)
  Stokely-Van Camp, Inc.
The colorfast shampoo
  Clairol, Inc.
Combines experience and innovation to
    solve its customers' problems, Dravo.
    A company of uncommon enterprise.
  Dravo Corp.
Come alive! (Pepsi-Cola)
  Pepsico, Inc.
Come to Kentucky! It's a profitable move!
  Kentucky Department of Commerce
Come to where the flavor is. . .come to
    Marlboro country (cigarettes)
  Philip Morris, Inc.

16

Come up to the Kool taste
    Brown and Williamson Tobacco Corp.
The comfort shave (Norelco)
    North American Philips Corp.
Comfortable, carefree cotton
    Cotton Producers Institute
Commitment to quality (machinery)
    Bucyrus-Erie Co.
The company for people who travel
    American Express Co.
The company for precious metals
    Handy and Harman
The company of specialists (filing equipment)
    Watson Mfg. Co., Inc.
The company with the "know-how"
    Metropolitan Furniture Adjusters
The company with the partnership
        philosophy
    American United Life Insurance Co.
The complete authority of packaging
    Modern Packaging
The complete brake lining service
    Raybestos-Manhattan, Inc.
The complete family of dog and cat foods
        from the world leader in nutrition
        (Friskies)
    Carnation Co.
The complete line of electric cooking
        equipment (Toastmaster)
    McGraw-Edison Co.
Complete line of mobile food service
        equipment
    Crescent Metal Products, Inc.
A complete source for fine office furniture
    Desks, Inc.
The computer with a future, System/360
    International Business Machines Corp.
Consider paper
    Champion Papers, Inc.
Consider the power of paper used with
        imagination
    Champion Papers, Inc.
Consistently better
    Apex Smelting Co.
Consult your doctor about your weight
        problem (Sego)
    Milk Products Div., Pet, Inc.
Consult your physician on matters of weight
        control (Metracal)
    Mead Johnson and Co.
Containers of distinction
    J. L. Clark Mfg. Co.
Contemporary fibers
    Celanese Corp.

Continuing research for lower cost drilling
    Hycelog, Inc.
Continuous filament textured nylon
        (Tycora)
    Textured Yarn Co., Inc.
Continuous flow packaging (R)
    Battle Creek Packaging Machinery, Inc.
Control with Dole (R)
    Dole Valve Co.
Controls temperature. . .precisely
    Fenwal, Inc.
Coordinated fashions for bed and bath
    Fieldcrest Mills, Inc.
Copies for communication. . .throughout the
        world
    American Photocopy Equipment Co.
Correct mistakes in any language (erasers)
    Weldon Roberts Rubber Co.
Corrugated packaging specialists
    Hoerner Boxes, Inc.
Costs less than trouble, UNBRAKO
    Precision Fastener Div., Standard Pressed
    Steel Co.
The costume jewelry of the home
    Mersman Tables
Cotton: You can feel how good it looks
    Cotton Producers Institute
Could it be the real thing? (pearls)
    Marvella, Inc.
Country charm quality (dairy products)
    Dean Foods Co.
The country garden soap for the "country
        complexion" (Cashmere Bouquet)
    Colgate-Palmolive Co.
The courage to change. The strength to grow.
    International Harvester Co.
Le couturier de la monte (watches)
    Universal Geneve
Cover the earth (paint)
    Sherwin-Williams Co.
Covers a world of sports
    Slazengers, Inc.
Craftsmen of fine solid wood furniture
    Davis Cabinet Co.
Creams your skin while you wash, Dove
    Personal Products Div., Lever Bros. Co.
Creates new dimensions in automatic
        packaging machinery!
    Circle Design and Mfg. Corp.
Creating a new world with electronics
    Hughes Aircraft Co.
. . .creating better ways to hold things
        together
    National Screw and Mfg. Co.

The creating fiber, Source
  Allied Chemical Corp.
Creating world-famed fishing tackle since
    1893
  South Bend Tackle Co., Div. Gladding
  Corp.
Creative ideas in glass
  American Saint Gobain Corp.
Creator of advanced writing instruments
  Micropoint, Inc.
Creators of chemicals for modern agriculture
  Geigy Chemical Corp.
Creators of dependability (gears, gear drives)
  Geartronics Corp.
Creators of 1,001 products for home
    decorating
  Conso Products Co., Div. Consolidated
  Foods Corp.
Creators of the world famous Stratolounger
    (furniture)
  Futorian Mfg. Corp.
The crown jewels of ignition (R)
  Filko Ignition
The crown jewels of ignition and carburetion
  Filko Ignition
The crowning touch of quality
  Red Cedar Shingle and Handsplit Shake
  Bureau
Cruising everywhere under the sun
  American President Lines
The custom crafted shotgun
  Charles Daly
Custom made luggage (Lark)
  Droutman Mfg. Co.
"Custom of course" (beads)
  Lew Smith
The customer is always No. 1
  National Car Rental System, Inc.
Customer satisfaction—our no. 1 job
  Detroit Steel Corp.
A cut above the commonplace
  Danish Blue Cheese
Cutting costs is our business
  Addressograph Multigraph Corp.

D

Dedicated to excellence
  American Motors Corp.
Dedicated to people on the move
  U.S. Van Lines, Inc.
"Dedicated to serving the families of the
    West and Hawaii. . .no one else"
  Sunset

Dedicated to the pursuit of excellence
  Rohr Corp.
Definitely Glenoit for happy persons
    (apparel)
  Glenoit Mills, Inc.
Definitive modern furniture
  Founders Furniture, Inc.
Delivers in the clutch, Lipe (motor truck
    parts)
  Lipe-Rollway Corp.
Depend on Potlach for everything in quality
    lumber
  Potlatch Forests, Inc.
The dependable automatics (washing
    machines)
  Maytag Co.
Dependable spark plugs
  Champion Spark Plug Co.
Dependability in the field. . .safety for the
    operator (agricultural machinery)
  Tryco Mfg. Co., Inc.
The dependability people (washing
    machines)
  Maytag Co.
Design/plus (office furniture)
  Steelcase, Inc.
"Designs for the world's best dressed"
  Mr. John
Designs that dreams are made of (interior
    decoration)
  M/B Designs, Inc.
Designs them. . .builds them!
  Chicago Bridge and Iron Co.
Determined to serve you best
  Eastern Air Lines, Inc.
Developers and producers of extraordinary
    materials
  The Beryllium Corp.
"Developing products for recreation through
    electronic research" (C)
  Byrd Industries, Inc.
A diamond is forever
  DeBeers Consolidated Mines, Ltd.
Die casting is the process. . .zinc, the metal
  St. Joseph Lead Co.
The difference is quality (guitars)
  Epiphone, Inc.
The difference is value (Datsun automobiles)
  Nissan Motor Co., USA
The different antacid (Gelusil)
  Warner-Lambert Pharmaceutical Co.
Discover extra coolness (Kool cigarettes)
  Brown and Williamson Tobacco Corp.

Discover the new in New York State
  New York State Department of
  Commerce
Discover what sound is all about
  James B. Lansing Sound, Inc.
The discovery company
  Union Carbide Corp.
Distinctive as your own finger print (anti-
  corrosive)
  Rust-Oleum Corp.
Distinctive designs in leather accessories
  Prince Gardner Co., Inc.
Distinctive floor coverings since 1917
  Ernest Treganowan
Distinguished furniture for distinguished
  offices
  Stow and Davis Furniture Co.
Diversified—worldwide
  Singer, Inc.
Do it tomorrow's way. . .with gas
  American Gas Association, Inc.
Does a lot for you
  Scovill Mfg. Co.
Does it better. . .for a wide range of indus-
  tries, Doughboy
  Doughboy Industries, Inc.
Does its share to help you share in a better
  future, Allis-Chalmers
  Allis-Chalmers Mfg. Co.
Does she. . .or doesn't she (R) (hair color)
  Clairol, Inc.
Dog food of champions (Ken-L-Biskit)
  Ken-L-Products Div., Quaker Oats Co.
"Dollar wise group insurance"
  Pan-American Life Insurance Co.
Don't be a pale face (suntan lotion)
  The Coppertone Corp.
Don't be satisfied with less than Lennox (air
  conditioning—heating)
  Lennox Industries, Inc.
Don't be vague. . .ask for Haig and Haig
  (Scotch whiskey)
  Renfield Importers, Ltd.
Don't just fertilize. . .Spencerize
  Spencer Chemical Div., Gulf Oil Corp.
Don't miss the magic of Rit (dyes)
  Best Foods Div., CPC International, Inc.
Don't say it can't be done. . .talk to Olin
  (cartons)
  Olin Mathieson Chemical Corp.
Don't say sun glasses—say C'Bon! (T)
  Polaroid Corp.
Don't stir without Noilly Prat (vermouth)
  Browne-Vintners Co.

Don't wait to inherit Spode (tableware)
  Spode, Inc.
Dream carved rings (Art Carved)
  J. R. Wood and Sons, Inc.
The drier liqueur (DOM B and B)
  Julius Wile Sons and Co., Inc.
Drink RC—for quick, fresh energy
  Royal Crown Cola Co.
Dutch name, world fame (Bols liqueurs)
  Brown-Forman Distillers Corp.
Dyeing with Rit is fast, fun, almost fool-
  proof!
  Best Foods Div., CPC International, Inc.
A dynamic force with paper
  Kimberly-Clark Corp.

E

Each week the facts add up to success
  Sports Illustrated
Easiest travel on earth
  Continental Trailways Bus System
Easy, delicious. . .versatile, nutritious
  Rice Council
The easy ones (cameras)
  Eastman Kodak Co.
Editorial excellence in action
  Pit and Quarry
8 companies running hard
  Trans Union Corp.
Electrics give more people more time for
  more important jobs
  Boston-Hunt Mfg. Co.
The elegant 8 year old (Walker's De Luxe
  bourbon)
  Hiram Walker, Inc.
11 kinds—better than most people make
  (Heublein cocktails)
  Heublein, Inc.
Eliminates drops that spot, Cascade
  (detergent)
  Procter and Gamble Co.
Enchanting ladies choose Dorothy Gray
  (cosmetics)
  Lehn and Fink Products Corp.
Energy chemicals
  Cities Service Co.
Engine life preserver
  Quaker State Oil Refining Corp.
Engineered for longer life (tractors)
  Minneapolis-Moline, Inc.
Engineered for the ultimate in precision
  (Kwik-Way Brake Service Centers)
  Cedar Rapids Engineering Co.

Engineered for value (control systems)
  Cutler Hammer, Inc.
"Engineered transportation" (motor truck
    bodies)
  Fruehauf Corp.
Engineering know-how. . .by Blaw-Knox
  Blaw-Knox Co.
Engineering with imagination (fountain
    pens)
  Scripto, Inc.
Engineers to the woodworking industry
  Wisconsin Knife Works, Inc.
Enjoy the rest of your life (Koolfoam
    pillows)
  American Latex Products Corp.
Enjoyable always and all ways
  Bacardi Imports, Inc.
Escape from the ordinary
  Oldsmobile Div., General Motors Corp.
Europe's foremost airline
  British European Airways
Europe's most helpful airline
  Sabena Belgian World Airlines
Every Bali has a bow
  Bali Brassiere Co.
Every day, Bemis develops a new packaging
    idea to serve you better
  Bemis Co., Inc.
Every pair shows the care of the shoemaker's
    hand (Bostonian)
  The Commonwealth Shoe and Leather Co.
Every woman alive wants Chanel No. 5
    (perfume)
  Chanel, Inc.
Every year, more Royal typewriters are
    bought in America than any other
    brand
  Royal Typewriter Co., Div. Litton
  Industries
Everybody appreciates the finest (Radi-
    Oven)
  Knapp-Monarch Co.
Everyday good. . .glass with flair
  Anchor Hocking Glass Corp.
Everyone knows, if it's Caryl Richards, it is
    just wonderful for your hair
  Caryl Richards, Inc.
Everything for the fireplace since 1827
  Wm. H. Jackson Co.
Everything hinges on Hager
  Hager Hinge Co.
Everything to wear
  Genesco, Inc.

Everything's better with Blue Bonnet on it
  Standard Brands, Inc.
Everywhere west
  Chicago, Burlington and Quincy Railroad
Exacting standards only
  Sommers Brass Co., Inc.
Excellence doubly safeguarded (Beefeater
    gin)
  Kobrand Corp.
Expensive shirts ought to look it (Excello)
  Kayser-Roth Corp.
The experienced cruise line
  Furness, Withy and Co., Ltd.
Expert's choice. . .since 1880
  Ithaca Gun Co., Inc.
The extra care airline
  United Air Lines, Inc.
The extraordinary fiber (Trevira)
  Hystron Fibers, Inc.

F

The fabric with reflex action (Expandra)
  Burlington Industries
Fabrics used in the most wanted women's
    and children's sportswear (Clan Crest)
  Glen Raven Mills
Fabrics with the character of quality
  Greenwood Mills, Inc.
Families that move the most call the world's
    largest mover
  Allied Van Lines, Inc.
A famous brand in glass
  Latchford Glass Co.
A famous camera from camera-famous West
    Germany
  Minox Corp.
Famous for candy flavors
  Fenn Bros., Inc.
Famous for power mowers for over 50 years
    (Toro)
  Wheel Horse Products, Inc.
Famous for products that really work
    (cleaning compounds)
  Glamorene Products Corp.
Famous for quality
  Brunswick Rubber Co.
Famous for quality the world over (R)
    (television)
  Philco Corp.
Famous. Smooth. Mellow. (Old Crow
    bourbon)
  National Distillers and Chemical Corp.

The fan-jet airline
  Northwest Airlines, Inc.
Far sighted planners choose Herman Nelson
  American Air Filter Co., Inc.
Farm implements with a future—yours!
  Brillion Iron Works, Inc.
Fashion loomed to last
  Magee Carpet Co.
Fashion luggage (Lady Baltimore)
  Baltimore Luggage Co.
The fashion shoe (Mademoiselle)
  Genesco, Inc.
...fashioned for those who enjoy extra-
    ordinary quality
  Gerber Legendary Blades
Fasten it better and faster with Bostitch
  Bostitch, Inc.
Favorite of the nation's bakers
  National Bakery Div., Package Machinery
  Co.
Feather touch control
  Acme Lite Products Co.
Feature rich (Aiwa tape recorders)
  Selectron International Co.
The fiber glass for finer fabrics
  PPG Industries, Inc.
The fiber you can trust
  Cotton Producers Institute
50 years of brighter tasting meals (Corning
    Ware)
  Corning Glass Works
The filter for the taste that's right (Viceroy)
  Brown and Williamson Tobacco Corp.
Find it faster in the Yellow Pages
  American Telephone and Telegraph Co.
Fine bootmakers since 1876
  Charles A. Eaton Co.
Fine cabinetmakers since 1886
  Karges Furniture Co.
Fine chemicals (Baker and Adamson)
  General Chemical Div., Allied Chemical
  Corp.
Fine coffee liqueur...from sunny Mexico
    (Kahlúa)
  Jules Berman and Associates, Inc.
Fine dinnerware (Vernonware)
  Vernon Div., Metlox Mfg. Co.
Fine fabrics made in America since 1813
  J. P. Stevens and Co., Inc.
Fine fashion jewelry
  Sarah Coventry, Inc.
Fine flooring
  Ruberoid Co.

Fine floors (Congoleum-Nairn)
  Congoleum Industries, Inc.
Fine food products
  Geo. A. Hormel and Co.
Fine furniture
  Henredon Furniture Industries, Inc.
Fine furniture
  George J. Kempler Co.
"The fine old innkeeping tradition in a
    modern setting" (R)
  Holiday Inns of America, Inc.
Fine letter papers
  Eaton Paper Corp.
Fine papers
  Crane and Co., Inc.
Fine photography for 40 years
  Minolta Corp.
Fine watchmakers since 1791 (Girard
    Perregaux)
  Jean R. Graef, Inc.
Fine whiskey on the mild side (Corby's)
  Jas. Barclay and Co., Ltd.
Finer seamless stockings
  Oleg Cassini, Inc.
The finest aluminum
  Mirro Aluminum Co.
The finest ice making unit ever made
  Henry Vogt Machine, Co.
Finest in china since 1735 (Richard Ginori)
  Pasmantier Co., Inc.
The finest in expanded vinyl fabric
    (Naugahyde)
  Uniroyal, Inc.
Finest in flooring since 1898
  Harris Hardwood Co.
Finest in sporting arms
  Browning Arms Co.
"The finest in the field" (R) (sporting goods)
  Rawlings Corp.
The finest in vinyl upholstery (Royal
    Naugahyde)
  Uniroyal, Inc.
The finest name in frozen foods
  Dunlany Foods, Inc.
The finest name in locks and hardware (Yale
    and Towne)
  Eaton Yale and Towne, Inc.
The finest name in pumps, Myers
  F. E. Myers and Bro., Inc.
The finest name in sleep (mattress)
  Englander Co., Inc.
The finest of natural cheeses—naturally from
    Kraft
  Kraft Foods Div., Kraftco Corp.

"The finest pads have purple bindings"
    The Universal Pad and Tablet Co.
The finest protection available for your
        family, your property and your
        business
    Fireman's Fund American Life Insurance
    Co.
Finest quality on wheels since 1885
        (materials handling)
    The Colson Corp.
The finest. . .the record proves it since 1900,
        Dual's (high fidelity sound equipment)
    United Audio Products, Inc.
The finest tribute. . .the most trusted
        protection
    Clark Metal Grave Vault Co.
The finest wines of France
    Barton and Guestier
Fire up with Firebird (gasoline)
    Pure Oil Co.
Fireplace specialists for four generations
    Edwin Jackson, Inc.
First airline in the Americas
    Avianca
First and finest in copper and brass. Fully
        integrated in aluminum
    Revere Copper and Brass, Inc.
First and foremost in microfilming since
        1928
    Recordak Corp.
First and foremost line of cleaning products
        (automobile service)
    Gunk Laboratories, Inc.
First choice in fishing tackle hardware
    Allan Mfg. Co.
First choice in food, lodging and service—
        nationwide!
    Holiday Inns of America, Inc.
The first computer (Univac)
    Sperry Rand Corp.
First family in drapery hardware since 1903
    Newell Mfg. Co.
First for fast service (automobile parts)
    Federal-Mogul Corp.
First in airfreight with airfreight first
    Flying Tiger Line, Inc.
First in automated materials handling
    Barrett Electronics Corp.
First in automation (machinery)
    The Cross Co.
First in banking
    Bank of America
First in carbonless papers
    National Cash Register Co.

First in cellulose
    Buckeye Cellulose Corp.
First in dependability (outboard motors)
    Johnson Div., Outboard Marine Corp.
First in engineered plastics (C)
    Hareg Industries, Inc.
First in epoxies. . .in the age of ideas
    CIBA Products Co.
First in fabric forming equipment
    Textile Machinery Div., Crompton and
    Knowles
First in fabrics for industry
    Industrial Fabrics Div., West Point—
    Pepperell, Inc.
First in fashion (carpets)
    Patcraft Mills, Inc.
First in grassland farming (agricultural
        machinery)
    New Holland Div., Sperry Rand Corp.
First in home service
    Watkins Products, Inc.
First in Latin America
    Pan American World Airways, Inc.
First in loans to business and industry
    Chase Manhattan Bank
First in marine propulsion
    Keikhaefer Mercury Div., Brunswick
    Corp.
First in outboards
    Evinrude Motors Div., Outboard Marine
    Corp.
First in powered equipment since 1918
        (compact tractor)
    Bolens Div., FMC Corp.
First in quality!
    Nunn-Bush Shoe Co.
First in quality conveyors and driers for the
        plastics industry
    Whitlock Associates, Inc.
First in resources/first in capability
    Enco Div., Humble Oil and Refining Co.
First in sporting arms
    Browning Arms Co.
First in urethane chemistry
    Mobay Chemical Co.
First in world records
    Ashaway Line and Twine Mfg. Co.
First magazine for women
    McCall's
First name for the martini, Beefeater
        (Beefeater gin)
    Kobrand Corp.
First name in cast steel!
    Farrell-Cheek Steel Co.

The first name in custom bedding
  Hein and Kopins, Inc.
First name in filing
  Oxford Filing Supply Co.
First name in herbicide research
  Amchem Products, Inc.
First name in paper punches
  Mutual Products Co., Inc.
First name in pneumatic protection
  C. A. Norgren Co.
The first name in seats. The last word in
    quality. (bathroom fixtures)
  Beneke Corp.
The first name in textile machinery
  Platts Bros., Ltd.
First name in tire valves for original
    equipment and replacement
  A. Schrader's Son, Div. Scovill Mfg. Co.
First new no-filter cigarette in years (York)
  Lorillard Corp.
First on famous waters
  Johnson Reels, Inc.
First on the Atlantic
  Pan American World Airways, Inc.
First on the Pacific
  Pan American World Airways, Inc.
First Pennsylvania means business
  First Pennsylvania Banking and Trust Co.
First 'round the world
  Pan American World Airways, Inc.
The first taste will tell you why
    (Fleischmann's whiskey)
  Fleischmann Distilling Corp.
First to develop the latest in bat developments
  Hanna Mfg. Co.
First to serve the farmer (agricultural
    machinery)
  International Harvester Co.
First with better ways to build (Gold Bond)
  National Gypsum Co.
First with the features women want most
    (domestic appliances)
  Hotpoint Div., General Electric Co.
First with the finest in wallcoverings. . .
    always!
  Timbertone Decorative Co., Inc.
The fish hook people
  O. Mustad and Son
A flair for elegance (television)
  Sylvania Electric Products, Inc.
Flavor so delicious only your figure knows
    they're low calorie (Wish-Bone salad
    dressings)
  Thos. J. Lipton, Inc.

Fly the friendly skies of United
  United Air Lines, Inc.
The folding furniture with the permanent
    look (chairs)
  Stakmore Co., Inc.
Fond of things Italiano? Try a sip of
    Galliano
  Liquor Div., McKesson and Robbins, Inc.
The food power (R) people
  Central Soya Co., Inc.
For a big difference in your profits. . .the line
    with the big difference
  Meilink Steel Safe Co.
For a good night's sleep (Nytol)
  Block Drug Co.
For a lifetime of proud possession
  Omega Watch Co.
For a sure tomorrow—insure enough today!
  American Hardware Mutual Insurance Co.
For a taste that's Springtime fresh (Salem
    cigarettes)
  R. J. Reynolds Tobacco Co.
For accuracy, Mossberg (firearms)
  O. F. Mossberg and Sons, Inc.
For all industry
  Snap-On Tools Corp.
For all kinds of insurance in a single plan,
    call your Travelers man
  The Travelers Insurance Cos.
For almost any product, aluminum makes it
    better and Kaiser aluminum makes
    aluminum work best
  Kaiser Aluminum and Chemical Corp.
For any air conditioning
  Trane Co.
For commercial cooking. . .gas is good
    business
  American Gas Association, Inc.
For connoisseurs by connoisseurs (interior
    design accessories)
  Mottahedeh and Sons
For doctor bills
  Blue Shield
For every business need
  Nekoosa-Edwards Paper Co.
For exacting service (machinery)
  Whitey Research Tool Co.
For gifts of love (R) (jeweler)
  N. Pfeffer
For good advice. . .and good products. . .
    depend on your Mobil dealer
  Mobil Oil Corp.
For good food and good food ideas
  Kraft Fords Div., Kraftco Corp.

For heating and cooling...gas is good business
  American Gas Association, Inc.
For imagination in communication, look to
  3M business products centers
  Minnesota Mining and Mfg. Co.
For improved production through measure-
  ment and control
  The Bristol Co.
For languages, Berlitz
  The Berlitz Schools of Language of
  America
For many converting purposes
  Nekoosa-Edwards Paper Co.
For modern industry
  New Departure-Hyatt Bearings Div.,
  General Motors Corp.
For more than a century makers of fine
  furniture in traditional and modern
  idiom
  John Widdicomb Co.
For oil marketing
  National Petroleum News
For people who travel. . .and expect to again
  and again (Starflite luggage)
  The Sardis Luggage Co.
For quality paper products you can't beat
  Marathon
  Marathon Div., American Can Co.
For quality western lumber products, look
  to T, W, and J
  Tarter, Webster and Johnson Div.,
  American Forest Products Corp.
For quality you can depend on. . .depend on
  Skelgas
  Skelly Oil Co.
For serving. . .it's Erving
  Erving Paper Mills
For special industrial requirements
  Nekoosa-Edwards Paper Co.
For that certain kind of woman (retail store)
  Peck and Peck
For the beautiful point of view (R)
  (windows)
  Woodco Corp.
For the best, Hunt
  Hunt Wesson Foods, Inc.
For the best combination of filter and good
  taste Kent satisfies best (cigarettes)
  Lorillard Corp.
For the climate of excellence (periodicals)
  Cahners Publishing Co., Inc.
For the decorator touch (Best Pleat Nip-tite)
  Conso Products Co., Div. Consolidated
  Foods Corp.

For the discriminating sportsman (fishing
  tackle)
  O. Mustad and Son
For the elegant petite (coats, suits)
  Lilli-Ann Corp.
For the finest, Golfcraft
  Golfcraft, Inc.
For the girl who knows value by heart
  (brassieres)
  The Loveable Co.
For the man on the move (clothing)
  McGregor-Doniger, Inc.
For the men in charge of change
  Fortune
For the private world of the bath
  House of Wrisley, Inc.
For the smart young woman
  Mademoiselle
For the taste that's right (Viceroy cigarettes)
  Brown and Williamson Tobacco Corp.
For the typical American size (R) (women's
  apparel)
  Leslie Fay, Inc.
For the woman who dares to be different
  (Emraude perfume)
  Coty Div., Chas. Pfizer and Co., Inc.
For the women who can afford the best.
  Even though it costs less. (Hazel
  Bishop cosmetics)
  Bishop Industries, Inc.
For those who can hear the difference
  (phonograph high fidelity equipment)
  Pickering and Co., Inc.
For those who think young (Pepsi-Cola)
  Pepsico, Inc.
For those who want every puff to taste as
  fresh as the first puff! (Montclair
  cigarettes)
  American Brands Co.
For twenty-five years, first in professional
  hair care
  Rayette-Faberge, Inc.
For women whose eyes are older than they
  are (makeup)
  John Robert Powers Products Co.
. . .for your family and business—your auto,
  home and everything you own.
  Aetna Insurance Co.
The forbidden fragrance (Tabu)
  Dana Perfumes, Inc.
Foremost brand in outdoor living
  American Thermos Products Co.
The foremost in drums
  Slingerland Drums Co.

Foremost in final control elements
Conoflow Corp.
Foremost name in indoor comfort (camping lanterns, stoves, etc.)
Coleman Co., Inc.
The fourth necessity
Metropolitan Life Insurance Co.
Freight by air
Slick Airways
Fresh ideas in meat. . .from Hormel
Geo. A. Hormel and Co.
A friend of the family
Air Canada
The friendly
Franklin Life Insurance Co.
Friendly, familiar, foreign and near
Ontario, Canada, Department of Tourism and Information
Friendly land of infinite variety
South Dakota Department of Highways
The friendly world of Hilton
Hilton Hotels Corp.
From contented cows
Carnation Co.
From natural gas and oil. . .heat, power, petrochemicals that mean ever wider service to man
Tenneco, Inc.
From the land of sky blue waters (Hamm's beer)
Theo. Hamm Brewing Co.
From the largest cellars in the world (Moët champagne)
Schieffelin and Co.
From the space age laboratories of Olympic
Olympic Radio and Television Div., Lear Siegler, Inc.
From the tractor people who make the big ones
Allis-Chalmers Mfg. Co.
From world leaders in nutrition (Friskies pet food)
Carnation Co.
From the world's most renowned cosmetic research laboratories
Revlon, Inc.
Full circle packaging
Alton Box Board Co.
Full service bank
Foundation for Commercial Banks
Functional papers
Thilmany Pulp and Paper Co.
Furniture of timeless beauty (C)
Romweber Industries

Furniture that's fun to live with
H. T. Cushman Mfg. Corp.
The future are made for you, North
American Rockwell and
North American Rockwell Corp.
The future belongs to those who prepare for it
The Prudential Insurance Co. of America
The future is building now at Garrett
Garrett AiResearch, The Garrett Corp.

G

Gas makes the big difference
American Gas Association, Inc.
Gateway to and from the booming West
Union Pacific Railroad
Gateway to and from your world markets
Union Pacific Railroad
Gateway to the world of fabrics (Westgate)
Reese B. Davis and Co., Inc.
A generation of worldwide acceptance (flooring)
Torginol of America, Inc.
The gentlemen of the moving industry
North American Van Lines, Inc.
Get better yields from your fields with Armour
Get going great—with Graco (automobile service equipment)
Gray Co., Inc.
Get it in glass
Glass Containers Mfrs. Institute
Get time from a timepiece, but if you want a watch, get a Hamilton.
Hamilton Watch Co.
Get your hands on a Toyota. You'll never let go. (automobiles)
Toyota Motor Distributors, Inc.
Getting results in rural America is *Farm Journal's* business
Farm Journal
The girl with the beautiful face (TM) (make-up)
Clairol, Inc.
The girl with the beautiful mouth (lipstick)
Clairol, Inc.
Give so more will live
Heart Fund
Give your dishwasher the best (Cascade)
Procter and Gamble Co.
Gives you more to work with, Janitrol (heating, air conditioning)
Janitrol Div., Midland-Ross Corp.

Giving industry a lift since 1878
    Shephard Niles Crane and Hoist Corp.
Go first class. . .go Phillips 66 (gasoline)
    Phillips Petroleum Co.
Go international...with all the comforts of
        Hilton
    Hilton Hotels Corp.
Go where you get choosing range
    United States Borax and Chemical Corp.
Go with the pick of the pros (power tools)
    Skil Corp.
The gold medal Kentucky bourbon since
        1872 (I. W. Harper)
    Schenley Industries, Inc.
The gold standard (automobile parts)
    Wix Corp.
Golden nugget jet service
    Alaska Airlines, Inc.
Golden nugget jets
    Alaska Airlines, Inc.
A good business letter is always better. . .
        written on a Gilbert paper
    Gilbert Paper Co.
The good food service
    Prophet Co.
Good kind to keep handy—because they stay
        soft (marshmallows)
    Kraft Foods Div., Kraftco Corp.
A good name in industry (gears, drives)
    The Falk Corp.
Good people
    Olsten Temporary Services
Good people to do business with
    Employers Mutual Liability Insurance Co.
    of Wisconsin
A good society is good business
    McGraw-Hill Publications Div., McGraw-
    Hill, Inc.
Good things from the garden (canned,
        frozen vegetables)
    Green Giant Co.
The good things of life
    Bankers Life Insurance Co. of Nebraska
Good things to eat come from 1 Mustard St.
    The R. T. French Co.
Good to the last drop (coffee)
    Maxwell House Div., General Foods Corp.
Got the deepweave filter and the taste that's
        right, Viceroy's
    Brown and Williamson Tobacco Co.
Le grande liqueur francaise (Benedictine
        D.O.M.)
    Julius Wile Sons and Co., Inc.

The grass people
    O. M. Scott and Co.
The great engineers
    Borg-Warner Corp.
The great highway performers (Corvair,
        Monza)
    Chevrolet Motor Div., General Motors
    Corp.
Great legs deserve Hanes, others need them.
    Hanes Hosiery Div., Hanes, Inc.
The great name in American ceramics
    Haeger Potteries, Inc.
A great name in oil
    Sinclair Oil Corp.
Great people to fly with
    Pakistan International Airlines
Great people to ship with
    Pakistan International Airlines
The greatest line in glassware!
    Anchor Hocking Glass Corp.
The greatest name in bourbon (Old Crow)
    National Distillers and Chemical Corp.
The greatest name in building (building
        materials)
    United States Gypsum Co.
Greatest name in color (movie film)
    Technicolor Corp.
The greatest name in golf (MacGregor)
    Brunswick Sports Co.
The greatest name in health insurance
    Mutual of Omaha Insurance Co.
The greatest name in socks (Interwoven)
    Kayser-Roth Corp.
Greatest name in the great outdoors. Fore-
        most name in indoor comfort. (camp-
        ing lanterns, stoves, etc.)
    Coleman Co., Inc.
The greatest tire name in racing
    Firestone Tire and Rubber Co.
The green cleans in-between. . .the white
        polishes bright
    Pro-phy-lac-tic Brush Co.
Grow, grow by the rail way
    Association of American Railroads
The growing world of Libby-Owens-Ford Co.
    Libby-Owens-Ford Co.
Grows more beautiful with use
    Wallace Silversmiths, Div. the Hamilton
    Watch Co.
The growth company
    Georgia Pacific Corp.
Growth leader of the aluminum industry
    Consolidated Aluminum Corp.

Guaranteed, the hardest working workwear
    H. D. Lee Co., Inc.
Guardian lighting (C)
    Guardian Light Co.

H

Hair color so natural only her hairdresser
    knows for sure (TM)
    Clairol, Inc.
Hand made to fit you (golf clubs)
    Kenneth Smith
The handcrafted T.V.
    Zenith Radio Corp.
Happy motoring! (R)
    Enco Div., Humble Oil and Refining Co.
Harp-maker to the world since 1889
    Lyon-Healy Co.
Has a better idea, Ford
    Ford Motor Co.
Has the strength of Gibralter, The Prudential
    The Prudential Insurance Co. of America
Have the genius to chill it (Chartreuse)
    Schiefflin and Co.
Head of the bourbon family (Old Grand-Dad)
    National Distillers and Chemical Corp.
Headquarters for hand valves
    Barksdale Valves
Headquarters for steam-cookers
    The Cleveland Range Co.
Heirloom quality pianos since 1896
    Kohler and Campbell, Inc.
The heart of a tune-up
    Champion Spark Plug Co.
The heart of the market
    Pennsylvania Power and Light Co.
Help make him all the dog he's meant to be
    (Ken-L-Biskit)
    Ken-L-Ration Products Div., Quaker Oats
    Co.
Help yourself as you help your country
    United States Savings Bonds
.. .helping people and business help them-
    selves
    Commercial Credit Co.
Helping people communicate
    Addressograph Multigraph Corp.
Helping your product speak for itself
    (marking equipment)
    Marken Machine Co.
Helps build strong bodies 12 ways! (Wonder
    bread)
    Continental Baking Co., Inc.

Helps you do things right (hardware)
    The Stanley Works
A heritage of quality, craftsmanship, service
    Virginia Mirror Co.
Hey man!. . .say Heyman
    Heyman Mfg. Co.
High fashion in fragrance from France
    Carven Parfums
High fidelity phono cartridges. . .world stan-
    dard wherever sound quality is para-
    mount
    Shure Bros., Inc.
High-performance tirepower
    Firestone Tire and Rubber Co.
His master's voice (phonograph records)
    RCA Corp.
Holds the world together (adhesives)
    H. B. Fuller Co.
Holiday all the way with. . .Canadian Pacific
    Railway
    Canadian Pacific Railway
Home-care know-how...at your doorstep!
    Amway Corp.
The home furnishings fiber (Herculon)
    Hercules, Inc.
The homes teamwork builds
    Inland Homes Corp.
Hosiery fashion on five continents
    Berkshire International Corp.
The hospitality state
    Mississippi
Host of the highways
    Howard Johnson Co.
Hot-line claims service
    Imperial Auto Insurance
Hottest brand going! (R) (Conoco gasoline)
    Continental Oil Co.
Hottest name in golf
    Kroydon Golf Corp.
The house of experience
    Mirro Aluminum Co.
The house of flavor (spices, flavorings)
    McCormick and Co., Inc.

I

I'd walk a mile for a Camel (cigarettes)
    R. J. Reynolds Tobacco Co.
Idea leader in storage systems
    Acme Steel Co.
Idea leader in strapping
    Acme Steel Co.
Ideas that work
    McLouth Steel Corp.

If babies were born trained, they wouldn't
need Diaprene Baby Powder
Breon Laboratories, Inc.

If it flows through pipe, chances are it's controlled by Fisher (valves, controls)
Fisher Governor Co.

If it folds. . .ask Howe
Howe Folding Furniture, Inc.

If it's a bag. . .we make it!
KOBI Polyethylene Bag Mfg. Co., Inc.

If it's a question of cleaning/conditioning. . .
ask Oakite
Oakite Products, Inc.

If it's Bordens it's got to be good (dairy
products)
Borden, Inc.

If it's chairs. . .it's Miele!
Ralph A. Miele, Inc.

If it's conveyed, processed or mined, it's a
job for Jeffrey
The Jeffrey Mfg. Co.

If it's paper
Dillard Paper Co.

If Miele doesn't have it. . .no one has! (chairs)
Ralph A. Miele, Inc.

"If someone makes it—we can mark it!"
Carter's Ink Co.

If this gold seal is on it—there's better meat
in it
Wilson and Co., Inc.

If you care enough to send the very best
Hallmark Cards, Inc.

If you could see inside oranges, you'd buy
Sunkist every time.
Sunkist Growers, Inc.

If you have an instinct for quality (Amelia
Earhart luggage)
Baltimore Luggage Co.

If you prize it. . .Krylon-ize it (spray paint)
Krylon Dept., Borden Chemical Co.

If you want more than time, get a Hamilton.
Hamilton Watch Co.

If you want to give more than time, give
Hamilton
Hamilton Watch Co.

Ignition starts with P and D
P. and D. Mfg. Co.

I'm particular (Pall Mall cigarettes)
American Brands Co.

Imagination in steel for the needs of today's
architecture
Granco Steel Products Co.

Important name in the box business
Owens-Illinois Inc., Forest Products Div.

"Important occasion dresses" (R)
Lorrie Deb Corp.

Important to important people
Advertising Age

Imported from Spain, of course. True sherry
is (Duff Gordon)
Munson G. Shaw Co., Div. National
Distillers and Chemical Corp.

The imported one (Beefeater gin)
Kobrand Corp.

Importers and makers of fine furniture
Leopold Colombo, Inc.

In a word, confidence
The Carpenter Steel Co.

In a word, it's Selig (furniture)
Selig Mfg. Co., Inc.

In advance of progress
Euclid Crane and Hoist Co.

In design and performance, always a year
ahead (machinery)
Prodex Div., Koehring Co.

In fast to hold fast
Duo-Fastener Corp.

In home, health, farm and industry, science
in action for you
American Cyanamid Co.

In industry world-wide (chemicals)
Swift and Co.

In metals, plastics and paper Budd works to
make tomorrow. . .today
Budd Co.

In plastics, it's Spencer...for action
Spencer Chemical Div., Gulf Oil Corp.

In products, performance, purpose. . .Essex
measures up! (automobile parts)
C-P Fittings Div., Essex Wire Corp.

In stainless, too, you can take the pulse of
progress at Republic
Republic Steel Corp.

In the air or outer space Douglas gets things
done
Douglas Aircraft Co., Inc. (Now
McDonnell Douglas Corp.)

The incomparable (Imperial whiskey)
Hiram Walker, Inc.

The independent supplier for independents
Ashland Oil and Refining Co.

The industrial resources company
Ashland Oil and Refining Co.

Industrious Maine, New England's big stake
in the future
Maine Department of Economic Development

Industry is on the move to Iowa
Iowa Development Commission
Industry-owned to conserve property and profits
Factory Mutual Liability Insurance Co. of America
Industry spokesman to CPI management
Chemical week
Industry's friendliest climate
Public Service of Indiana, Inc.
Industry's helping hand
Rex Chainbelt, Inc.
Industry's leading insurance brokers
Marsh and McLennan, Inc.
The industry's market place
Electronics
Industry's partner in production
E. F. Houghton and Co.
Innovations that squeeze the waste out of distribution
Southern Railway Co.
"The innovators"
Torrington Co.
Innovators in the design and manufacture of quality labelling equipment
Phin, Inc.
Innovators of research-engineered products
Bostrom Corp.
"Inspection is our middle name"
Hartford Steam Boiler Inspection and Insurance Co.
Inspirations lead to new value in paper and packaging, Westvaco
Westvaco Corp.
Install confidence. . .install Thermoid (automobile equipment)
Thermoid Div., H. K. Porter Co., Inc.
Instant elevatoring (T)
Otis Elevator Co.
Instant news service (R)
Dow Jones and Co.
Instruments mean accuracy first, Taylor
Taylor Instrument Cos.
Instruments worthy of the masters since 1857 (pianos, organs)
W. W. Kimball Co.
Insurers of energy systems
Hartford Steam Boiler Inspection and Insurance Co.
Interested personal service—always—when you buy from Eastman (office equipment)
Eastman Chemical Products, Inc.

The international authority on visual merchandising
Display World
The international one (home entertainment equipment)
Toshiba America, Inc.
Internationally known mark of quality (shirts)
Manhattan Industries, Inc.
Invented by a doctor—now used by millions of women
Tampax, Inc.
Iron horse quality (agricultural equipment)
Matthews Co.
Is at work in the fields of the future, North American Aviation
North American Aviation, Inc. (now North American Rockwell Corp.)
Is experience, Garrett
Garrett AiResearch, the Garrett Corp.
Is go. . .go with it, McCord (automobile parts)
McCord Corp.
Is material handling, Clark
Clark Equipment Co.
Is more truck...day in, day out, Chevrolet
Chevrolet Motor Div., General Motors Corp.
Is saving a lot of people a lot of time, Univac (electronic data processing)
Sperry Rand Corp.
It bends with the heat (thermostatic bimetal)
W. M. Chace Co.
It floats (Ivory soap)
Procter and Gamble Co.
It gets there right in Wirebounds
Wirebound Box Mfg. Association
It leaves you breathless (R) (Smirnoff vodka)
G. F. Heublein and Bro.
It makes a dust magnet of your dust soap or cloth (Endust)
Drackett Co.
It pays to be in the news
Architectural and Engineering News
It pays to be particular about your oil
Wolf's Head Oil Refining Co., Inc.
It pays to insure with the "Blue Chip" company
Connecticut Mutual Life Insurance Co.
It pays to make it Corbin—throughout! (door lockset)
P and F Corbin Div., Emhart Corp.
It speaks for itself (Audiotape)
Audio Devices, Inc.

It takes a man to help a boy
  Big Brother
It's a National (R)
  National Tank Co., Div. Combustion
  Engineering, Inc.
It's a snap with Dot
  Carr Fastener Co.
It's always a pleasure (I. W. Harper bourbon)
  Schenley Industries, Inc.
It's built to sell when it's built of wood
  National Lumber Mfrs. Association
It's fun to own a gift by Rival (household
    products)
  Rival Mfg. Co.
It's good business to do business with
    Mallory (electronic instruments)
  P. R. Mallory and Co., Inc.
. . .it's good to have a great bank behind you
  Manufacturers Hanover Trust Co.
It's matchless (heating)
  Hunter Div., Robbins and Meyers, Inc.
Its name indicates its character
  The Lincoln National Life Insurance Co.
It's nature's freshness—indoors (air condi-
    tioning, heating)
  Lennox Industries, Inc.
It's no secret...Schilling flavor makes all the
    difference in the world!
  Schilling Div., McCormick and Co., Inc.
It's not Jockey brand if it doesn't have the
    Jockey boy
  Jockey Menswear Div., Cooper's, Inc.
"It's smart to buy right" (Highland Scotch
    Mist)
  Heublein, Inc.
It's the contacts that count (commercial
    refrigeration)
  Americo Contact Plate Freezers, Inc.
It's the going thing
  Ford Motor Co.
It's the very finest because it's Rubee
  Rubee Furniture Mfg. Corp.
It's the water (Olympia beer)
  Olympia Brewing Co.
It's uncanny (Knorr soups)
  Best Foods Div., CPC International, Inc.
It's what's inside that counts
  Explosives Div., Atlas Chemical Indus-
  tries, Inc.
It's worth it. . .it's Bud (beer)
  Annheuser-Busch, Inc.
It's worth the difference (underwear)
  Munsingwear, Inc.

It's your guarantee of quality (Con-tac cold
    remedy)
  Menley and James Laboratories

J

Jamaica's legendary liqueur (Tia Maria)
  W. A. Taylor and Co.
Jet action washers
  Frigidaire Div., General Motors Corp.
The jet that justifies itself
  North American Rockwell Corp.
The jet with the extra engine
  Western Air Lines, Inc.
The jewelers' quality watch
  Vantage Products, Inc.
"Jewelry for the home" (lamps)
  Greene Bros., Inc.
Jewelry of tradition for the contemporary
    man
  Swank, Inc.
Join with Bostik for better bonding
  B. B. Chemical Div., United Shoe
  Machinery Corp.
Just enough! (Montclair cigarettes)
  American Brands Co.
Just everyday things for the home made
    beautiful by Stevens (linens)
  J. P. Stevens and Co., Inc.
. . .just for the sun of it
  T. S. Hanseatic German Atlantic Line
Just has to be good, Borden's (dairy
    products)
  Borden, Inc.
Just smooth, very smooth (Johnnie Walker
    Red Label scotch)
  Canada Dry Corp.
Just wear a smile and a Jantzen (bathing
    suits)
  Jantzen, Inc.

K

Keep a cupboard full of cans
  National Steel Corp.
Keep Missouri in the center of your thinking
  Missouri Commerce and Industrial
  Development Commission
Keep your eye on Elliott (tools)
  Elliott Co. Div., Carrier Corp.
Keep your eye on Maidenform (brassieres)
  Maidenform, Inc.
. . .keeping tradition alive (furniture)
  Meldan Co., Inc.

Keeps the shape (synthetic fabric)
    Pellon Corp.
Keeps you in the driver's seat, Genie! (garage
        door opener)
    The Alliance Mfg. Co., Inc.
Keeps you in trim, John Lees (frames,
        mouldings)
    Cullman Products Corp.
Keeps you years ahead, Roberts (machinery)
    Roberts Co.
The "Kid Glove Treatment!" (R)
    Evans Transportation Equipment Div.,
    Evans Products Co.
The kind you cook up fresh...and quick
        (home cooked dinners)
    Kraft Foods Div., Kraftco Corp.
King of the kitchen (towels)
    Startex Mills, Inc.
The kitchen people with different ideas
    I-X-L Co., Inc.
Know the best by this mark
    Jackson China Co.
Knowledgeable people buy Imperial
        (whiskey)
    Hiram Walker, Inc.
Known by the company it keeps (Seagram's
        Canadian V.O.)
    Seagram Distillers Co.
Known for extra care
    United Air Lines, Inc.
Known in millions of homes (high fidelity
        sound equipment)
    Nutone, Inc.
Known 'round the world for quality in
        sporting goods and tires
    Dunlop Tire and Rubber Corp.
Known the world over as the world's best
        (luggage)
    Karl Seeger
Knows how to please him, Hanes (hosiery)
    Hanes Corp.
Knows the territory, Chessie
    Chesapeake and Ohio Railway

L

Label protects your table, The Wilson
    Wilson and Co., Inc.
The label to ask for
    Davidow Suits, Inc.
Lamps of elegance
    Frederick Cooper Lamps, Inc.
Land of elbow room and elbow grease
    Omaha Public Power District

Land of enchantment
    Department of Development, New Mexico
The land that was made for vacations
    Wisconsin Vacation and Travel Service
Landmark for hungry Americans
    Howard Johnson Co.
Largest selling pain reliever (Anacin)
    Whitehall Labs. Div., American Home
    Products Corp.
Lasting impressions begin with Oxford papers
    Oxford Paper Co.
The lawn people
    O. M. Scott and Co.
Lead the Ship 'n Shore life (blouses)
    Ship 'n Shore, Inc.
The leader around the world
    Cocker Machine and Foundry Co.
Leader in adhesive technology
    H. B. Fuller Co.
Leader in bathroom fashion
    Showerfold Dor Corp.
Leader in business insurance
    New York Life Insurance Co.
Leader in computer graphics
    California Computing Products, Inc.
A leader in dental research
    Squibb Beech-Nut, Inc.
Leader in prefinished hardwoods
    E. L. Bruce Co.
The leader in solid-state high-fidelity
        components
    Harmon-Kardon, Inc.
Leader in the field. Choice of the leaders.
        (pumps)
    Gilbarco, Inc.
Leader in the manufacture of custom built-in
        refrigeration
    Revco, Inc.
Leader in vibration/shock/noise control
    Lord Mfg. Co.
Leaders by design
    Precision Valve Corp.
Leaders go to Carnes for the newest in air
        distribution equipment
    Carnes Corp.
Leaders in lawn research
    O. M. Scott and Co.
Leaders in thermal engineering design
    Struthers Thermo-Flood Corp.
Leadership built on the research and experi-
        ence of over 48,000 store installations
        (store equipment)
    Bulman Corp.

Leadership in low-cost/high-reliability digital
    magnetic tape handling
    Datamec Corp.
The leadership line (physical fitness
    equipment)
    Battle Creek Manufacturers, Inc.
Leadership through accomplishment
    (thermostats)
    Therm-O-Disc, Inc.
Leadership through creative engineering
    (machinery)
    McCulloch Corp.
Leadership through design (high fidelity
    sound equipment)
    Mercury Record Corp.
Leadership through quality (utensil handling
    equipment)
    The Steril-Sil Co.
Leading direct sellers of fine fashion jewelry
    Sarah Coventry, Inc.
Leading innovators in polymer chemistry
    Goodrich-Gulf Chemicals, Inc.
Leading maker of watches of the highest
    character for almost a century
    Longines-Wittnauer Watch Co.
The leading name in dictionaries since 1847
    (Merriam-Webster)
    G. and C. Merriam Co.
Leading name in truck transportation
    Consolidated Freightways, Inc.
Leading writer of workmen's compensation,
    all forms of liability, crime, accident
    and health insurance
    American Mutual Liability Insurance Co.
Leads in automatic log computation (elec-
    tronic data processing)
    Schlumberger, Ltd.
Leads in quiet bearings that last longer,
    Hoover
    Hoover Bearing Div., Hoover Ball and
    Bearing Co.
Leads the industry in quality and dependa-
    bility (cabinets, vending machine parts)
    Universal Metal Products Div., UMC
    Industries, Inc.
Leave the driving to us
    Greyhound Corp.
Leave the moving to us
    Greyhound Corp.
Leaves you breathless, Smirnoff vodka
    G. F. Heublein and Bro.
Legsize stockings (Belle Sharmeer)
    Wayne Gossard Corp.

Let Hertz put you in the driver's seat
    Hertz Corp.
Let Lyon guard your goods (R)
    Lyon Van Lines, Inc.
Let this seal be your guide to quality (wines,
    liqueurs)
    Julius Wile Sons and Co.
Let us help put Armour idea chemicals to
    work for you
    Armour and Co.
Let your fingers do the walking (The Yellow
    Pages)
    American Telephone and Telegraph Co.
Let yourself go. . .Plymouth
    Plymouth Div., Chrysler Corp.
Let's find better ways. . .we'll follow through
    Strapping Div., Signode Corp.
Let's talk Maxitorq (machinery)
    The Carlyle Johnson Co.
Lets you take the weekends easy the year
    around! (garden tractor)
    Deere and Co.
Life at sea is like nothing on earth
    Pacific and Orient Lines
The lifeline of your equipment (industrial
    hose)
    Aeroquip Corp.
Lifelong security through programmed
    protection
    Monarch Life Insurance Co.
The light moisturizing bath oil for dry skin
    (Tender Touch)
    Helene Curtis Industries, Inc.
The light that never fails
    Metropolitan Life Insurance Co.
The "light" touch in automation and control
    (electronic instruments)
    Clairex Corp.
The lighter that works
    Zippo Mfg. Co.
Lightest smoke of all (Carlton cigarettes)
    American Brands Co.
The line and design for creative window
    planning
    Malta Mfg. Co.
The line that moves (automobile parts)
    Murray Corp.
The line with the carbon gripper (paper)
    Codo Mfg. Co.
The lipstick without the dye
    Ar-ex Products, Inc.
Live better electrically
    Edison Electric Institute

Live modern for less with gas
American Gas Association, Inc.
The live ones! (periodicals)
Cahners Publishing Co., Inc.
Living insurance
Equitable Life Assurance Society of the
United States
A living tradition in furniture
Heritage Furniture, Inc.
Localized for you (Texaco Sky Chief
gasoline)
Texaco, Inc.
Long distance is the next best thing to being
there
American Telephone and Telegraph Co.
Look ahead, look South
Southern Railway Co.
Look ahead with lead
Lead Industries Association, Inc.
Look ahead with living insurance
The Equitable Life Assurance Society of
the United States
Look-alikes aren't cook-alikes
Idaho Potato Growers, Inc.
Look for more from Morton
Morton Chemical Co., Div. Morton
International, Inc.
Look for the label with the Big Red "1"
(One-A-Day vitamins)
Miles Laboratories, Inc.
Look for the red ball (shoes)
Mishawaka Rubber Co., Inc.
Look for the Tinnerman "T", the mark of
total reliability (fastening devices)
Tinnerman Products, Inc.
Look for this famous name in the oval
(Philadelphia Brand cream cheese)
Kraft Foods Div., Kraftco Corp.
The look of quality
La Barge Mirrors, Inc.
Look risqué from the ankles down
Risqué Shoes Div., Brown Shoe Co.
Look to Eastman to look your best!
Plastic Shelving Div., Eastman Chemical
Products, Inc.
Look to Eberhard Faber for the finest...first!
(pencils)
Eberhard Faber, Inc.
Look to MFG for the shape of things to
come
Molded Fiber Glass Companies, Inc.
Look to Olds for the new
Oldsmobile Div., General Motors Corp.

Look to 3M for imagination in image-making
Duplicating Products Div., Minnesota
Mining and Mfg. Co.
Look what Plymouth's up to now
Plymouth Div., Chrysler Corp.
Looks out for you
Sentry Life Insurance Co.
Lubrication is a major factor in cost control
Texaco, Inc.
The luggage that knows its way around the
world
Samsonite Corp.
Luggage that sets the pace for luxury
Samsonite Corp.
Luxury acrylic fiber (Creslan)
American Cyanamid Co.
Luxury and comfort with utmost safety
United Air Lines, Inc.
The luxury of velvet with the worry left out
(Islon)
Textiles Div., Monsanto Co.
"Luxury for less" (R)
Ramada Inns, Inc.

M

Machines at work around the world
Joy Mfg. Co.
Machines for total productivity
Gisholt Machine Co.
Machines should work. People should think.
Office Products Div., International
Business Machines Corp.
Machines that build for a growing America
Caterpillar Tractor Co.
Machines that make data move
Teletype Corp.
Made for the professional! (R) (gasket
sealant)
Permatex Co., Inc.
Made with the extra measure of care
(Cordova guitars)
David Wexler and Co.
The magazine farm families depend on
Farm Journal
The magazine for all manufacturing
Factory
The magazine for professional builders
NAHB Journal of Homebuilding
The magazine of architectural technology
Building Construction
The magazine of broadcast advertising
Sponsor

The magazine of business leaders around the
world
Fortune
The magazine of business leadership
Fortune
Magazine of mass feeding, mass housing
Institutions
The magazine of methods, personnel and
equipment
Administrative Management
The magazine of the American market
Look
The magazine of Western living
Sunset
The magazine of world business
International Management
A magazine only a homemaker could love
Family Circle
The magazine that moves the men who move
the merchandise
Progressive Farmer
The magic of Masland carpets (R)
C. H. Masland and Sons
The magnificent (television)
Magnavox Co.
Make hard jobs easy (tools)
K-D Mfg. Co.
Make no mistake about figurework: call
Friden (office machines)
Friden Div., Singer Co.
Make Sunsweet your daily good health habit
Sunsweet Growers, Inc.
Make the capital choice
Port Authority of the City of St. Paul
Make the seasons come to you (Crystal Tips
ice machine)
McQuay, Inc.
Make your own luck with Heddon (fishing
tackle)
James Heddon and Sons
Maker of America's number 1 cat food (Puss
'n Boots)
Quaker Oats Co.
Maker of the world's first cordless electric
tools
The Black and Decker Mfg. Co.
Maker of the world's most wanted pens
Parker Pen Co.
Makers of fine shoes for men and women
Florsheim Shoe Co.
Makes good eating sense, Mazola (margarine)
Best Foods Div., CPC International, Inc.

Makes it authentic, Amerock (lumber,
building materials)
Amerock Corp.
Makes it better for you, Scott
Scott Paper Co.
Makes it easy, Skil (tools)
Skil Corp.
Makes its own gravy (Gravy Train dog food)
General Foods Corp.
Makes only particleboard and only the best,
Duraflake
Duraflake Co.
Makes practically everything best, Peerless
Peerless Roll Leaf Co.
Makes products better, safer, stronger,
lighter.
Fiber Glass Div., PPG Industries, Inc.
Makes the glass that makes the difference,
PPG
PPG Industries, Inc.
Makes the going great, Pan Am
Pan American World Airways, Inc.
Makes things run better, Gulf
Gulf Oil Corp.
Makes your husband feel younger, too. . .just
to look at you! (Loving Care hair color)
Clairol, Inc.
Making music possible for everyone
(Guitaro)
Oscar Schmidt International, Inc.
Making petroleum do more things for more
people
Atlantic Richfield Co.
Making things happen with petroleum energy
Atlantic Richfield Co.
Making today's medicines with integrity. . .
seeking tomorrow's with persistence
A. H. Robins Co.
The man from A. G. Becker is always worth
listening to (investments)
A. G. Becker and Co., Inc.
A man you can lean on, that's Klopman
(fabrics)
Klopman Mills, Inc.
Management publication of the housing
industry
House and Home
Manning the frontiers of electronic progress
Autonetics Div., North American Rock-
well Corp.
Manufacturers of creative building products
Caradco, Inc.

Manufacturers of equipment to make coal a
    better fuel
    McNally Pittsburgh Mfg. Corp.
Manufacturers of quality drapery hardware
    since 1903
    Silent Gliss, Inc.
Manufacturers of quality hardwood products
    since 1872
    Connor Lumber and Land Co.
Manufacturers of world's most widely used
    personal communications transmitters
    E. F. Johnson Co.
Mark it for the market. . .the Weber way
    Weber Marking Systems, Inc.
Mark of excellence
    General Motors Corp.
Mark of excellence (silversmiths)
    Oneida, Ltd.
The mark of quality (shavers)
    Schick Electric, Inc.
The mark of quality in tobacco products
    Brown and Williamson Tobacco Corp.
Mark of quality throughout the world
    (television)
    Admiral Corp.
The mark of total reliability ("Speednuts")
    Tinnerman Products, Inc.
"Market-directed"
    McGraw-Hill Publications Div., McGraw-
    Hill, Inc.
Marketing methods since 1850 (plastics)
    Industrial Marketing Div., Jas. H.
    Matthews and Co.
Marks practically everything best, Peerless
    Peerless Roll Leaf Co.
The massive men's market in print
    True
Master crafted
    Eljer Plumbingware Div., Wallace-Murray
    Corp.
Master craftsmen since 1890 (furniture)
    Biggs Antique Co., Inc.
Master designers of modern centrifugal
    pumps
    Morris Machine Works
Master jeweler
    Monet Jewelers
Master navigators through time and space
    A. C. Sparkplug Div., General Motors
    Corp.
Master of color finishes since 1858 (paint)
    Martin Senour Co.
Master of color since 1858
    Martin Senour Co.

Masterworkers in machinery for printing and
    converting
    Mecca Machinery Co.
Mastery of precision optics
    Varo Optical, Inc.
Matched tools for unmatched performance
    Baash-Ross Div., Joy Mfg. Co.
Matchless quality. . .superior service. . .endur-
    ing excellence (vacuum cleaners)
    Electrolux Corp.
Matchless valves for exacting service
    Whitey Research Tool Corp.
The material difference in building (Geon
    vinyls)
    B. F. Goodrich Chemical Co.
Materials and methods make the difference
    in modern building, Gold Bond
    National Gypsum Co.
Maximum capacity (Ca̅ Pac automobile parts)
    Wells Mfg. Corp.
Maximum refrigeration efficiency
    Dole Refrigeration Co.
Means better made, Rubbermaid (household
    products)
    Rubbermaid, Inc.
Means controls, Abex
    Abex Corp.
Means craftsmanship, Scandia
    Scandia Packaging Machinery Co.
Means distinction, convenience, innovation,
    protection, inventory control, service,
    C.C.A.
    Container Corp. of America
Means diesel, Cummins
    Cummins Engine Co., Inc.
Means more under-car business, Moog
    Moog Industries, Inc.
Means music to millions, Wurlitzer
    Wurlitzer Co.
Means profits for business
    State of Louisiana Department of Com-
    merce and Industry
Means progress. . .through catalysis, Houdry
    Houdry Process and Chemical Co.
Means Swissmanship, Hermes...A step be-
    yond craftsmanship (typewriters)
    Paillard, Inc.
Measure of quality (rice)
    Uncle Ben's, Inc.
Measure up with the best
    The Lufkin Rule Co.
Meats that wear the Armour star are the
    meats the butcher brings home
    Armour and Co.

Meets tomorrow's challenges today, Canon
(cameras)
Canon, Inc.
Men care for people, MONY
Mutual of New York
Men who know valves know Powell
The Wm. Powell Co.
The merchant-minded mill with variety and
reliability
Riegel Paper Corp.
Metallurgy is our business
Vanadium-Alloys Steel Co.
Miles ahead (road machinery)
The Galion Iron Works and Mfg. Co.
The mini-brutes (Opel Kadett)
Buick Motor Div., General Motors Corp.
Missile quality ball bearings
MPB, Inc.
Mix fun and history in Virginia
Virginia Department of Conservation and
Economic Development
The modern aid to appetite control (Slim-
Mint gum)
Thompson Medical Co., Inc.
Modern masters of time
Seiko Time Corp.
The modern mattress (Koylon)
Uniroyal, Inc.
The modern way to grow (sprinklers)
National Rain Bird Sales and Engineering
Corp.
Moist as homemade (Duncan Hines cake
mixes)
Procter and Gamble Co.
The Money Truck
Mack Trucks, Inc.
More and more the complete source for your
store (furniture, equipment)
The H.O.N. Co.
More choose Metropolitan. Millions more
than any other company.
Metropolitan Life Insurance Co.
The more colorful nylon (Caprolan)
Allied Chemical Corp.
More dentists use Lavoris than any other
mouthwash. Shouldn't you?
Vick Chemical Co.
More doors fold on Fold-Aside than any
other kind.
Acme Appliance Mfg. Co.
More fun per ton than any other line
Italian Line

More ideas from the Armstrong world of
interior design
Armstrong Cork Co.
The more living you do, the more you need
Samsonite (furniture)
Samsonite Corp.
More music for the money
Kay Musical Instrument Co.
More people buy Cessna twins than any
other make
Cessna Aircraft Co.
More people fly Cessna airplanes than any
other make
Cessna Aircraft Co.
More people have bought Pipers than any
other plane in the world
Piper Aircraft Corp.
More people put their confidence in Carrier
air conditioning than in any other
make
Carrier Corp.
More people ride on Goodyear tires than on
any other brand
Goodyear Tire and Rubber Co.
More power from more research
Gould-National Batteries, Inc.
More savings with Symons (building
materials)
Symons Mfg. Co.
More than a truck line—a transportation
system
Interstate Motor Freight System
More years to the gallon (Dutch Boy paints)
Pigments and Chemicals Div., National
Lead Co.
The more you learn about photography, the
more you count on Kodak.
Eastman Kodak Co.
The most beautiful copies of all
Chas. Bruning Co.
The most beautiful kitchens of them all
H. J. Scheirich Co.
The most complete line of electronic ovens
Raytheon Co.
The most elegant name in cosmetics
(DuBarry)
Lambert-Hudnut Mfg. Labs, Inc.
The most experienced food processor in the
world
Libby McNeill and Libby
The most famous name in rattan furniture
Ficks Reed Co.

Most famous name on drums
    Ludwig Drum Co.
The most important magazine to the
    world's most important people
    Time
The most in dry cleaning (One Hour
    Martinizing)
    Martin Equipment Sales, American
    Laundry Machinery Industries
The most prized eye cosmetics in the world
    Maybelline Co.
The most progressive name in steel
    Nippon Kokan
"A most remarkable airline"
    Continental Air Lines, Inc.
The most respected name in fishing tackle
    Zebco Div., Brunswick Corp.
Most respected name in power (engines)
    Briggs and Stratton Corp.
The most treasured name in perfume
    Chanel, Inc.
The most trusted name in electronics
    RCA Corp.
The most trusted name in furniture
    Drexel Enterprises, Inc.
Most trusted name in modeling
    Hawk Model Co.
The most trusted name in sound
    RCA Corp.
The most trusted name in television
    RCA Corp.
Most trusted trademark in the valve world
    Jenkins Bros.
The most useful magazine in metalworking
    American Machinist
Motivating men to sell your product is our
    business
    Maritz, Inc.
"The motor carrier with more Go-How"
    (TM)
    Eastern Express, Inc.
Mountain grown
    Almaden Vineyards, Inc.
Moves the people that move the world,
    United
    United Van Lines, Inc.
Moving up
    U.S. Van Lines, Inc.
Moving with care...everywhere (R)
    United Van Lines, Inc.
Multiple copies without carbons (NCR
    paper)
    National Cash Register Co.

The muscles of automation, Sheffer
    cylinders
    The Sheffer Corp.
Music's most glorious voice
    Hammond Organ Co.

N

The name again. . .Nationwide Life
    Nationwide Life Insurance Co.
. . .the name for fine rattan furniture
    Whitecraft, Inc.
The name for quality
    Planters Peanuts Div., Standard Brands,
    Inc.
The name for quality athletic goods
    Nocona Athletic Goods Co.
The name for quality hobby kits
    Monogram Models, Inc.
The name indicates the quality (office
    supplies)
    Keener Rubber, Inc.
The name is Crane
    Crane Co.
The name known in millions of American
    homes (ranges, ovens)
    Nutone, Inc.
The name of the game is living. Explore a
    new home today.
    National Association of Homebuilders
The name quality made famous (Zoom 8
    camera)
    Minolta Corp.
The name that means quality (Trade Wind
    ventilating hood)
    Robbins and Myers, Inc.
The name that means temperature control
    Robertshaw Controls Co.
The name that protects your name
    Watts Regulator Co.
The name that's known is Firestone—all
    over the world
    Firestone Tire and Rubber Co.
The name to look for
    Golfcraft, Inc.
A name to remember (building materials)
    Pen Metal Co., Inc.
A name you can trust (drugs, pharmaceuti-
    cals)
    Squibb Beech-Nut, Inc.
The name you can trust in margarine
    (Mazola)
    Best Foods Div., CPC International, Inc.

Named for the original American professionals
Indian Archery Corp.
The nation's big name in archery
Ben Pearson, Inc.
The nation's going-est railroad
Norfolk and Western Railway
The nation's innkeeper (R)
Holiday Inns of America, Inc.
The nation's largest airline
United Air Lines, Inc.
The nation's largest-selling drawing pencils and leads
Eagle Pencil Co.
The nation's printing papers
Howard Paper Mills Div., St. Regis Paper Co.
Nationwide, worldwide depend on. . .
Trans World Airlines, Inc.
The natural lift (Instant Postum)
General Foods Corp.
Naturally it's delicious. . .it's made by Bordens (dairy products)
Borden, Inc.
Never lets go (automobile parts)
Hammer Blow Tool Co.
"Never wear a white shirt before sundown," says Hathaway (R)
C. F. Hathaway Co.
New advances in office copying keep coming from Kodak
Eastman Kodak Co.
New concepts in corrugated packaging machinery
Huntingdon Industries, Inc.
New dimensions in driving on the safer Kelly road
The Kelly-Springfield Tire Co.
A new high in auto test equipment. . .a new high for you
Sun Electric Corp.
New ideas for happier homemaking (small appliances)
The West Bend Co.
New ideas in automation control
Photoswitch Div., Electronics Corp. of America
New leader in the lively art of electronics
Motorola, Inc.
New steels are born at Armco
Armco Steel Corp.
New taste enjoyment, new smoking convenience. . .anywhere, anytime (Roi-Tan Little Cigars)
American Brands, Inc.

Newest look in laminates (Enjay Nevamer)
Enjay Chemical Co. Div., Humble Oil and Refining Co.
News of consequence for people of consequence
U.S. News and World Report
The newsweekly that separates fact from opinion
Newsweek
Nicest next to you (undergarments)
H. W. Gossard Co.
Nickel. . .its contribution is quality
International Nickel Co.
99 44/100% pure (R) (Ivory soap)
Procter and Gamble Co.
The no. 1 buy in the design field
Product Engineering
No. 1 heavy-duty sales leader
Motor Truck Div., International Harvester Co.
No. 1 in V-belts and hose
The Gates Rubber Co.
The no. 1 men's service magazine
Argosy
The no. 1 name in billiards
Brunswick Corp.
No. 1 name in bowling
Brunswick Corp.
No. 1 source of gummed papers
Dennison Mfg. Co.
No one is in a better position to solve your lubrication problems
Manzel Div., Houdaille Industries
No sash hardware installs faster than Grand Rapids hardware
Grand Rapids Hardware Co.
No Scotch improves the flavour of water like Teacher's
Schieffelin and Co.
No-stick cooking with no-scour clean-up (Teflon)
E. I. duPont de Nemours and Co.
No water needed (Phillips' Milk of Magnesia tablets)
Glenbrook Laboratories Div., Sterling Drug, Inc.
No wonder more women rely on Ivory Liquid to help keep their hands soft, young-looking.
Procter and Gamble Co.
The nobility of Italian wines
Marchesi L and P Antinori

Not just good...but wonderful (R)
    Johnston Pies Co. Div., Ward Foods, Inc.
—not only light but deliciously light (peanut
    oil)
    Planters Peanuts Div., Standard Brands,
    Inc.
Not the biggest—but the best (Seven Seas
    slacks)
    Anthony Gesture
Nothing but nylon makes you feel so female
    Textiles Div., Monsanto Co.
Nothing but Spandex makes you look so
    female
    Textiles Div., Monsanto Co.
Nothing else quite measures up (Walker's
    De Luxe bourbon)
    Hiram Walker, Inc.
Now everybody can have Xerocopies
    Xerox Corp.
Now's the time to get away to it all
    Southwest Sun Country Association
Number 1 in acceptance (automobile parts)
    Airtex Products, Inc.

O

Obviously it must be Western Union
    Western Union Telegraph Co.
Of America's great sources of energy, only
    National serves you in so many ways
    National LP-Gas Market Development
    Council
Of the world, 'Capitol'
    Capitol Records, Inc.
Office help—temporary or permanent
    American Girl Service
Official tailors to the West
    H. D. Lee Co., Inc.
Often imitated, never duplicated (Davis
    tennis rackets)
    Victor Sports, Inc.
The oldest and largest tree saving service in
    the world
    The Davey Tree Expert Co.
Oldest in permanent type wall coverings
    Frederic Blank and Co., Inc.
On rearing children from crib to college
    Parents Magazine
On the job wherever a client's interest is at
    stake (insurance broker)
    Marsh and McLennan, Inc.
On the range
    Williams Gun Sight Co.

On-time-delivery is our #1 concern
    Reading Railroad
The one and only
    Hammond Organ Co.
The one bed frame people ask for by name
    Harvard Mfg. Co.
The one cigarette for everyone who smokes
    (Kent)
    Lorillard Corp.
The one great name in valves
    The Lunkheimer Co.
100% cotton. The fiber you can trust.
    National Cotton Council
100% guaranteed temporary office help
    Kelly Services, Inc.
One of America's great weeklies
    Railway Age
One of the many fine products that come
    from 40 years of thinking new (Gold
    Bond building materials)
    National Gypsum Co.
One of the great watches of our time
    Waltham Watch Co.
The one-man gang (R) (materials handling
    equipment)
    Towmotor Corp.
One of the many quality home-improvement
    products made by J.M.
    Johns Manville Corp.
One of the oldest names in textiles. . .for the
    newest development in synthetics
    Conmark Plastics Div., Cohn-Hall-Marx
    Co.
One proven design throughout the line
    builds greater value into every engine
    Detroit Diesel Engine Div., General
    Motors Corp.
One source, one standard—nationwide
    temporary employees)
    Kelly Services, Inc.
The "one-stop" creative lighting source
    Petelco Div., Pyle-National Co.
The one to watch for new developments
    Goodrich-Gulf Chemicals, Inc.
The ones professionals reach for, Ingersoll-
    Rand power tools
    Ingersoll-Rand Co.
Only Elgin gives you Elgineering (water
    conditioning)
    Elgin Softener, Inc.
Only her hairdresser knows for sure (hair
    color)
    Clairol, Inc.

The only name for both fuel and water
    pumps
    Airtex Products Co.
The only nicer water comes from clouds
    Servisoft Div., Water Treatment Corp.
The only 100% coverage line for cars,
    trucks, tractors, stationary engines
    Victor Mfg. and Gasket Co.
Only the rich can afford poor windows
    Andersen Corp.
The only truck bodies built like a trailer
    Fruehauf Corp.
Only when the finest is good enough
    (building materials)
    Globe Steel Products Corp.
The original and largest-selling in the world
    (cocktail mixes)
    Holland House Brands, Inc.
The original masonry wall reinforcement
    with the truss design
    Dur-O-Wal Div., Cedar Rapids Block Co.
The original polyethylene coated freezer
    wrap (Polywrap)
    St. Regis Paper Co.
The original reinforced plastic hose
    Supplex Co.
Original research serving the physician
    (drugs, pharmaceuticals)
    Sandoz, Inc.
The original self-adhesive pin-feed labels
    (Avery Tabulabels)
    Avery Label Co., Div. Avery Products
    Corp.
Originator and perfecter of the garbage
    disposer
    In-Sink-Erator Mfg. Co.
Originator and world's largest builder of
    narrow aisle trucks
    Raymond Handling Equipment, Ltd.
The originator of cultured pearls
    K. Mikimoto, Inc.
Originators and designers of ultrasonic seal-
    ing equipment
    Ultra Sonic Seal, Inc.
Originators and pioneers of allsteel stamping
    press operation
    Verson Allsteel Press Co.
Originators of prefinished hardwood flooring
    The Cromar Co.
Originators of the world-famous Utility
    (TM) ball pen
    Lindy Pen Co.
The other computer company
    Honeywell, Inc.

Our business is the intelligent use of com-
    puters
    Electronic Data Systems
Our concern is people
    Aetna Insurance Co.
Our integrity is your security
    American Warehousemen's Association
Our products are your protection
    Schwab Safe Co., Inc.
Our readers manage the country
    Successful Farming
"Our work is child's play"
    Fisher-Price Toys, Inc.
Outselling all others. . .by far (wrecking
    machinery)
    Ernest Holmes Co.
Outstanding—and they are mild (Pall Mall
    cigarettes
    American Brands, Inc.
Oven-tempered for flexible strength!
    (Reynolds Wrap)
    Reynolds Metals Co.
Over one billion dollars annually for industry
    (financial)
    Walter E. Heller and Co.
Own your share of American business
    New York Stock Exchange Members

P

Pace setting engineered systems to control
    materials in motion
    The Louis Allis Co.
Pacemakers in flexible package-makers
    Mira-Pak, Inc.
Packages better. . .for a wide range of indus-
    tries, Doughboy
    Doughboy Industries, Inc.
Packaging materials for American industry
    Cellu-Craft Products Co.
Packaging that builds and holds sales
    Alton Box Board Co.
Pain is the test that Bayer meets best
    Bayer Aspirin, Glenbrook Laboratories
    Div., Sterling Drug, Inc.
The paper people
    Brown Co.
Papers for the printer who puts quality first
    S. D. Warren Co., Div. Scott Paper Co.
Partners in progress around the world
    First National City Bank
The pattern people
    Simplicity Pattern Co., Inc.

The pause that refreshes
   The Coca-Cola Co.
The peak of Swiss watchmaking perfection
   Rado Watch Co.
Pennies more in cost. . .worlds apart in
      quality (J and B scotch)
   James Moroney, Inc.
People have faith in *Reader's Digest*
   Reader's Digest
The people movers
   Budd Co.
The people who bring you the machines that
   <u>work</u> (agricultural machinery)
   International Harvester Co.
The people who care about people who move
   Fernstrom Storage and Van Co.
The people who invented a nicer way to
      cruise
   Holland-American Line
The people who keep improving flame
      (cigarette lighters)
   Ronson Corp.
People who know buy Bigelow (carpets)
   Bigelow-Sanford, Inc.
People you can depend on to power
      America's progress
   Investor-owned Electric Light and Power
   Companies
Perfection in projection since 1909
   Da-Lite Screen Co., Inc.
Performance insurance (Ca Pāc automobile
      parts)
   Wells Mfg. Corp.
The performance line (machinery)
   HPM Div., Kolhring Co.
The perfume of romance (Chanel No. 22)
   Chanel, Inc.
Personalized cosmetic services
   Luzier, Inc.
Personalized service that makes the big
      difference
   A. L. Mechling Barge Lines, Inc.
Phone power in action (Bell Telephone
      System)
   American Telephone and Telegraph Co.
Pick a Perrine today (fishing tackle)
   Aladdin Laboratories, Inc.
Pioneer and pacemaker in essential fields of
      industry
   Firestone Tire and Rubber Co.
Pioneer in powder and molten metallurgy
   Firth Sterling, Inc.

Pioneer in the development and construction
      of electric industrial trucks
   Elwell-Parker Electric Co.
A pioneer in the leasing field (automobile)
   Emkay, Inc.
The pioneer of low fares to Europe
   Icelandic Airlines, Inc.
Pioneered the continuous extrusion process
      in 1880 (plastics machinery)
   John Royle and Sons
Pioneering in ideas for industry
   United States Gypsum Co.
Pioneers in automated lithography
   H. S. Crocker Co., Inc.
Pioneers in colored glass technology
   Houze Glass Corp.
Pioneers in hydride chemistry
   Metal Hydrides, Inc.
Pioneers in plastics
   Hopp Plastics Div., Hopp Press, Inc.
Pioneers in plastics
   Flex-O-Film, Inc.
Pioneers in pneumatic bar feeding
   Lipe-Rollway Corp.
Pioneers in polycoatings
   H. P. Smith Paper Co.
Pioneers in precision (control equipment)
   Leeds and Northrup Co.
Pioneers of disposers dedicated to quality
   National Commercial Disposers
Pipeliners of energy
   Texas Eastern Transmission Corp.
The place to go (Spain)
   Spanish National Tourist Office
The place where you keep your checking
      account
   Foundation for Commercial Banks
Plastics make a difference, Celanese
   Celanese Plastics Co., Div. Celanese Corp.
Play to win with Wilson
   Wilson Sporting Goods Co.
Please! Only <u>you</u> can prevent forest fires.
   The Advertising Council
Plus packaging
   Ekco Containers, Inc.
Plus values
   Chemical Div., General Mills, Inc.
Pool products from a name you know—
      Purex (Guardex)
   Purex Corp., Ltd.
Pop goes the Piper (Piper-Heidsieck cham-
      pagne)
   Renfield Importers, Ltd.

Portable power for progress
  Battery Div., Sonotone Corp.
Power across land and sea
  ASEA Electric Inc.
The power behind the leading products
    (motors)
  Bodine Elec. Co.
Power for progress
  Consolidated Edison Co.
Power for progress (public utility)
  The Southern Co.
The power to please (public utility)
  Florida Power Corp.
"Power to spare" (Everready flashlight
    batteries)
  Union Carbide Corp.
"Power without powder"
  Crosman Arms Co., Inc.
Powered by Howard (R) (motors)
  Howard Industries, Inc.
Practical in design. Dependable in action.
    (agricultural machinery)
  New Holland Div., Sperry Rand Corp.
Precision fishing reels since 1883
  Martin Reel Co.
The precision line
  Fellows Gear Shaper Co.
Precision machinery since 1880
  Warner and Swasey Co.
Precision typewriters
  Olympia Div., Inter-Continental Trading
  Corp.
Precisioneered by Edelmann (automobile
    testing equipment)
  E. Edelmann and Co.
Preferred for America's most distinguished
    homes (furniture)
  Romweber Industries
Prescription medicines around the world
  Eli Lilly and Co.
The pressure cooker people
  National Presto Industries, Inc.
The priceless ingredient, Squibb quality
    (drugs, pharmaceuticals)
  Squibb Beech-Nut, Inc.
Pride of Cognac since 1724 (Remy Martin)
  Renfield Importers, Ltd.
Prime source for weighing equipment and
    technology
  Toledo Scale Co.
The pro line (tape recorders)
  Roberts Div., Rheem Mfg. Co.
Probing deeper to serve you better
  Ford Motor Co. Research Laboratories

The problem solver people (TM) (automobile
    service equipment)
  Champ-Items, Inc.
The problem solvers (G.E. computers)
  General Electric
Producers of all basic urethane chemicals
  Allied Chemical Corp.
Producers of quality steel for industry and
    construction
  Laclede Steel Co.
Producers of zinc for American industry
  St. Joseph Lead Co.
Products made to measure
  Daniel Orifice Fitting Co.
Products of wood technology for construc-
    tion and industry
  Pope and Talbot, Inc.
Products that extend and protect man's
    physical senses
  American Optical Co.
The products with the pluses
  Dodge Mfg. Corp.
Products you can depend on. . .day in. . .day
    out (materials handling)
  NVF Co.
Products you can trust from people you
    know (surgical dressings)
  Will Ross, Inc.
Professional cosmetics for lovlier hair color
  Roux Labs, Inc.
The professionals
  Bekins Van and Storage Co.
"The profit line" (automobile lubrication
    equipment)
  The Shaler Co.
Progress begins with digging
  Marion Power Shovel Co.
Progress for industry worldwide
  Combustion Engineering, Inc.
Progress in the world of time
  Westclox Div., General Time Corp.
Progress is our most important product
  General Electric Co.
Progress through precision
  Torrington Co.
A progressive past. A golden future.
  Wilson Sporting Goods Co.
Progressive products for fluid control
    (metering valves)
  Manatrol Div., Perry-Fay Co.
Progressive products through chemical
    research
  Hysol Div., Dexter Corp.

Promise her anything but give her Arpege
    (perfume)
    Lanvin-Charles of the Ritz, Inc.
Promoting high standards in the public
    interest
    New York Stock Exchange
Proprietary pharmaceuticals made to ethical
    standards (Con-tac cold remedy)
    Menley and James Labs
Protecting the nation—through hometown
    agents
    Great American Insurance Cos.
Protecting the new in your pneumatics
    Wilkerson Corp.
Protection in a new light
    Monumental Life Insurance Co.
Protection in depth
    Liberty Mutual Insurance Co.
Proud bird with the golden tail
    Continental Air Lines, Inc.
Proved throughout industry for over 40
    years (anti-corrosive)
    Rust-Oleum Corp.
The prune juice with the fruit juice appeal
    (Del Monte)
    California Packing Corp.
P.S. And it's especially great as a hand lotion
    (Dermassage)
    S. M. Edison Chemical Co.
P.S. The last word in "automatic control" is
    still Robertshaw
    Robertshaw Controls Co.
P.S.—Personal service (casualty insurance)
    Aetna Insurance Co.
The pumportation people
    Gray Co., Inc.
Purposeful growth in power transmission
    Diamond Chain Co.
The pursuit of excellence
    International Flavors and Fragrances, Inc.
Put a Burke where they lurk (fishing lures)
    Flexo-Products Div., McClellan Industries
Put a tiger in your tank (Enco)
    Humble Oil and Refining Co.
Put Alliance in your appliance
    The Alliance Mfg. Co., Inc.
Put errors out of business
    Victor Computer Corp.
Put quality first and everything follows
    Fuji Electric Co., Ltd.
Put your money where the market is
    Modern Machine Shop
Puts its quality in writing
    Eberhard Faber, Inc.

Puts the "go" in ignition
    Tungsten Contact Mfg. Co.
Puts you ahead in offset duplicating
    (Ektalith)
    Eastman Kodak Co.
Puts you in the driver's seat, Hertz
    Hertz Corp.
Putting ideas to work. . .in machinery, chemi-
    cals, defense, fibers and films
    FMC Corp.
Putting the "push" in America's finest
    aerosols (Genetron)
    Allied Chemical Corp.
Putting you first, keeps us first
    Chevrolet Motor Div., General Motors
    Corp.

Q

Quality all the way (commercial kitchen
    equipment)
    The Hobart Mfg. Co.
Quality at your feet (R)
    Brown Shoe Co.
Quality electronic components
    Allen-Bradley Co.
The quality equipment line (automobile
    parts)
    Bishman Mfg. Co.
Quality fastening products for industry
    Simmons Fastener Corp.
Quality first. . .from America's first penmaker
    Esterbrook Pen Co.
Quality food products used with confidence
    (commercial)
    Procter and Gamble Co.
Quality foods (commercial)
    John Sexton Co.
The quality goes in before the name goes on
    (R) (television)
    Zenith Radio Corp.
Quality is standard equipment
    Mosler Safe Co.
The quality line (automobile parts)
    Wagner Electric Corp.
The quality line that's easy to find (auto-
    mobile parts)
    Dorman Products, Inc.
Quality-made by Illinois Shade
    Illinois Shade Div., Slick Industrial Co.
The quality mark to look for (glass)
    Libbey-Owens-Ford Co.

Quality motor control
  Allen-Bradley Co.
The quality name in air conditioning and
    refrigeration
  York Corp.
A quality name in forest products
  Long-Bell Lumber Co.
Quality papers for industry since 1889
  Sonoco Products Co.
Quality parts for auto makers and owners
  Holley Carburetor Co.
Quality products for quality living (building
    materials)
  Mirawal Co.
Quality products known throughout the
    world for engineered quality (restau-
    rant equipment, supplies)
  Bastian-Blessing Co.
Quality runs deep, Rust-Oleum (anti-
    corrosive)
  Rust-Oleum Corp.
Quality seals build the reputation of profes-
    sional mechanics
  Chicago Rawhide Mfg. Co.
Quality shows through
  Drew Furniture Co.
Quality since 1846
  Philadelphia Carpet Co.
Quality. . .the best economy of all
  Sun Oil Co.
Quality through craftsmanship (radio receiv-
    ing apparatus)
  The Hallicrafters Co.
Quality toys with a purpose (Tinkertoy)
  Toy Tinkers Div., A. G. Spalding and
  Bros., Inc.
Quality trucks always cost less
  Chevrolet Motor Div., General Motors
  Corp.
Quality turns on Timken
  Timken Roller Bearing Co.
Quality you can trust
  Crown Central Petroleum Corp.
Quality you can trust. Value you can recog-
    nize. (electrical appliances, house-
    wares)
  Iona Mfg. Co.
The quick brown fox (Smith-Corona type-
    writers)
  SCM Corp.
The quick kind you cook up fresh (home
    cooked dinners)
  Kraft Foods Div., Kraftco Corp.

R

The railroad of "creative crews"
  Milwaukee Road
The railroad of planned progress. . .geared to
    the nation's future
  Rock Island Lines
"The railroad that runs by the customer's
    clock"
  Nickel Plate Railroad
The railroad that's always on the move
    toward a better way
  Santa Fe System Lines
"The railroad is the right way"
  French National Railroads
A rainbow of distinctive flavors (Hiram
    Walker's cordials)
  Hiram Walker-Gooderham and Worts, Ltd.
Reach for the Campbell's. It's right on your
    shelf.
  Campbell Soup Co.
Reach her when home is on her mind
  American Home
Read and preferred by construction men
  Construction Methods and Equipment
A real cigarette (Camel)
  R. J. Reynolds Tobacco Co.
Real farm sausage from a real Wisconsin farm
  Jones Dairy Farm
Real gusto in a great light beer (Schlitz)
  Jos. Schlitz Brewing Co.
The real thing from Florida (orange juice)
  Florida Citrus Commission
Really cares about people who care, Tussy
    (deodorant)
  Lehn and Fink Products Corp.
Really cares about the sorcery of scent,
    Tussy
  Lehn and Fink Products Corp.
Recommended by dentists surveyed 9 to 1
    over all toothpastes combined
    (Polident)
  Block Drug Co., Inc.
Recordings for the connoisseur
  Vanguard Recording Society, Inc.
The red nylon ring of reliability
  Elastic Stop Nut Corp. of America
The reels of champions
  Penn Fishing Tackle Mfg. Co.
Re-equip/equip and profit
  Ammco Tools, Inc.
Re-equip/equip and profit with Bear (auto-
    mobile service equipment)
  Bear Mfg. Co.

Refrigeration is our business. . .our only
business
Norcold, Inc.
The registered symbol of quality since 1908
(R) (plastics molding)
Garfield Mfg. Co.
Relax, you're on Air-India
Air-India
Reliables. . .the powerful performers, Reo
(power lawn, garden equipment)
Wheel Horse Products Co.
Reliability in rubber, asbestos, sintered
metal, specialized plastics
Raybestos-Manhattan, Inc.
Relief is just a swallow away (Alka Seltzer)
Miles Laboratories, Inc.
Rely on T I
Texas Instruments, Inc.
Rely on us
Louisville and Nashville Railroad
The remarkable new carpet that's flooring
the country (Densylon)
Commercial Carpet Corp.
Remember: no one is paid to play Titleist
(golf balls)
Acushnet Co.
Research in the service of medicine
G. D. Searle and Co.
The responsibility of being the best (Wild
Turkey bourbon)
Austin Nichols and Co., Inc.
Restituimus—"We restore". . .since 1854
Phoenix of Hartford Insurance Cos.
The retailer's line
National Blank Book Co.
Rhymes with increase (Cantrece) (synthetic
fabric)
E. I. duPont de Nemours and Co.
The rice people, Uncle Ben's
Uncle Ben's, Inc.
"The right business form for every form of
business"
Moore Business Forms, Inc.
The right hand of production
Industrial Distributors, Ltd.
The right hoist for every application
Harnischfeger Corp.
The right tool for the right job
True Temper Corp.
Road to the future
New York Central System
The rocket action car
Oldsmobile Div., General Motors Corp.

The roll specialists (paper, paper products)
Eastern Specialties Co., Inc.
Round the calendar comfort (air condition-
ing, heating)
Lennox Industries, Inc.
The round tire that rolls 3,000 miles further
(Atlas Plycron)
General Tire and Rubber Co.
Route of the incomparable empire builder
Great Northern Railway
Route of the Vista-Dome North Coast Limited
Northern Pacific Railway
Royal family of home fashions (linens)
Cannon Mills, Inc.
The royalty of lamps
The Stiffel Co.
Rugs, carpets since 1825
Bigelow-Sanford, Inc.
A rum to remember, Ronrico
General Wine and Spirits Co.
"Run away to sea with P and O"
Pacific and Orient Lines

S

Safe as America
United States Savings Bonds
The safe way out
Von Duprin Div., Vonnegut Hardware
Co., Inc.
Sail a happy ship
Holland-American Line
The salt of the earth
Potash Co. of America
Sane toys for healthy kids
Lionel Toy Corp.
Sanitize your dishes sparkling clean (dish-
mobiles)
Frigidaire Div., General Motors Corp.
Satisfies best (Kent cigarettes)
Lorillard Corp.
Saving ways in doorways (rolling doors)
The Kinnear Mfg. Co., Inc.
Say it with flowers
Florists' Transworld Delivery Association
Say Seagrams and be sure (7 Crown)
Seagrams Distillers Co.
Science for the world's well-being (R) (drugs,
pharmaceuticals)
Chas. Pfizer and Co., Inc.
The seal mechanics see most, use most
Chicago Rawhide Mfg. Co.

The search ends at Wellington Sears (textiles)
  West Point-Pepperell, Inc.
The seat of the in house (bathroom fixtures)
  Magnolia Products, Inc.
Security is our business (insurance)
  United of Omaha
See America best by car
  American Petroleum Institute
See how much better an airline can be
  Eastern Air Lines, Inc.
See what air can do for you (compressors)
  Gardner-Denver Co.
See what air-conditioning is doing now. . .See
    Gardner-Denver
  Gardner-Denver Co.
See what happens when you start using
    American ingenuity
  Standard Oil Div., American Oil Co.
Sell at the decision level
  Business Week
Sell Simpson and be sure (building materials)
  Simpson Timber Co.
Sell the man who talks to the farmer just
    before the sale
  Farm Store Merchandising
Selling and advertising to business and
    industry
  Industrial Marketing
Sells easy. . .sells fast. . .makes resales (build-
    ing materials)
  Insulite Div., Minnesota and Ontario
  Paper Co.
Sells hard wherever hardware sells
  Hardware Age
"Send me a man who reads!" (C)
  International Paper Co.
The sensible spectaculars
  American Motors Corp.
Serves the man who makes a business of
    agriculture, Cyanamid
  American Cyanamid Co.
Serves the South, Southern
  Southern Railroad Co.
Serves you first (R)
  Independent Insurance Agent
Service-backed shop equipment
  Snap-On Tools Corp.
Service first
  Houston Lighting and Power Co.
"Service guaranteed for life" (fishing tackle)
  The Garcia Corp.
SERVICE, in the broadest sense, is the dif-
    ference (public utility)
  Century Electric Co.

Service is the difference (public utility)
  Century Electric Co.
The service shop authority
  Motor Service
Service that never sleeps
  Reynolds Aluminum Supply Co.
Service to medicine (R)
  Wyeth Laboratories Div., American Home
  Products Corp.
Serving America's schools, homes, commerce
    and industry (publishing)
  Rand McNally and Co.
Serving industry constructively since 1902
  Miller Freeman Publications
Serving the Golden Empire
  Southern Pacific Co.
Serving man's need for knowledge. . .in many
    ways (publishing)
  McGraw-Hill, Inc.
Serving the big river region
  Texas Gas Transmission Corp.
Serving the businessman in the blue denim
    suit (Master Mix)
  Central Soya Co., Inc.
Serving you (Bell Telephone System)
  American Telephone and Telegraph Co.
Serving you around the world. . .around the
    clock
  The St. Paul Insurance Cos.
Sets the standard in world-wide insurance
    brokerage service, J and H
  Johnson and Higgins
Sets the standards for the gasketing industry,
    FEL-PRO
  Felt Products Mfg. Co., Inc.
Setting new standards in sound (phonograph
    high fidelity systems)
  Electro-Voice, Inc.
Seven leagues ahead (R) (ovens)
  Thermador Electrical Mfg. Co., Div. Norris
  Industries, Inc.
7-Up your thirst away
  The Seven-Up Co.
Shapemakers to the world's most beautiful
    women
  Treo Co., Inc.
Shares the risk. . .to assure performance,
    Bodine (machines)
  Bodine Corp.
Sharing greatly in America's growth
  General Telephone and Electronics Corp.
Sharing the responsibilities of modern
    medicine
  Stanlabs, Inc.

She has it made (TM) (lipstick)
    Clairol, Inc.
"Sheeting action" (Cascade detergent)
    Procter and Gamble Co.
The shoe with a memory (Johnston and
        Murphy)
    Genesco, Inc.
The shoe with the beautiful fit (Naturalizer)
    Brown Shoe Co., Inc.
Shot from guns (breakfast cereal)
    Quaker Oats Co.
Shows the way! (building materials)
    Masonite Corp.
Sign of a better future for you
    Shell Oil Co.
"Sign of happy travel" (motels)
    Downtowner Corp.
Sign of the leader in lawn/garden equipment
    Wheel Horse Products Co.
Sign of the right time
    Zodiac Watch Co.
The sign of tomorrow. . .today
    General Tire and Rubber Co.
The silent drapery track (R)
    Silent Gliss Inc.
Silent partners in famous foods (R) (color-
        ing, flavoring)
    Stange Co.
Simply say Delco (storage batteries)
    General Motors Corp.
Since 1720, a family heritage of careful boat
        building
    C. P. Leek and Sons, Inc.
Since 1808, a tradition in factoring and
        financing
    William Iselin and Co., Inc.
Since 1833. . .Better vision for better living
    American Optical Co.
Since 1846, the quality of elegance underfoot
    Philadelphia Carpet Co.
Since 1847, the trusted and authoritative
        name in dictionaries
    G and C Merriam Co.
Since 1857. . .the standard of excellence in
        men's footwear (Foot-Joy)
    Brockton Footwear, Inc.
Since 1867 maker of watches of the highest
        character
    Longines-Wittnauer Watch Co.
Since 1867. . .the first name in materials
        handling
    The Louden Machinery Co.

Since 1874 stringed instrument house of the
        masters
    William Lewis and Son
Since 1886. . .scientifically designed for prac-
        tical use (fertilizer, agricultural equip-
        ment)
    John Blue Co., Inc.
Since 1904 fine plumbing fixtures
    Eljer Plumingware Div., Wallace-Murray
        Corp.
Since 1921. . .the engine builders source
    Muskegon Piston Ring Co.
Since 1922, leader in motivating people
    E. F. MacDonald Co.
Since 1928—industry leadership in heating
        and air conditioning
    Fraser and Johnston Co.
Six and a half billion dollars of protection
        for our policy holders
    Great-West Life Assurance Co.
The skier's tailor since 1929
    White Stag Mfg. Co.
A skilled hand in chemistry. . .at work for
        you
    Nopco Chemical Co.
Sleeping on a Sealy is like sleeping on a cloud
    Sealy Mattress Co.
The small business that got big serving small
        business
    Sentry Insurance Co.
Smart, smooth, sensibly priced (Gilbey's
        vodka)
    National Distillers and Chemical Corp.
Smoke all 7 (Viceroy cigarettes)
    Brown and Williamson Tobacco Co.
Smoked with hickory (hams)
    Rath Packing Co.
Smokes fresher—and tastes better than any
        other cigarette, Newport
    Lorillard Corp.
Smoothing industry's pathway for nearly
        half a century
    Messinger Bearings, Inc.
So beautifully practical (ovens, ranges)
    Jenn-Air Corp.
So glamorous you have to be told they're
        hypo-allergenic (Almay cosmetics)
    Schieffelin and Co.
So high in fashion. . .so light in weight
    Ventura Travelware, Inc.
So long as the rig is on the location
    Drilling

47

So new! So right! So obviously Cadillac.
Cadillac Motor Car Div., General Motors
Corp.
So soft. . .it comes in a tub (Chiffon mar-
garine)
Anderson, Clayton and Co.
Soft whiskey (Calvert Extra)
Calvert Distillers Co., Div. The House of
Seagram, Inc.
Softness freshens your taste, Salem
R. J. Reynolds Tobacco Co.
Softness is Northern (toilet paper)
Marathon Div., American Can Co.
Sold by more dealers than any other brand
(mufflers)
A. P. Parts Corp.
Solid comfort seating
Hampden Specialty Products Co.
Soothes. Cleanses. Refreshes. (eyedrops)
Murine Co., Inc.
The sound approach to quality (phonograph
high fidelity equipment)
Kenwood Electronics, Inc.
The sound investment (pianos)
D. H. Baldwin Co.
The source for answers to wire problems
Page Steel and Wire Div., American Chain
and Cable Co.
The South's oldest makers of fine furniture
White Furniture Co.
Spanning the spectrum of packaging
(Reynolds Aluminum)
Reynolds Metals Co.
Special chemicals for industry
Carlisle Chemical Works, Inc.
Specialist in enamel papers/printing paper
Consolidated Paper Co.
The specialist in plate steels
Lukens Steel Co.
Specialists in digital technology
California Computer Products, Inc.
Specialists in farmstead mechanization
(agricultural machinery)
New Holland Div., Sperry Rand Corp.
Specialists in filing supplies and equipment
since 1894
The Weis Mfg. Co.
Specialists in financing
Associates Investment Co.
Specialists in fluid power control
Waterman Hydraulics Corp.
Specialists in frozen food packaging
Iceland Products, Inc.

Specialists in high polymers
Polyvinyl Chemicals, Inc.
Specialists in international jet service to
Texas or South America
Braniff Airways, Inc.
Specialists in making water behave
Anderson Chemical Co., Inc.
Specialists in process and energy control
The Foxboro Co.
Specialists in seating—and seating only—
since 1947
Harter Corp.
Specialists in skin care
Chap Stick Co.
Specialists in solving unusual heating
problems
Glas-Col Apparatus Co.
Specialists in the application of adhesives
(paper)
The Brown-Bridge Mills, Inc.
Specialty chemicals for industry
Carlisle Chemical Works, Inc.
The specialty steel company
Latrobe Steel Co.
Specify Spicer (automobile parts)
Spicer Div., Dana Corp.
Speed. Simplicity. Versatility. (business
machines)
Dura Corp.
"Speed with economy"
Yale Express System, Inc.
Speedy is its middle name (Alka-Seltzer)
Miles Laboratories, Inc.
Spirited new scent of the sixties (Richard
Hudnut Sportsman)
Cosmetics and Toiletries Div., Warner-
Lambert Pharmaceutical Co.
Sports isn't just fun and games
Sports Illustrated
The sportsman's car (BMW)
Bavarian Motor Works
Sportswear for sportsmen
Jantzen, Inc.
Stampede of power (Exide storage batteries)
ESB, Inc.
Standard of the plotting industry
California Computer Products, Inc.
Standard of the world
Cadillac Motor Car Div., General Motors
Corp.
The star's address, CBS
Columbia Broadcasting System, Inc.
Start with—stay with Knox
Knox Gelatine, Inc.

State of excitement
  Oregon Highway Dept.
Stay fit for fun with Phillips (Phillips' Milk
    of Magnesia)
  Glenbrook Labs Div., Sterling Drug, Inc.
Stays on till you take it off (Coty 24 Hour
    lipstick)
  Coty, Div., Chas. Pfizer and Co., Inc.
A step ahead of tomorrow
  Zurn Industries, Inc.
Stops rust! (R) (anti-corrosive)
  Rust-Oleum Corp.
A store a woman should look into
  Hoffritz for Cutlery
Store more. . .better. . .at less cost
  Vidmar, Inc.
The straight-talk tire people
  B. F. Goodrich Tire Co.
The strength of Gibraltar
  Prudential Insurance Co. of America
Style authority in wrought iron (furniture)
  Lee L. Woodward Sons, Inc.
The successful ones (agricultural hybrids)
  P-A-G Div., W. R. Grace and Co.
Sugar's got what it takes
  Sugar Information, Inc.
Sunlane (R) cruises to Europe
  American Export Isbrandtsen Lines, Inc.
Super-moisturizes dry skin zones instantly!
    (Dermassage)
  S. M. Edison Chemical Co.
Super service . . . .
  T.I.M.E. Freight, Inc.
The superior brake fluid
  Wagner Electric Corp.
Superior performance through design
    simplicity
  Triangle Package Machinery Co.
Sure has a way with water, Calgon Corpora-
    tion
  Calgon Corp.
The sure test. . .Scott (machinery)
  Scott Testers, Inc.
The surprise of Formica products (interior
    decoration)
  Formica Corp.
The surprising state
  State of Washington
Swisscare. Worldwide.
  Swiss Air Transport Co., Ltd.
Swiss-care world-wide on the privately
    owned airline of Switzerland.
  Swiss Air Transport Co., Ltd.

Symbol of accuracy since 1870
  Marlin Firearms Co.
Symbol of excellence (gasoline pumps)
  Tokheim Corp.
Symbol of excellence in West German optics
    (Zeiss Ikon)
  Carl Zeiss, Inc.
Symbol of quality (R)
  Potlatch Forests, Inc.

T

Takes a load off your mind, Big Joe (mate-
    rials handling)
  Big Joe Mfg. Co.
Takes good care of you, BOAC
  British Overseas Airway Corp.
Takes many shapes to serve you, O-I Plas-
    technics (packaging)
  Ownes-Illinois Glass Co.
Takes the burden out of keeping up your
    home, Bird (building materials)
  Bird and Son, Inc.
Takes the guessing out of dressing (R)
  Wembley Ties, Inc.
Talk things over, get things done. . .by long
    distance! (Bell Telephone System)
  American Telephone and Telegraph Co.
Talk to the right people in the right places
  Time
The talked-about jewelry
  Castlecliff, Inc.
The tape that won't hurt coming off
    (Micropore)
  Minnesota Mining and Mfg. Co.
The tapeway to stereo (R)
  Sony Corp. of America
Taste as good as they make you feel (Tums)
  Lewis-Howe Co.
Taste that beats the others cold (Pepsi-Cola)
  Pepsico, Inc.
The taste that sets the trend
  Harper's Bazaar
The taste that's right (Viceroy cigarettes)
  Brown and Williamson Tobacco Corp.
Tastes better than any other menthol ciga-
    rette (Newport)
  Lorillard Corp.
Tastes good. . .like a cigarette should, Winston
  R. J. Reynolds Tobacco Co.
Tastes great. . .tastes mild, Chesterfield King
    (cigarettes)
  Liggett and Meyers, Inc.

Tastes great. . .yet it smokes so mild (Chester-
field cigarettes)
    Liggett and Meyers, Inc.
Tastes so good and so good for you (Cream
of Rice)
    Grocery Store Products Co.
Taxpaying servant of a great state
    New Jersey Public Service Electric and
    Gas Co.
A team of specialists
    Cameron Machine Co.
Temperatures made to order
    Harrison Radiator Div., General Motors
    Corp.
The tender-textured gelatin (Royal)
    Standard Brands, Inc.
The tender tuna with the delicate taste
    Star Kist Foods, Inc.
Test drive total performance '65
    Ford Motor Co.
Thank goodness for Banquet cooking bag
foods
    Banquet Canning Div., F. M. Stamper Co.
Thank goodness for Banquet frozen foods
    Banquet Canning Div., F. M. Stamper Co.
Thanks for using coast line
    Atlantic Coast Line Railroad
That Bud. . .that's beer!
    Anheuser-Busch, Inc.
There are imitations—be sure the brand is
    Tabasco (food sauce)
    McIlnenny Co.
There are imitations, of course (fabric)
    Viyella International, Ltd.
There is no equal (mass feeding equipment)
    Lowerator Div., American Machine and
    Foundry Co.
"There is nothing better in the market" (Old
    Forester bourbon)
    Brown-Forman Distillers Corp.
"There is nothing finer than a Stromberg-
    Carlson" (radios)
    Stromberg-Carlson Corp.
There should be a Lee in your future
    Lee Machinery Corp.
There's a good future with Mobil
    Mobil Oil Co.
There's a need-keyed billfold for you
    Amity Leather Products Co.
There's a quality about a home with Hen-
    redon
    Henredon Furniture Industries, Inc.

There's a world of difference in Webster
dictionaries
    G. and C. Merriam and Co.
There's no obligation. . .except to those you
love
    Metropolitan Life Insurance Co.
There's no place like this showplace!
    Chicago Merchandise Mart
These names assure you the best in pneu-
    matic, hydraulic and electronic com-
    ponents
    Bellows-Valvair Div., International Basic
    Economy Corp.
They always eat better when you remember
the soup
    Campbell Soup Co.
They fit (Round-the-Clock stockings)
    National Mills Div., U.S. Industries
Things go better with Coke
    The Coca-Cola Co.
The things we'll do to make you happy
    Trans World Airlines
Think ahead—think SCM (typewriters)
    SCM Corp.
Think copper
    Anaconda Co.
Think original, think Dellinger (carpets)
    Dellinger, Inc.
Think straight. . .think Rollway
    Rollway Bearing Co.
Think system
    Scientific Anglers, Inc.
Thinks ahead with textiles, Sandoz (dyes)
    Sandoz, Inc.
This is living. . .this is Marriott
    Marriott Motor Hotels, Inc.
This is no place for "second best" (Hell-
    mann's mayonnaise)
    Best Foods Div., CPC International, Inc.
This is the center of industrial America
    Ohio Edison-Pennsylvania Power
This is the dream you can be—with Maiden-
    form (brassieres)
    Maidenform, Inc.
This is the open world of LOF glass
    Libbey-Owens-Ford Co.
This is the way to run a railroad
    Northern Pacific Railway
This one means business (airplanes)
    Hawker Siddeley Group, Ltd.
Those heavenly carpets by Lees
    James Lees and Sons Co.

Thoughtfully designed with a woman in
    mind (Bowlene cleaner)
    The Climalene Co.
Three steps to safety (brake lining)
    Grey Rock Div., Raybestos-Manhattan,
    Inc.
Thundering power in the eye of the market
    Metalworking News
A title on the door rates a Bigelow on the
    floor
    Bigelow-Sanford, Inc.
To be sure you're right. . .insist on Merriam-
    Webster (dictionaries)
    G. and C. Merriam Co.
To energize your sales curve, put power
    behind it
    Power
To feel new power, instantly, install new
    Champions now and every 10,000
    miles
    Champion Spark Plug Co.
To get more that's good. . .trust Swanson
    (frozen dinners)
    Campbell Soup Co.
To serve something fancy start with some-
    thing fancy (Flav-R-Pac)
    Stayton Canning Co., Co-op
To "test with the best" (automobile parts
    service)
    Imperial Eastman Corp.
"Tobacco is our middle name" (C)
    American Brands, Inc.
Today's finest-designed for tomorrow's
    needs (camera equipment)
    Charles Beseler Co.
Today's ideas. . .engineered for tomorrow
    (machinery)
    Powermatic, Inc.
Today's leader in tomorrow's look (radio
    receiving apparatus)
    Panasonic
Tomorrow is a friend of Dunbar (R)
    Dunbar Furniture Corp.
Tomorrow's skin care—today
    Coty Div., Chas. Pfizer and Co., Inc.
The tone heard 'round the world (musical
    instruments)
    Wm. S. Haynes Co.
The tool box of the world
    Stanley Tool Div., Stanley Works
Top quality for 50 years
    General Tire and Rubber Co.
Tops everything for lasting beauty (Nevamar)
    National Plastics Products Co.

Tops them all 'Cap' Resina
    Resina Automatic Machinery Co., Inc.
Total capability in fire protection (alarm
    system)
    Grinnell Corp.
Total communications from a single source
    through Sylvania (Sylvania Electric
    Products, Inc.)
    General Telephone and Telegraph Co.
Total environmental control (cold storage)
    Tectrol Div., Whirlpool Corp.
Total performance
    Ford Motor Co.
Total quality (pianos, organs)
    W. W. Kimball Co.
Total transportation (motor truck bodies)
    Fruehauf Corp.
The touch of tomorrow in office living
    (office equipment)
    The Globe-Wernicke Co.
The tough breed of tire
    The B. F. Goodrich Co.
The tough pumping problems go to Aldrich
    Aldrich Pump Co.
The tractor people, Allis-Chalmers
    Allis-Chalmers Mfg. Co.
The traveler's world
    Venture
Treasured American glass
    Viking Glass Co.
Tri-sure the world over (packaging)
    American Flange and Mfg. Co., Inc.
The true old-style Kentucky bourbon (Early
    Times)
    Brown-Forman Distillers Corp.
Trust in Phillips is world-wide
    Phillips Research Laboratories
Trust your car to the man who wears the star
    Texaco, Inc.
The trusted and authoritative name in dic-
    tionaries (Merriam-Webster)
    G. and C. Merriam Co.
The trusted name in household products
    since 1917
    Gem, Inc.
Trusted name. . .proved by medical research
    and the experience of millions (Niagra
    Cyclo-Massage)
    Niagra Therapy Mfg. Corp.
A trustworthy name in electrical protection
    (Buss fuses)
    Bussmann Mfg. Div., McGraw-Edison Co.
The tuned car
    Buick Motor Div., General Motors Corp.

12 kinds–better than most people make
(Heublein cocktails)
Heublein, Inc.

The 21st century company
Gulf and Western Industries, Inc.

The "Twin Formula" head cold tablet
(Vics Tri-Span)
Vick Chemical Co.

Twin names in quality towels (Martex and
Fairfax)
West Point-Pepperell, Inc.

Two layers of softness. . . and one is purest
white (Aurora toilet paper)
Marathon Div., American Can Co.

The two most trusted names in meat (Swift's
Premium)
Swift and Co.

Two scotches of exceptional character
("Black and White")
Fleischmann Distilling Corp.

U

The unbeatable way to jet home
Western Air Lines, Inc.

The uncola–7-Up
The Seven-Up Co.

Unique in all the world (Thunderbird)
Ford Motor Co.

"Unlocking new concepts in architectural
hardware since 1839" (keys)
Russwin-Emhart Corp.

Unmistakably. . .America's premium quality
beer
Falstaff Brewing Corp.

Unquestionably the world's finest stereo-
phonic console
Pilot Radio Corp.

The "Unstoppables"
Kaiser Jeep Corp.

Unusually reliability and service. . .the usual
at Kopp Glass
Kopp Glass, Inc.

Unwind your way to Europe
Italian Line

Up, up and away (S.M.)
Trans World Airlines, Inc.

"Us Tareyton smokers would rather fight
than switch!"
American Brands, Inc.

Use-engineered for cleaning, protecting and
processing
DuBois Chemical Div., W. R. Grace and
Co.

Used where performance counts
Grant Oil Tool Co.

Useful products for family living
Hamilton Cosco, Inc.

V

The vacation way to Hawaii
Matson Navigation Co.

Vacationing in San Antonio is a family affair
San Antonio Municipal Information
Bureau

Value-engineered papers from the mills of
Mosinee
Mosinee Paper Mills Co.

Value engineering favors zinc
American Zinc Institute

"Value" is a good word for Benefit Trust
Life
Benefit Trust Life Insurance Co.

Value keeps you years ahead, Roberts
(machinery)
Roberts Co.

Verified insulation performance
Owens-Corning Fiberglas Corp.

The very best in floor care products (vacuum
cleaners)
Eureka Williams Co.

The very best in temporary help
Manpower, Inc.

The very good washer (RCA Whirlpool)
Whirlpool Corp.

Vital link in America's supply line
Transamerican Freight Lines, Inc.

W

Wash easier, dry faster, absorb more, wear
longer (Curity diapers)
Textile Div., The Kendall Co.

Watch Hughson. . .for progress through creative research
Hughson Chemical Co., Div. Lord Corp.

The way the best lemons sign their name
Sunkist Growers, Inc.

The way to get there
Iberia Airlines of Spain

We care about color (carpets)
Simon Manges and Son, Inc.

We know where you're going
Air France

"We like it here"
Wisconsin Div. of Economic Development

We mass produce quality! (tubing)
Atlas Bradford Co.

We move families, not just furniture
Allied Van Lines, Inc.
We pamper passengers throughout mid-
central U.S.A.
Lake Central Airlines, Inc.
We take better care of your car
Standard Oil Co.
We try harder (automobile leasing)
Avis, Inc.
We want you to hear more music (high
fidelity equipment)
Harmon Kardon, Inc.
Wear tested for your comfort (Jarman shoes)
Genesco, Inc.
"Weavers of the world's finest netting"
Victory Sports Net Div., The Fishnet and
Twine Co.
The weekly news magazine
Time
Welcome aboard
United Air Lines, Inc.
"Well dressed/wool dressed"
American Wool Council
We'll wait. Grant's 8 (R) (scotch)
Austin, Nichols and Co., Inc.
We're synergistic
Sperry Rand Corp.
We've just begun to grow
Keene Corp.
What next from Alcoa!
Aluminum Co. of America
What Scandinavian men have (Teak toilet
goods)
Shulton, Inc.
What you want is a Wollensak (tape recorder)
Revere-Wollensak Div., Minnesota Mining
and Mfg. Co.
What's happening. In business. To business.
Nation's Business
What's new? Ask. . .Cutler (control systems)
Cutler-Hammer, Inc.
What's new for tomorrow is at Singer today!
(TM)
Singer Co.
The wheels of transportation help turn the
wheels of industry
Union Pacific Railroad
The wheels that go everywhere
American Trucking Associations, Inc.
When a Studio Girl enters your home a new
kind of beauty brightens your life
(cosmetics)
Helene Curtis Industries, Inc.

When distribution is the question, UBL has
the answers
Union Barge Line Corp.
When it comes to color, come to Cyanamid
American Cyanamid Co.
When it comes to cooking for dogs—Rival
has no rival
Rival Pet Foods, Div. Associated Product,
Inc.
When it rains, it pours
Morton Salt Co.
When it's Domino Sugar, you're sure it's
pure!
American Sugar Refining Co.
When so much depends on a valve. . .so many
depend on LimiTorque
LimiTorque Corp.
When something happy happens—it's Bulova
time
Bulova Watch Co., Inc.
When you care enough to send the very best
Hallmark Cards, Inc.
When you mix with CinZano you mix with
the best (vermouth)
Schieffelin and Co.
When you make your move—make sure it's a
planned move (industrial development)
Central Illinois Light Co.
When you start with metal. . .finish with
Duracron!
PPG Industries, Inc.
When you're out to beat the world (tennis
shoes)
Converse Rubber Co.
When you've got to be right (bearings)
SKF Industries, Inc.
Whenever good impressions count, rely on
carbonizing papers by Schweitzer
Peter J. Schweitzer Div., Kimberly-Clark
Corp.
Where banking is a pleasure
Trust Company of Georgia
Where beautiful young ideas begin (cosmet-
ics)
Helene Curtis Industries, Inc.
Where beauty is material
The Masland Duraleather Co.
Where big ideas turn into aluminum extru-
sions
Superior Industries, Inc.
Where big things are happening
Commonwealth of Kentucky

Where bold new ideas pay off for profit-
minded farmers
New Idea Farm Equipment Co.
Where engraving is still an art
Roehlen Engraving Works
Where every carpet is custom made
Dellinger, Inc.
Where everything is done in plastics (molds)
American Insulator Corp.
Where experience guides exploration (indus-
trial chemicals)
Dow Corning Corp.
Where flame technology creates new products
Oxides Div., Cabot Corp.
Where free enterprise is still growing
Indiana Dept. of Commerce
Where good government is a habit
North Carolina Dept. of Conservation and
Development
Where great ideas are meant to happen
Arvin Industries, Inc.
Where ideas unlock the future
The Bendix Corp.
"Where inches count"
Acme National Refrigeration Co.
Where new ideas bring you better packaging
Reynolds Metals Co.
Where new ideas take shape in aluminum
Reynolds Metals Co.
Where only the plane gets more attention
than you
Iberia Air Lines of Spain
Where outstanding performance is standard
New York Shipbuilding Corp.
Where people and ideas create security for
millions
Connecticut General Life Insurance Co.
Where people make the difference
Connecticut General Life Insurance Co.
Where people make the difference
Toronto-Dominion Bank
Where pride of craftsmanship comes first
Empire Furniture Corp.
Where progress is a daily practice
Oil Center Tool Div., FMC Corp.
Where quality is a family tradition (agricul-
tural machinery)
Gehl Bros. Mfg. Co.
Where quality is a tradition (building
products)
Dierks Forest, Inc.
Where quality is a tradition...and an obliga-
tion (electrical control equipment)
Square D Co.

Where quality is built in, not added on
American Motors Corp.
Where quality is produced in quantity
Sterling Faucet Co.
Where quality is traditional
Old Colony Envelope Co.
Where quality makes sense
House Beautiful
Where research and development make excit-
ing ideas
General Tire and Rubber Co.
Where research is planned with progress in
mind (R)
Universal Oil Products Co.
Where telling the world means selling the
world
Life International
Where the action is! (fishing tackle)
Zebco Div., Brunswick Corp.
Where the big idea is innovation
United States Steel Corp.
Where the brightest ideas come to light
General Electric Co.
Where the data movement started and start-
ling moves are made
Teletype Corp.
Where the newest in packaging is happening
today
Milprint, Inc.
Where the nicest people meet the nicest
things
Stanley Home Products, Inc.
Where there's a window...there's a place for
Thermopane
Libby-Owens-Ford Co.
Where there's life...there's Bud (R) (beer)
Anheuser-Busch, Inc.
Where today's theory is tomorrow's remedy
(drugs, pharmaceuticals)
Merck, Sharpe and Dohme Div., Merck
and Co., Inc.
Where what you want to know comes first
Columbia Broadcasting System, Inc.
Where what's happening gets its start
Amoco Chemical Corp.
Where you are always number one (insurance)
The Glen Falls Group
Where you save does make a difference (R)
The Savings and Loan Foundation, Inc.
Where your dollar works harder...grows big-
ger!
Insured Savings and Loan Associations
Where your "resort dollar" buys more
Stardust Hotel and Golf Club

Where your sealing is unlimited (building
   products)
   Standard Products Co.
Wherever electricity is distributed and con-
   trolled
   Square D Co.
Wherever fruit grows, our machinery goes
   Elliott Mfg. Co., Inc.
Wherever you go, there it is! (Hiram Walker
   bourbon)
   Hiram Walker, Inc.
Wherever you go you look better in Arrow
   (shirts)
   Cluett, Peabody and Co.
Wherever you look. . .you see Budd
   Budd Co.
The white viking fleet
   Swedish American Line
Wholesale floor coverings of distinction
   Manuel Feldman Co., Inc.
Who changed it? (machinery)
   H. K. Porter, Co., Inc.
"Who we serve proves how we serve" (elec-
   trical contractors)
   Fishback and Moore, Inc.
Wide-track
   Pontiac Motor Div., General Motors Corp.
Wide world of entertainment
   American Broadcasting Co.
Wide world of recreation, The Starcraft
   (boats, camping trailers)
   Starcraft Co.
Will bring peace of mind to you and your
   family
   The Guardian Life Insurance Co. of
   America
Will enrich and safeguard your retirement
   years, Guardian
   The Guardian Life Insurance Co. of
   America
Window beauty is Andersen
   Andersen Corp.
Wines of California since 1882 (Christian
   Bros.)
   Fromm and Sichel, Inc.
Wire for industry
   Keystone Steel and Wire Co.
With Graflex, the payoff is in the picture
   Graflex, Inc.
"Woman's best friend" (Polly-Flex house-
   wares)
   Republic Molding Corp.
The word for champagne, Mumm's
   G. H. Mumm and Co.

Words to go to sleep by (Perfect Sleeper
   Mattress)
   Serta Associates, Inc.
Working funds for industry
   Walter E. Heller and Co.
Working wonders with wire
   E. H. Titchener Co.
Works best under pressure (cylinders)
   Hydro-Line Mfg. Co.
"Works with you—works for you" (physical
   fitness equipment)
   Battle Creek Manufacturers, Inc.
Works wonders, Bayer (aspirin)
   Glenbrook Labs, Div., Sterling Drug Co.
World champions of worth! (agricultural
   machinery)
   Hesston Corp., Inc.
World-famous Spanish sherries (Williams and
   Humbert dry sack)
   Julius Wile Sons and Co., Inc.
The world is smaller when you fly a Beech-
   craft
   Beech Aircraft Corp.
World leader in commercial refrigeration
   Tyler Refrigeration Div., Clark Equip-
   ment Co.
World leader in filtration
   Great Lakes Carton Corp.
World leader in heavy duty trucks
   White Motor Co.
World leader in luxury cigars (Gold Label)
   Gradiaz, Annis Div., General Cigar Co.
World leader in packaged power (storage
   batteries
   ESB Inc.
World leader in recorded sound (Command
   Records)
   ABC Records, Inc.
World leader in transport refrigeration
   Thermo King Corp.
World leader of the valve industry since 1846
   The Wm. Powell Co.
World leader on highway and speedway
   Monroe Auto Equipment Co.
World leaders in duplicating supplies since
   1906
   Frankel Mfg. Co.
World leaders in the development of pulp
   and paper mills for use of local fibers
   Parsons and Whittemore, Inc.
A world of engineering experience
   Globe Hoist Co.
World of experience (electronic instruments)
   Collins Radio Co.

A world of furniture made in a way that
makes a world of difference
Kroehler Mfg. Co.

A world of paper products—from frozen
food cartons to printing paper
International Paper Co.

A world of profits awaits the well informed
Dow Theory Forecasts, Inc.

World leaders in duplicating supplies since
1906
Frankel Mfg. Co.

World renowned for perfection in sound
James B. Lansing Sound, Inc.

World standard
Bell Helicopter Co.

The world's best climate makes the world's
best rum (Puerto Rican rums)
Schieffelin and Co.

World's best seller
Reader's Digest

World's biggest seller! (motorcycles)
American Honda Motor Co., Inc.

World's broadest line of thermoplastic sheet
materials, Seilon
Plastics Div., Seiberling Rubber Co.

World's easiest-to-use dictating machines
Steno Cord Dictation Systems

World's finest
Autocar Div., White Motor Co.

World's finest (filters)
J. A. Baldwin Mfg. Co.

World's finest (Garrard phonograph high
fidelity equipment)
British Industries Corp.

"The world's finest"
Goya Guitars, Inc.

World's finest
Phillipson Rod Co.

The world's finest bourbon since 1795
James B. Beam Distilling Co.

World's finest cottons
Supima Association of America

World's finest golf clubs and accessories
Bristol Pro-Golf, Inc.

The world's finest name in silver care
W. J. Hagerty and Sons, Ltd., Inc.

World's finest mink
United Mink Producers Association

World's finest petrochemical products
Gulf Oil Corp.

The world's finest the world over (mass feeding equipment)
Vulcan-Hart Corp.

World's first and largest manufacturer of
deep fat frying equipment
J. C. Pitman and Sons, Inc.

The world's "first family" of changers and
tape decks
B S R (USA) Ltd.

World's first family of jets
Boeing Co.

World's first mass produced tractor
Ford Tractor Div., Ford Motor Co.

World's first—world's finest
Valvoline Oil Co. Div., Ashland Oil and
Refining Co.

World's foremost heavy-duty ignition line
(Blue Streak)
Standard Motor Parts, Inc.

World's foremost rebuilders of automotive
parts
Kimco Auto Products, Inc.

World's friendliest airline (Panagra)
Pan-American—Grace Airways, Inc.

World's largest air cargo carrier
Pan American World Airways, Inc.

The world's largest airline
Air France

The world's largest and finest
Lindsay Ripe Olive Co.

World's largest and most experienced manufacturer of magnetic pickups (phonograph high fidelity equipment)
Pickering and Co., Inc.

World's largest builder of organs and pianos
Wurlitzer Co.

World's largest charter airline
World Airways, Inc.

World's largest citrus plant
Pasco Packing Co.

World's largest commercial oven manufacturer since 1888
Middleby-Marshall Oven Co.

World's largest creator of preschool toys
Fisher-Price Toys, Inc.

World's largest exclusive fly line manufacturer
Scientific Anglers, Inc.

World's largest exclusive manufacturer of
electric industrial trucks
Lewis-Shepard Co.

World's largest exclusive manufacturer of
golf balls
Plymouth Golf Ball Co.

The world's largest independent airline
World Airways, Inc.

World's largest maker of tufted carpets and rugs
E. T. Barwick, Inc.

World's largest maker of V-belts
Gates Rubber Co.

World's largest manufacturer and designer
Bead Design Studio

World's largest manufacturer of blister packaging machinery
Packaging Industries, Ltd., Inc.

World's largest manufacturer of fine carbonizing papers
Peter J. Schweitzer Div., Kimberly-Clark Corp.

The world's largest manufacturer of fine kitchen cabinets
Colonial Products Co.

World's largest manufacturer of gasoline pumps and service station equipment
Wayne Pump Co.

World's largest manufacturer of glass tableware
Anchor Hocking Glass Corp.

World's largest manufacturer of industrial rubber products
Uniroyal, Inc.

World's largest manufacturer of mirrors
Carolina Mirror Corp.

World's largest manufacturer of painters' and glaziers' tools—since 1872
Red Devil, Inc.

The world's largest manufacturer of reach-in refrigerators and freezers
Victory Metal Mfg. Co.

World's largest manufacturer of school supplies and stationery
Westab, Inc.

World's largest manufacturer of staplers for home and office
Swingline, Inc.

World's largest manufacturer of steel shipping containers
Rheem Mfg. Co.

World's largest manufacturer of ventilating louvers
Louver Mfg. Co., Inc.

World's largest mattress maker
Simmons Co.

World's largest producer of automotive wheels, hubs and drums
Kelsey-Hayes Co.

World's largest producer of bath scales (Counselor)
The Brearley Co.

World's largest producer of commercial heavy-duty truck drive axles
Axle Div., Eaton Mfg. Co.

World's largest producer of non-powder guns and ammo
Daisy/Heddon Div., Victor Comptometer Corp.

World's largest roof truss system
Sanford Truss, Inc.

World's largest selling air conditioners
Fedders Corp.

World's largest ski maker
Northland Ski Mfg. Co.

World's largest specialized publisher
Gulf Publishing Co.

World's leading direct-by-mail vitamin and drug company
Hudson National, Inc.

World's leading manufacturer of plastic products for 35 diversified industries
Colorite Plastics, Inc.

World's leading supplier of diamonds for industry
DeBeers Consolidated Mines, Ltd.

The world's most beautiful china
Minton, Inc.

The world's most beautiful organs
Story and Clark Piano Co.

The world's most broadly based electronics company
RCA Corp.

World's most complete fishing tackle line
Horrocks-Ibbutson Co.

World's most complete line of sporting arms and accessories
Savage Arms Div., Emhart Corp.

World's most complete transportation system
Canadian Pacific Railway

World's most dependable air freight service
Airborne Freight Corp.

The world's most distinctive digging machines are Davis
Davis Mfg., Inc.

World's most experienced airline
Pan American World Airways, Inc.

World's most experienced detergent engineers
Ing. Mario Ballestra and Co.

World's most experienced ski maker
Northland Ski Mfg. Co.

The world's most honored watch (R)
Longines-Wittnauer Watch Co.

World's most perfect high fidelity components
Empire Scientific Corp.

The world's most precious simulated pearls
Majorica

World's most wanted lure (fishing tackle)
Rapala Div., Nordic Enterprises, Inc.

World's most widely used brand of colds
medication (Vicks (R) VapoRub)
Vick Chemical Co.

World's number one weed killers (Weedone)
Amchem Products, Inc.

World's oldest and largest manufacturer of
electric blankets
Northern Electric Co.

The world's 100,000-mile durability champion (Mercury Comet)
Ford Motor Co.

World's second largest manufacturer of
cameras and films
Agfa-Gevaert, Inc.

World's strongest padlocks
Master Lock Co.

World's worst beauty soap. World's best
hand soap (Lava)
Procter and Gamble Co.

World-wide competence in control
Taylor Instrument Cos.

Worldwide electronics telecommunications
International Telephone and Telegraph
Corp.

World-wide engineering, manufacturing and
construction
Dorr-Oliver, Inc.

World-wide suppliers of the finest ball pen
inks
Formulabs, Inc.

The world-wide water conditioning people
Culligan, Inc.

Worth changing brands to get
The Pure Oil Co.

Wouldn't you really rather have a Buick?
Buick Motor Div., General Motors Corp.

Writing papers that create an impression
Montag, Inc., Div. Westab, Inc.

Y

The yarn with the "crepe" built in (Enka
Crepeset)
American Enka Corp.

Years from now you'll be glad its Norge
(domestic appliances)
Norge Div., Borg-Warner Corp.

"Yes, I know. . .Marie Brizard" (liqueur)
Schieffelin and Co.

You can be sure if it's Westinghouse
Westinghouse Electric Corp.

You can count on Continental to take care
of you
Continental Steel Corp.

You can count on Kemper care under the
Kemper flag
Kemper Insurance Co.

You can depend on it
National Oil Fuel Institute, Inc.

You can depend on the integrity and quality
of Smith-Douglass (fertilizer)
Smith-Douglass Div., Borden Chemical Co.

You can get all types of insurance under the
Travelers umbrella
The Travelers Insurance Cos.

You can rely on America's oldest and most
experienced custom finisher (interior
decoration)
Synthetics Finishing Corp.

You can take the pulse of progress at
Republic Steel
Republic Steel Corp.

You can trust the man who sells this brand
(Swift's Premium)
Swift and Co.

You can't afford to be without Swagelok
Crawford Fitting Co.

You can't buy a better brake lining to save
your life!
Grey-Rock Div., Raybestos-Manhattan,
Inc.

You can't do better than Sears
Sears Roebuck and Co.

You can't get any closer (Norelco shaver)
North America Philips Corp.

You can't get the whole picture in just a day
or two
San Francisco Convention and Visitors
Bureau

You cook better automatically with a
Tappan
Tappan Co.

"You don't have to be a millionaire to play
like one"
Walter Hagen Golf Equipment Co.

You expect more from Standard and you get
it
Standard Oil Div., American Oil Co.

You expect the best from Hanson. . .and you
get it (hardware)
Henry L. Hanson Co.

You fence for keeps with Red Brand
    Keystone Steel and Wire Co.
You feel so cool, so clean, so fresh. . .
    Tampax, Inc.
You furnish the print. . .we'll furnish the part
    (laminated plastics)
    Synthane Corp.
You get more from American
    American Laundry Machinery Industries
You have a friend at Chase Manhattan
    The Chase Manhattan Bank
You haven't seen your country if you
    haven't seen Alaska
    Alaska Travel Div., Department of Eco-
    nomic Development and Planning
You live better automatically with Tappan
    (domestic appliances)
    Tappen Co.
You never heard it so good (Sony Super-
    scope)
    Superscope, Inc.
You sleep on it. . .not in it!
    Serta Mattress Co.
You'll find the woman's touch in every
    Purex product
    Purex Corp., Ltd.
The young point of view in shoes (Life
    Stride)
    Brown Shoe Co.
Younger by design (Van Heusen shirts)
    Phillips-Van Heusen Corp.
Your air commuter service in 12 busy states
    Allegheny Airlines, Inc.
Your anywhere anything anytime network
    American Telephone and Telegraph Co.
Your assurance of quality in tape compo-
    nents
    Viking of Minneapolis, Inc.
Your assurance of the best (TM)
    W. A. Sheaffer Pen Co.
Your assurance that this fabric has been pre-
    tested for performance by Celanese
    (Arnel)
    Celanese Corp.
Your best bet for the best bits
    Rock Bit Div., Timken Roller Bearing Co.
Your best bet over the long haul
    D. C. Trucking Co., Inc.
Your best single source for quality drive
    train replacement parts
    Borg-Warner Corp.
Your face never had it so clean! (1006
    lotion)
    Bonne Bell, Inc.

Your guardian for life
    Guardian Life Insurance Co.
Your Hartford agent does more than he
    really has to
    The Hartford Insurance Group
Your investment success is our business
    Francis I. duPont and Co.
Your job is well powered when it's Ford
    powered
    Industrial Engine Dept., Ford Div., Ford
    Motor Co.
Your key to hospitality (Old Fitzgerald)
    Stitzel-Weller Distillery, Inc.
Your kitchen companion since 1899 (house-
    hold products)
    Dazey Products Co.
Your morning is as good as your mattress
    Sealy Mattress Co.
Your one-source solution to every filing
    problem
    The Smead Mfg. Co.
Your packaging deserves Crown quality
    Crown Cork and Seal Co., Inc.
Your paper problems are in good hands with
    Marathon
    Marathon Div., American Can Co.
Your partner in packaging progress
    Ball Bros. Co., Inc.
Your printer's performance starts with fine
    papers
    Crocker Hamilton Papers, Inc.
Your symbol of quality and service
    Firestone Tire and Rubber Co.
Your thirst away, 7-Up
    The Seven-Up Co.
Your world of ideas and products
    MPA Magazines
You're better off with Bostitch (office supplies)
    Bostitch Div., Textron, Inc.
You're better off with Pan Am
    Pan American World Airways, Inc.
You're in good hands with Allstate
    Allstate Insurance Co.
You're in the Pepsi generation
    Pepsico, Inc.
You're miles ahead with General Tire
    General Tire and Rubber Co.
You're right with Lufkin
    The Lufkin Rule Co.
You've got good things going for you with
    service by Investors-Owned Electric
    Light and Power Companies
    Investors-Owned Electric Light and
    Power Cos.

Subject categories are derived, in large part, from *Business Periodicals Index* and cross-references are utilized throughout. As in the alphabetical section, brand names and product definitions, where necessary, are identified in parentheses.

One-example headings have been eliminated, and one-of-a-kind slogans have been listed under related subjects. Therefore, the user is advised to check both specific and general headings. For example:

"Don't be a paleface" (suntan lotion) will be found under **Cosmetics.**

"The best anti-freeze since mink" (Zerex) will be found under **Auto Parts.**

Adhesives
Best glue in the joint (Elmer's)
    Borden Chemical Div., Borden, Inc.
The best in tapes has "Able" on the label
    Arno Adhesive Tapes, Inc.
Holds the world together
    H. B. Fuller Co.
Join with Bostik for better bonding
    B. B. Chemical Div., United Shoe
    Machinery Corp.
Leader in adhesive technology
    H. B. Fuller Co.

Agricultural Chemicals
Boost profits with the competitive edge
    Tyler Corp.
Creators of chemicals for modern agriculture
    Geigy Chemical Corp.
Get better yields from your fields with
    Armour
    Armour and Co.
The salt of the earth
    Potash Co. of America
Serves the man who makes a business of
    agriculture, Cyanamid
    American Cyanamid Co.

Agricultural Machinery
The big job matched line
    Massey-Ferguson, Inc.
Dependability in the field. . .safety for the
    operator
    Tryce Mfg. Co., Inc.

Does its share to help you share in a better
    future, Allis-Chalmers
    Allis-Chalmers Mfg. Co.
Engineered for longer life
    Minneapolis-Moline, Inc.
Farm implements with a future—yours!
    Brillion Iron Works, Inc.
First in grassland farming
    New Holland Div., Sperry Rand Corp.
First in powered equipment since 1918
    Bolens Div., FMC Corp.
First to serve the farmer
    International Harvester Co.
From the tractor people who make the big
    ones
    Allis-Chalmers Mfg. Co.
Iron horse quality
    Matthews Co.
The people who bring you the machines that
    work
    International Harvester Co.
Practical in design. Dependable in action.
    New Holland Div., Sperry Rand Corp.
Since 1886. . .scientifically designed for prac-
    tical use
    John Blue Co., Inc.
Specialists in farmstead mechanization
    New Holland Div., Sperry Rand Corp.
The tractor people, Allis-Chalmers
    Allis-Chalmers Mfg. Co.
Where bold new ideas pay off for profit-
    minded farmers
    New Idea Farm Equipment Co.

Where quality is a family tradition
    Gehl Bros. Mfg. Co.
World champions of worth!
    Hesston Corp., Inc.
World's first mass produced tractor
    Ford Tractor Div., Ford Motor Co.

Air Conditioning

Don't be satisfied with less than Lennox
    Lennox Industries, Inc.
For any air conditioning
    Trane Co.
It's nature's freshness—indoors
    Lennox Industries, Inc.
Leaders go to Carnes for the newest in air
    distribution equipment
    Carnes Corp.
More people put their confidence in Carrier
    air conditioning than in any other
    make
    Carrier Corp.
The quality name in air conditioning and
    refrigeration
    York Corp.
Round the calendar comfort
    Lennox Industries, Inc.
See what air-conditioning is doing now. . .See
    Gardner-Denver
    Gardner-Denver Co.
Since 1928—industry leadership in heating
    and air conditioning
    Fraser and Johnston Co.
World's largest selling air conditioners
    Fedders Corp.

Air Freight

Air-freight specialists
    Flying Tiger Line, Inc.
Airline of the professionals
    American Airlines, Inc.
Determined to serve you best
    Eastern Air Lines, Inc.
First in airfreight with airfreight first
    Flying Tiger Line, Inc.
Freight by air
    Slick Airways
Great people to ship with
    Pakistan International Airlines
World's largest air cargo carrier
    Pan American World Airways, Inc.
World's most dependable air freight service
    Airborne Freight Corp.

Air Guns—see Firearms

Airlines

À votre service
    Air France
The airline that knows the South Pacific best
    Air New Zealand
The airline that measures the midwest in
        minutes
    Ozark Air Lines, Inc.
The airline that treats you like a maharajah
    Air-India
The airline with the big jets
    Delta Air Lines, Inc.
The Alaska flag line
    Pacific Northern Airlines
All over the world BOAC takes good care of
        you
    British Overseas Airway Corp.
America's leading airline
    American Airlines, Inc.
Australia's round-the-world jet airline
    QANTAS
The calm beauty of Japan at almost the
        speed of sound
    Japan Air Lines
Coast to coast to coast
    National Airlines, Inc.
Europe's foremost airline
    British European Airways
Europe's most helpful airline
    Sabena Belgian World Airlines
The Extra Care Airline
    United Air Lines, Inc.
The fan-jet airline
    Northwest Airlines, Inc.
First airline in the Americas
    Avianca
First in Latin America
    Pan American World Airways, Inc.
First on the Atlantic
    Pan American World Airways, Inc.
First on the Pacific
    Pan American World Airways, Inc.
First 'round the world
    Pan American World Airways, Inc.
Fly the friendly skies of United
    United Air Lines, Inc.
A friend of the family
    Air Canada
Golden nugget jet service
    Alaska Airlines, Inc.
Golden nugget jets
    Alaska Airlines, Inc.

Great people to fly with
    Pakistan International Airlines
The jet with the extra engine
    Western Air Lines, Inc.
Known for extra care
    United Air Lines, Inc.
Makes the going great, Pan Am
    Pan American World Airways, Inc.
"A most remarkable airline"
    Continental Air Lines, Inc.
The nation's largest airline
    United Air Lines, Inc.
Nationwide, worldwide depend on. . .
    Trans World Airlines, Inc.
The pioneer of low fares to Europe
    Icelandic Airlines
Proud bird with the golden tail
    Continental Air Lines, Inc.
Sailing the South Pacific Skies
    UTA French Airlines
See how much better an airline can be
    Eastern Air Lines, Inc.
Specialists in international jet service to
        Texas or South America
    Braniff Airways, Inc.
Swisscare. Worldwide.
    Swiss Air Transport Co., Ltd.
Swiss-care world-wide on the privately
        owned airline of Switzerland
    Swiss Air Transport Co., Ltd.
Takes good care of you, BOAC
    British Overseas Airway Corp.
The things we do to make you happy
    Trans World Airlines, Inc.
The unbeatable way to jet home
    Western Air Lines, Inc.
Up up and away (S.M.)
    Trans World Airlines, Inc.
The way to get there
    Iberia Air Lines of Spain
We know where you're going
    Air France
We pamper passengers throughout mid-
        central U.S.A.
    Lake Central Airlines, Inc.
Welcome aboard
    United Air Lines, Inc.
Where only the plane gets more attention
        than you
    Iberia Air Lines of Spain
World's friendliest airline—Panagra
    Pan American—Grace Airways, Inc.
The world's largest airline
    Air France

World's largest charter airline
    World Airways, Inc.
The world's largest independent airline
    World Airways, Inc.
World's most experienced airline
    Pan American World Airways, Inc.
Your air commuter service in 12 busy states
    Allegheny Airlines, Inc.
You're better off with Pan Am
    Pan American World Airways, Inc.

Airplanes
Accustomed to the finest. . .you'll find it in a
        Beechcraft
    Beech Aircraft Corp.
The business jet that's backed by an airline
        (Fan Jet Falcon)
    Business Jets Div., Pan American World
    Airways, Inc.
The jet that justifies itself (Sabreliner)
    North American Rockwell Corp.
More people buy Cessna twins than any
        other make
    Cessna Aircraft Co.
More people fly Cessna airplanes than any
        other make
    Cessna Aircraft Co.
More people have bought Pipers than any
        other plane in the world
    Piper Aircraft Corp.
This one means business (The DH 125)
    Hawker Siddeley Group, Ltd.
The world is smaller when you fly a Beech-
        craft
    Beech Aircraft Corp.
World standard
    Bell Helicopter Co.
World's first family of jets
    Boeing Co.

Airplanes, Business—*see* **Airplanes**

Airplanes, Light—*see* **Airplanes**

Aspirin—*see* **Medicines, Proprietary**

Automobile Accessories—*see* **Automobile
    Parts**

Automobile Batteries—*see* **Storage Batteries**

Automobile Insurance—*see* **Insurance**

Automobile Lease and Rental Services
America's largest leasing system
    Ford Authorized Leasing System

Anywhere in the wide world
  Hertz Corp.
The biggest should do more. It's only right.
  Hertz Corp.
Car plan management and leasing specialists
  Peterson, Howell and Heather
The customer is always No. 1
  National Car Rental System, Inc.
Let Hertz put you in the driver's seat
  Hertz Corp.
A pioneer in the leasing field
  Emkay, Inc.
Puts you in the driver's seat, Hertz
  Hertz Corp.
We try harder
  Avis, Inc.

Automobile Parts

Assurance of quality
  National Automotive Parts Association
Be profit wise. . .(Sell only Buss) (fuses)
  Bussman Mfg. Div., McGraw-Edison Co.
Best anti-freeze since mink (Zerex)
  E. I. duPont de Nemours and Co.
Built stronger to last longer
  Powell Muffler Co.
Control with Dole (R)
  Dole Valve Co.
The crown jewels of ignition (R)
  Filko Ignition
The crown jewels of ignition and carburetion
  Filko Ignition
Famous for quality
  Brunswick Rubber Co.
First for fast service
  Federal-Mogul Corp.
First name in tire valves for original equip-
    ment and replacement
  A. Schrader's Son
The gold standard (filters)
  Wix Corp.
The heart of a tune-up
  Champion Spark Plug Co.
Ignition starts with P and D
  P and D Mfg. Co.
In products, performance, purpose. . .Essex
    measures up!
  C-P Fittings Div., Essex Wire Corp.
Install confidence. . .install Thermoid
  Thermoid Div., H. K. Porter Co., Inc.
Is go. . .go with it, McCord
  McCord Corp.
The line that moves
  Murray Corp.

Made for the professional! (R)
  Permatex Co., Inc.
Maximum capacity (CāPac)
  Wells Mfg. Corp.
Means more under-car business, Moog
  Moog Industries, Inc.
Never lets go
  Hammer Blow Tool Co.
Number 1 in acceptance
  Airtex Products, Inc.
The only 100% coverage line for cars, trucks,
    tractors, stationary engines.
  Victor Manufacturing and Gasket Co.
Performance insurance (CāPac)
  Wells Mfg. Corp.
Puts the "go" in ignition!
  Tungsten Contact Mfg. Co.
The quality equipment line
  Bishman Mfg. Co.
"Quality parts for the auto makers and
    owners"
  Holley Carburetor Co.
Quality seals build the reputation of profes-
    sional mechanics
  Chicago Rawhide Mfg. Co.
Re-equip/Equip and profit with. . .
  Bear Mfg. Co.
The seal mechanics see most, use most
  Chicago Rawhide Mfg. Co.
Sets the standards for the gasketing industry,
    FEL-PRO
  Felt Products Mfg. Co., Inc.
Simply say Delco (storage batteries)
  General Motors Corp.
Since 1921. . .the engine builders source!
  Muskegon Piston Ring
Sold by more dealers than any other brand
    (mufflers)
  A. P. Parts Corp.
Specify Spicer
  Spicer Div., Dana Corp.
Temperatures made to order
  Harrison Radiator Div., General Motors
  Corp.
World leader on highway and speedway
  Monroe Auto Equipment Co.
World's finest (filters)
  J. A. Baldwin Mfg. Co.
World's foremost heavy-duty ignition line
    (Blue Streak)
  Standard Motor Parts, Inc.
World's foremost rebuilders of automotive
    parts
  Kimco Auto Products, Inc.

World's largest maker of V-Belts
Gates Rubber Co.
World's largest producer of automotive
wheels, hubs and drums
Kelsey-Hayes Co.
Your best single source for quality drive train
replacement parts
Borg-Warner Corp.

Automobiles
America's favorite fun car (Mustang)
Ford Motor Co.
America's most distinguished motorcar
(Lincoln Continental)
Ford Motor Co.
Best year yet to go Ford!
Ford Motor Co.
The bold engineering comes from. . .
Ford Motor Co.
—Built means better built, Ford
Ford Motor Co.
"Built tough for you"
Toyota Motor Distributors, Inc.
Dedicated to excellence
American Motors Corp.
The difference is valves—Datsun
Nissan Motor Co., USA
Escape from the ordinary
Oldsmobile Div., General Motors Corp.
Get your hands on a Toyota. . .you'll never
let go
Toyota Motor Distributors, Inc.
The great highway performers (Corvair,
Monza)
Chevrolet Motor Div., General Motors
Corp.
Has a better idea, Ford
Ford Motor Co.
It's the going thing
Ford Motor Co.
Let yourself go. . .Plymouth
Plymouth Div., Chrysler Corp.
Look to Olds for the new
Oldsmobile Div., General Motors Corp.
Look what Plymouth's up to now
Plymouth Div., Chrysler Corp.
Mark of excellence
General Motors Corp.
The mini-brutes (Opel Kadett)
Buick Motor Div., General Motors Corp.
Putting you first, keeps us first
Chevrolet Motor Div., General Motors
Corp.

The rocket action car
Oldsmobile Div., General Motors Corp.
The sensible spectaculars
American Motors Corp.
So new! So right! So obviously Cadillac!
Cadillac Motor Car Div., General Motors
Corp.
The sportsman's car (BMW)
Bavarian Motor Works
Standard of the world
Cadillac Motor Car Div., General Motors
Corp.
Test drive total performance '65
Ford Motor Co.
Total performance
Ford Motor Co.
The tuned car
Buick Motor Div., General Motors Corp.
Unique in all the world (Thunderbird)
Ford Motor Co.
The "unstoppables"
Kaiser Jeep Corp.
Where quality is built in, not added on
American Motors Corp.
Wide-track
Pontiac Motor Div., General Motors Corp.
The world's 100,000-mile durability cham-
pion (Mercury Comet)
Ford Motor Co.
Wouldn't you really rather have a Buick?
Buick Motor Div., General Motors Corp.

Automobile Service Stations
As you travel ask us (R)
Standard Oil Div., American Oil Co.
For good advice. . .and good products. . .
depend on your Mobil dealer
Mobil Oil Corp.
There's a good future with Mobil (employ-
ment)
Mobil Oil Corp.
Trust your car to the man who wears the star
Texaco, Inc.
Sign of a better future for you (employment)
Shell Oil Co.
We take better care of your car
Standard Oil Div., American Oil Co.
You expect more from Standard and you get
it.
Standard Oil Div., American Oil Co.

Automobile Service Stations—Equipment
First and foremost line of cleaning products
Gunk Laboratories, Inc.

Get going great—with Graco
  Gray Co., Inc.
A new high in auto test equipment. . .a new
    high for you!
  Sun Electric Corp.
Precisioneered by Edelmann
  E. Edelmann and Co.
The problem solver people (TM)
  Champ-Items, Inc.
"The profit line"
  The Shaler Co.
To "test with the best"
  Imperial Eastman Corp.

Automobile Tires—see Tires, Automobile

Baby Products
"Babies are our business. . .our only business"
    (R)
  Gerber Products Co.
If babies were born trained, they wouldn't
    need Diaparene Baby Powder
  Breon Laboratories, Inc.
Wash easier, dry faster, absorb more, wear
    longer (Curity diapers)
  Textile Div., The Kendall Co.

Ball Point Pens—see Fountain Pens

Banks and Banking
All the bank you'll ever need in Texas
  Texas National Bank of Commerce of
  Houston
The bank for bankers and businessmen
  Irving Trust Co.
The bank that means business in California
  Crocker-Citizens National Bank
The bank that works hardest for you
  Chemical Bank, New York
The bank with the international point of
    view
  Bank of the Southwest
The bankers who do a little more for you
  United California Bank
Building with Chicago and the nation since
    1863
  First National Bank of Chicago
First in banking
  Bank of America
First in loans to business and industry
  Chase Manhattan Bank
First Pennsylvania means business
  First Pennsylvania Banking and Trust Co.
Full service bank
  Foundation for Commercial Banks

. . .It's good to have a great bank behind you
  Manufacturers Hanover Trust Co.
Partners in progress around the world
  First National City Bank
"The place where you keep your checking
    account"
  Foundation for Commercial Banks
Where banking is a pleasure
  Trust Co. of Georgia
Where people make the difference
  Toronto-Dominion Bank
You have a friend at Chase Manhattan
  Chase Manhattan Bank

Barge Lines
When distribution is the question UBL has
    the answers
  Union Barge Line Corp.
Personalized service that makes the big dif-
    ference
  A. L. Mechling Barge Lines, Inc.

Bath Preparations—see Toilet Goods

Bathing Suits—see Women's Apparel

Bathroom Fixtures—see Plumbing Fixtures

Batteries—see Electric Batteries

Bearings
America's leading bearing specialists since
    1925
  Detroit Aluminum and Brass Co.
For modern industry
  New Departure—Hyatt Bearings Div.,
  General Motors Corp.
Leads in quiet bearings that last longer,
    Hoover
  Hoover Bearing Div., Hoover Ball and
  Bearing Co.
Missile quality ball bearings
  MPB, Inc.
Quality turns on Timken
  Timken Roller Bearing Co.
Smoothing industry's pathway for nearly
    half a century
  Messinger Bearings, Inc.
Think straight. . .think Rollway
  Rollway Bearing Co.
When you've got to be right
  SKF Industries, Inc.

Beer—see also Liquors
America's original sparkling malt liquor
    (Champale)
  Metropolis Brewery of New Jersey, Inc.

America's premium quality beer
    Falstaff Brewing Corp.
The beer that made Milwaukee famous
    Jos. Schlitz Brewing Co.
Brewed only in Milwaukee (Miller High Life)
    Miller Brewing Co.
The champagne of bottle beer (Miller High Life)
    Miller Brewing Co.
From the land of sky blue waters (Hamm's)
    Theo. Hamm Brewing Co.
It's the water (Olympia)
    Olympia Brewing Co.
It's worth it. . .it's Bud
    Anheuser-Busch, Inc.
Real gusto in a great light beer
    Jos. Schlitz Brewing Co.
That Bud. . .that's beer!
    Anheuser-Busch, Inc.
Unmistakably. . .America's premium quality beer
    Falstaff Brewing Corp.
Where there's life. . .there's Bud (R)
    Anheuser-Busch, Inc.

Bedding
Coordinated fashions for bed and bath
    Fieldcrest Mills, Inc.
Enjoy the rest of your life (Koolfoam pillows)
    American Latex Products Corp.
The first name in custom bedding
    Hein and Kopins, Inc.

Beverages
America's most modern cola (Diet-Rite)
    Royal Crown Cola Co.
America's No. 1 low-calorie cola (Diet-Rite)
    Royal Crown Cola Co.
Beginning a second century of leadership (Chase and Sanborn Coffee)
    Standard Brands, Inc.
Brighten up with Instant Tender Leaf Tee
    Standard Brands, Inc.
The brighter tasting tea (Instant Tender Leaf)
    Standard Brands, Inc.
The brisk tea
    Thos. J. Lipton, Inc.
The coffee served at the Waldorf-Astoria (Savarin)
    S. A. Schonbrunn and Co., Inc.
The coffee-er coffee (Savarin)
    S. A. Schonbrunn and Co., Inc.

Come alive! (Pepsi-Cola)
    Pepsico, Inc.
Drink RC for quick, fresh energy
    Royal Crown Cola Co.
For those who think young (Pepsi-Cola)
    Pepsico, Inc.
Good to the last drop (coffee)
    Maxwell House Div., General Foods Corp.
How can just 1 calorie taste so good! (Tab)
    Coca-Cola Co.
The natural lift (Instant Postum)
    General Foods Corp.
The pause that refreshes
    Coca-Cola Co.
The prune juice with the fruit juice appeal (Del Monte)
    California Packing Corp.
The real thing from Florida (orange juice)
    Florida Citrus Commission
Taste that beats the others cold (Pepsi-Cola)
    Pepsico, Inc.
Things go better with Coke
    Coca-Cola Co.
The uncola
    The Seven-Up Co.
Your thirst away, 7-Up
    The Seven-Up Co.
You're in the Pepsi generation
    Pepsico, Inc.

Boats and Boating
America's most popular boats
    Starcraft Co.
Another carefree Johnson
    Johnson Motors Div., Outboard Marine Co.
First in dependability
    Johnson Motors Div., Outboard Marine Co.
First in marine propulsion
    Keikhaefer Mercury Div., Brunswick Corp.
First in outboards
    Evinrude Motors Div., Outboard Marine Co.
Since 1720, a family heritage of careful boat building
    C. P. Leek and Sons, Inc.

Bowling Equipment—see Sporting Goods

Brakes
The complete brake lining service
    Raybestos-Manhattan, Inc.

Engineered for the ultimate in precision
(Kwik-Way Brake Service Centers)
Cedar Rapids Engineering Co.
The quality line
Wagner Electric Corp.
The quality line that's easy to find
Dorman Products, Inc.
Three steps to safety
Grey-Rock Div., Raybestos-Manhattan, Inc.

Building Materials—*see also* **Houses**
The action line
Evans Products Co.
The brightest name in aluminum
Nichols Aluminum Co.
Chief of the mouldings
Ponderosa Mouldings, Inc.
The classic name in the building field
Bird and Son, Inc.
. . .Creating better ways to hold things together
National Screw and Mfg. Co.
Creative ideas in glass
American Saint Gobain Corp.
The crowning touch of quality
Red Cedar Shingle and Handsplit Shale Bureau
Depend on Potlatch for everything in quality lumber
Potlatch Forests, Inc.
First in epoxies. . .in the age of ideas
CIBA Products Co.
First with better ways to build (Gold Bond)
National Gypsum Co.
For quality Western lumber products, look to T, W, and J
Tarter, Webster and Johnson Div., American Forest Products Corp.
The greatest name in building
United States Gypsum Co.
It's built to sell when it's built of wood
National Lumber Manufacturers Association
Keeps you in trim, John Lees
Cullman Products Corp.
Leader in prefinished hardwoods
E. L. Bruce Co.
Look to MFG for the shape of things to come
Molded Fiber Glass Companies, Inc.
Makes it authentic, Amerock
Amerock Corp.

Makes only particleboard and only the best, Duraflake
Duraflake Co.
Makes products better, safer, stronger, lighter
Fiber Glass Div., PPG Industries, Inc.
Makes the glass that makes the difference, PPG
PPG Industries, Inc.
Manufacturers of creative building products
Caradco, Inc.
Manufacturers of quality hardwood products since 1872
Connor Lumber and Land Co.
The material difference in building (Geon vinyls)
B. F. Goodrich Chemical Co.
Materials methods make the difference in modern building, Gold Bond
National Gypsum Co.
More savings with Symons
Symons Mfg. Co.
A name to remember
Pen Metal Co., Inc.
One of the many fine products that comes from 40 years of thinking new (Gold Bond)
National Gypsum Co.
One of the many quality home-improvement products made by J. M.
Johns Manville Corp.
Only when the finest is good enough
Globe Steel Products Corp.
Products of wood technology for construction and industry
Pope and Talbot, Inc.
A quality name in forest products
Long-Bell Lumber Co.
Quality products for quality living
Mirawal Co.
The red nylon ring of reliability
Elastic Stop Nut Corp. of America
Sell Simpson and be sure
Simpson Timber Co.
Sells easy. . .sells fast. . .makes resales
Insulite Div., Minnesota and Ontario Paper Co.
Symbol of quality (R)
Potlatch Forests, Inc.
Takes the burden out of keeping up your home, Bird
Bird and Son
Verified insulation performance
Owens-Corning Fiberglas Corp.

Where quality is a tradition
  Dierks Forests, Inc.
Where your sealing is unlimited
  Standard Products Co.
World's largest roof truss system
  Sanford Truss, Inc.

Buildings
"Builds walls for keeps, Smitty"
  Elwin G. Smith and Co., Inc.
Instant elevatoring (T)
  Otis Elevator Co.
The original masonry wall reinforcement
    with the truss design (Dur-O-Wal)
  Cedar Rapids Block Co.

Bus Travel—see Motor Bus Travel

Business Airplanes—see Airplanes

Business Insurance—see Insurance

Business Machines—see Office Equipment

Cameras and Equipment
Brings out the expert in you (automati-
    cally!), Bell and Howell
  Bell and Howell Co.
Builds photographic instruments a little
    better than they really have to be,
    Bell and Howell
  Bell and Howell Co.
The camera you never leave at home
  Minox Corp.
Classics of optical precision (Schneider
    lenses)
  Burleigh Brooks, Inc.
The easy ones
  Eastman Kodak Co.
A famous camera from camera-famous West
    Germany
  Minox Corp.
Fine photography for 40 years
  Minolta Corp.
Meets tomorrow's challenges today, Canon
  Canon, Inc.
The more you learn about photography, the
    more you count on Kodak
  Eastman Kodak Co.
The name quality made famous (Zoom 8)
  Minolta Corp.
Perfection in projection since 1909
  Da-Lite Screen Co., Inc.
Today's finest—designed for tomorrow's
    needs (Topcon Super D)
  Charles Beseler Co.

With Graflex, the payoff is in the picture
  Grayflex, Inc.
World's second largest manufacturer of
    cameras and films
  Agfa-Gevaert, Inc.

Campers and Coaches, Truck—see Recreation

Camping Equipment and Supplies—see Recreation

Carpets
America's finest power-loomed rug
  Karastan Rug Mills Div., Fieldcrest Mills,
  Inc.
The answer is wool. . .it costs less in the long
    run
  Wool Carpets of America
Artistry in carpets
  Painter Carpet Mills, Inc., Div. Collins and
  Aikman
Carpets of distinction
  Patcraft Mills, Inc.
Fashion loomed to last
  Magee Carpet Co.
First in fashion
  Patcraft Mills, Inc.
The magic of Masland Carpets
  C. H. Masland and Sons
People who know buy Bigelow
  Bigelow-Sanford, Inc.
Quality since 1846
  Philadelphia Carpet Co.
The remarkable new carpet that's flooring
    the country (Densylon)
  Commercial Carpet Corp.
Rugs, carpets since 1825
  Bigelow-Sanford, Inc.
Since 1846, the quality of elegance under-
    foot
  Philadelphia Carpet Co.
Think original, think Dellinger
  Dellinger, Inc.
Those heavenly carpets by Lees
  James Lees and Sons Co.
A title on the door rates a Bigelow on the
    floor
  Bigelow-Sanford, Inc.
We care about color
  Simon Manges and Son, Inc.
World's largest maker of tufted carpets and
    rugs
  E. T. Barwick Industries, Inc.

Casualty Insurance—see Insurance

Chairs

Best buy Boling
  Boling Chair Co.
The chair that stands by itself
  Stakmore Co., Inc.
Chairs for all business
  Boling Chair Co.
The folding furniture with the permanent
    look
  Stakmore Co., Inc.
If it's chairs. . .it's Miele!
  Ralph A. Miele, Inc.
If Miele doesn't have it. . .no one has!
  Ralph A. Miele, Inc.
Specialists in seating—and seating only—since
    1927
  Harter Corp.

Cheese—see Dairy Products

Chemical Industry

Another example of how Monsanto moves
    on many fronts to serve you
  Monsanto Co.
Ask Allied Chemical
  Allied Chemical Corp.
Basic chemicals and cost-cutting ideas
  Chemical Div., PPG Industries, Inc.
Basic in catalyst chemistry
  American Cyanamid Co.
Basic producers from mine to finished
    product
  Industrial Chemicals Marketing Div.,
  Tennessee Corp.
Basic provider of chemicals in volume
  Abbott Laboratories
Basic to America's progress
  Allied Chemical Corp.
Best-selling aerosols are powered with Freon
    propellents
  Freon Products Div., E. I. duPont de
  Nemours and Co.
Better things for better living through
    chemistry
  E. I. duPont de Nemours and Co.
The bright new silicates for industry
  Allegheny Industrial and Chemical Co.
Energy chemicals
  Cities Service Co.
Fine chemicals (Baker and Adamson)
  General Chemical Div., Allied Chemical
  Corp.
First in urethane chemistry
  Mobay Chemical Co.

First name in herbicide research
  Amchem Products, Inc.
Go where you get choosing range
  United States Borax and Chemical Corp.
In home, health, farm and industry, science
    in action for you
  American Cyanamid Co.
In industry world-wide
  Swift and Co.
Leading innovators in polymer chemistry
  Goodrich-Gulf Chemicals, Inc.
Let us help put Armour idea chemicals to
    work for you
  Armour and Co.
Look for more from Morton
  Morton Chemical Co., Div. Morton Inter-
  national, Inc.
Means progress. . .through catalysis, Houdry
  Houdry Process and Chemical Co.
The one to watch for new developments
  Goodrich-Gulf Chemicals, Inc.
Pioneers in hydride chemistry
  Metal Hydrides, Inc.
Plus values
  Chemical Div., General Mills, Inc.
Producers of all basic urethane chemicals
  Allied Chemical Corp.
Progressive products through chemical
    research
  Hysol Div., Dexter Corp.
Putting the "push" in America's finest aero-
    sols (Genetron)
  Allied Chemical Corp.
A skilled hand in chemistry. . .at work for
    you
  Nopco Chemical Co.
Special chemicals for industry
  Carlisle Chemical Works, Inc.
Specialists in high polymers
  Polyvinyl Chemicals, Inc.
Specialists in making water behave
  Anderson Chemical Co., Inc.
Specialty chemicals for industry
  Carlisle Chemical Works, Inc.
Use-engineered for cleaning, protecting and
    processing
  DuBois Chemical Div., W. R. Grace and
  Co.
Watch Highson. . .for progress through creative
    research
  Highson Chemical Co., Div. Lord Corp.
Where experience guides exploration
  Dow Corning Corp.

Where flame technology creates new products
    Oxides Div., Cabot Corp.
Where what's happening gets its start
    Amoco Chemicals Corp.
World's most experienced detergent engineers
    Ing. Mario Ballestra and Co.

Cigarette Lighters
Automatically better
    Ronson Corp.
The lighter that works
    Zippo Mfg. Co.
The people who keep improving flame
    Ronson Corp.

Cigarettes
The best tobacco makes the best smoke
    (Camel)
    R. J. Reynolds Tobacco Co.
Come to where the flavor is. . .come to
    Marlboro country
    Philip Morris, Inc.
Come up to the Kool taste
    Brown and Williamson Tobacco Corp.
Discover extra coolness (Kool)
    Brown and Williamson Tobacco Corp.
The filter for the taste that's right! (Viceroy)
    Brown and Williamson Tobacco Corp.
The first new no-filter cigarette in years
    (York)
    Lorillard Corp.
For a taste that's Springtime fresh (Salem)
    R. J. Reynolds Tobacco Co.
For the best combination of filter and good
    taste Kent satisfies best
    Lorillard Corp.
For the taste that's right (Viceroy)
    Brown and Williamson Tobacco Corp.
For those who want every puff to taste as
    fresh as the first puff! (Montclair)
    American Brands, Inc.
Get the deepweave filter and the taste that's
    right, Viceroy's
    Brown and Williamson Tobacco Corp.
I'd walk a mile for a Camel
    R. J. Reynolds Tobacco Co.
I'm particular (Pall Mall)
    American Brands, Inc.
Just enough! (Montclair)
    American Brands, Inc.
Lightest smoke of all (Carlton)
    American Brands, Inc.
The mark of quality in tobacco products
    Brown and Williamson Tobacco Corp.

The one cigarette for everyone who smokes!
    (Kent)
    Lorillard Corp.
Outstanding—and they are mild! (Pall Mall)
    American Brands, Inc.
A real cigarette (Camel)
    R. J. Reynolds Tobacco Co.
Satisfies best (Kent)
    Lorillard Corp.
Smoke all 7 (Viceroy)
    Brown and Williamson Tobacco Corp.
Smokes fresher—and tastes better than any
    other menthol cigarette, Newport
    Lorillard Corp.
Softness freshens your taste, Salem
    R. J. Reynolds Tobacco Co.
The taste that's right (Viceroy)
    Brown and Williamson Tobacco Corp.
Tastes better than any other menthol ciga-
    rette! (Newport)
    Lorillard Corp.
Tastes good. . .like a cigarette should, Winston
    R. J. Reynolds Tobacco Co.
Tastes great. . .tastes mild, Chesterfield King
    Liggett and Meyers, Inc.
Tastes great. . .yet it smokes so mild (Chester-
    field)
    Liggett and Meyers, Inc.
"Tobacco is our middle name" (C)
    American Brands, Inc.
"Us Tareyton smokers would rather fight
    than switch!"
    American Brands, Inc.

Cigars
America's best tasting little cigar (Between
    the Acts)
    Lorillard Corp.
The cigar that never lasts long enough
    Antonio y Cleopatra)
    American Brands, Inc.
New taste, new smoking convenience. . .any-
    where, anytime (Roi-Tan Little Cigars)
    American Brands, Inc.
World leader in luxury cigars (Gold Label)
    Gradiaz, Annis Div., General Cigar Co.

Citrus—see **Food and Food Ingredients**

Cleaning Compounds
By the world's largest maker of dishwasher
    detergents (Electrasol)
    Economics Laboratories, Inc.
Cleans like a white tornado (TM) (Ajax)
    Colgate-Palmolive Co.

Eliminates drops that spot, Cascade
Procter and Gamble Co.
Famous for products that really work
Glamorene Products Corp.
Give your dishwasher the best (Cascade)
Procter and Gamble Co.
If it's a question of cleaning/conditioning. . .
ask Oakite
Oakite Products, Inc.
"Sheeting action" (Cascade)
Procter and Gamble Co.
Thoughtfully designed with a woman in
mind (Bowlene)
The Climalene Co.
The world's finest name in silver care
W. J. Hagerty and Sons, Ltd., Inc.

Cleaning Machines
. . .Certifies the most in dry cleaning (One
Hour Martinizing)
Martin Equipment Sales, American
Laundry Machinery Industries
The most in dry cleaning (One Hour
Martinizing)
Martin Equipment Sales, American
Laundry Machinery Industries
You get more from American
American Laundry Machinery Industries

Clocks—see Watches

Coffee—see Beverages

Communications
All around the world
Western Union International, Inc.
Long distance is the next best thing to being
there (Bell System)
American Telephone and Telegraph Co.
Manufacturers of world's most widely used
personal communications transmitters
E. F. Johnson Co.
The star's address, CBS
Columbia Broadcasting System, Inc.
Obviously it must be Western Union
Western Union Telegraph Co.
Phone power in action (Bell System)
American Telephone and Telegraph Co.
Serving you (Bell System)
American Telephone and Telegraph Co.
Talk things over, get things done. . .by long
distance! (Bell System)
American Telephone and Telegraph Co.

Where what you want to know comes first
(CBS radio network)
Columbia Broadcasting System, Inc.
Wide world of entertainment
American Broadcasting Co.
Your anywhere, anything, anytime network
American Telephone and Telegraph Co.

Computers—see Electronic Data Processing

Construction Equipment—see Building Materials

Construction Machinery—see Machines and Machinery

Control Equipment—see also Valves
Controls temperature. . .precisely
Fenwal, Inc.
Engineered for value (control systems)
Cutler-Hammer, Inc.
Feather touch control
Acme Lite Products Co.
For improved production through measure-
ment and control
The Bristol Co.
Foremost in final control elements
Conoflow Corp.
If it flows through pipe, chances are it's
controlled by Fisher
Fisher Governor Co.
Leadership through accomplishment
(thermostats)
Therm-O-Disc, Inc.
Means Control, Abex
Abex Corp.
The name that means temperature control
Robertshaw Controls Co.
The name that protects your name
Watts Regulator Co.
Pace setting engineered systems to control
materials in motion
The Louis Allis Co.
Pioneers in precision
Leeds and Northrup Co.
Products made to measure
Daniel Orifice Fitting Co.
Progressive products for fluid control
Manatrol Div., Perry-Fay Co.
P.S. The last word in "automatic control" is
still Robertshaw
Robertshaw Controls Co.
Quality motor control
Allen-Bradley Co.

Rely on T I
 Texas Instruments, Inc.
These names assure you the best in pneu-
  matic, hydraulic and electronic compo-
  nents
 Bellows-Valvair Div., International Basic
 Economy Corp.
What's new? Ask. . .Cutler
 Cutler-Hammer, Inc.
When so much depends on a valve. . .so many
  depend on LimiTorque
 LimiTorque Corp.
Where quality is a tradition. . .and an obliga-
  tion
 Square D Co.
Wherever electricity is distributed and con-
  trolled
 Square D Co.
World-wide competence in control
 Taylor Instrument Companies

Copying Processes
Copies for communication throughout the
  world
 American Photocopy Equipment Co.
For imagination in communication, look to
  3M business product centers
 Minnesota Mining and Mfg. Co.
Look to 3M for imagination in image-making
 Duplicating Products Div., Minnesota
 Mining and Manufacturing Co.
The most beautiful copies of all
 Chas. Bruning Co.
New advances in office copying keep coming
  from Kodak
 Eastman Kodak Co.
Now everybody can have Xerocopies
 Xerox Corp.

Corporate
And the future are made for you, North
  American Rockwell
 North American Rockwell Corp.
Applying advanced technology to bring you
  exciting new products
 Eaton, Yale and Towne, Inc.
Better ideas from UOP
 Universal Oil Products Co.
Building business is our business
 Tenneco, Inc.
Builds for the future, Mannesmann
 Mannesmann—Export Corp.
Capability has many faces at Boeing
 Boeing Co.

Check with Koppers
 Koppers Co., Inc.
Combines experience and innovation to solve
  its customers' problems, Dravo. A
  company of uncommon enterprise.
 Dravo Corp.
A company of uncommon enterprise
 Dravo Corp.
The courage to change. The strength to grow.
 International Harvester Co.
Dedicated to the pursuit of excellence
 Rohr Corp.
The discovery company
 Union Carbide Corp.
Diversified-worldwide
 Singer Co.
Does a lot for you
 Scovill Mfg. Co.
Does it better. . .for a wide range of industries,
  Doughboy
 Doughboy Industries, Inc.
8 Companies running hard
 Trans Union Corp.
The Foodpower (R) people
 Central Soya Co., Inc.
The future is building now at Garrett
 Garrett AiResearch, The Garrett Corp.
The great engineers
 Borg-Warner Corp.
The growing world of Libby-Owens-Ford
 Libby-Owens-Ford Co.
The growth company
 Georgia-Pacific Corp.
. . .Helping people communicate
 Addressograph-Multigraph Corp.
In metals, plastics and paper Budd works to
  make tomorrow. . .today
 Budd Co.
In the air or outer space Douglas gets things
  done
 Douglas Aircraft Co., Inc. (now McDonnell-
 Douglas Corp.)
"The Innovators"
 Torrington Co.
Is at work in the fields of the future, North
  American Aviation
 North American Aviation, Inc. (now
 North American Rockwell Corp.)
Is experience, Garrett
 Garrett AiResearch, The Garrett Corp.
Means distinction, convenience, innovation,
  protection, inventory control, service,
  C.C.A.
 Container Corp. of America

73

The <u>name</u> is Crane
    Crane Co.
A natural resource company
    Cities Service Co.
The people movers
    Budd Co.
Progress for industry worldwide
    Combustion Engineering, Inc.
Progress is our most important product
    General Electric Co.
Progress through precision
    Torrington Co.
Putting ideas to work. . .in machinery, chemi-
    cals, defense, fibers and films
    FMC Corp.
Reliability in rubber, asbestos, sintered
    metal, specialized plastics
    Raybestos-Manhattan, Inc.
"Send me a man who reads!" (C)
    International Paper Co.
Sharing greatly in America's growth
    General Telephone and Electronics Corp.
Specialists in process and energy control
    The Foxboro Co.
A step ahead of tomorrow
    Zurn Industries, Inc.
The 21st century company
    Gulf and Western Industries, Inc.
We're synergistic
    Sperry Rand Corp.
We've just begun to grow
    Keene Corp.
What's new for tomorrow is at Singer today
    Singer Co.
Where great ideas are meant to happen
    Arvin Industries, Inc.
Where ideas unlock the future
    Bendix Corp.
Wherever you look. . .you see Budd
    Budd Co.
World-wide engineering, manufacturing and
    construction
    Dorr-Oliver, Inc.
You can be sure if it's Westinghouse
    Westinghouse Electric Corp.

Corrosion and Anti-Corrosives

Distinctive as your own finger print
    Rust-Oleum Corp.
Proved throughout industry for over 40
    years
    Rust-Oleum Corp.
Quality runs deep, Rust-Oleum
    Rust-Oleum Corp.

Stops rust! (R)
    Rust-Oleum Corp.

Cosmetics—*see also* Hair Preparations; and Toilet Goods

The authority in the exciting world of
    beauty
    Max Factor and Co.
Beauty designers (Dermetics)
    Turner Hall Corp.
Don't be a pale face
    The Coppertone Corp.
Enchanting ladies choose Dorothy Gray
    Lehn and Fink Products Corp.
For the women who can afford the best. Even
    though it costs less. (Hazel Bishop)
    Bishop Industries, Inc.
From the world's most renowned cosmetic
    research laboratories
    Revlon, Inc.
For women whose eyes are older than they
    are
    John Robert Powers Products Co.
The girl with the beautiful face (TM)
    Clairol, Inc.
The girl with the beautiful mouth (TM)
    Clairol, Inc.
The lipstick without the dye
    Ar-ex Products, Inc.
The most elegant name in cosmetics
    (DuBarry)
    Lambert-Hudnut Mfg. Labs, Inc.
The most prized eye cosmetics in the world
    Maybelline Co.
Personalized cosmetic services
    Luzier, Inc.
She has it made (TM)
    Clairol, Inc.
. . .So glamorous you have to be <u>told</u> they're
    hypo-allergenic (Almay)
    Schieffelin and Co.
Specialists in skin care
    Chap Stick Co.
Stays on till you take it off (Coty 24 Hour
    lipstick)
    Coty Div., Chas. Pfizer and Co., Inc.
Tomorrow's skin care—today
    Coty Div., Chas. Pfizer & Co., Inc.
When a Studio Girl enters your home a new
    kind of beauty brightens your life
    Helene Curtis Industries, Inc.
Where beautiful young ideas begin
    Helene Curtis Industries, Inc.

Your face never had it so clean! (1006 lotion)
    Bonne Bell, Inc.

Cotton Fabrics—*see* **Textile Fabrics**

Dairy Products
The cheese with the paper between the slices
    N. Dorman and Co.
Country charm quality
    Dean Foods Co.
A cut above the commonplace
    Danish and Blue Cheese
The finest of natural cheeses—naturally from Kraft
    Kraft Foods Div., Kraftco Corp.
From contented cows
    Carnation Co.
If it's Bordens, it's got to be good
    Borden, Inc.
Just has to be good, Borden's
    Borden, Inc.
Look for this famous name in the oval
    (Philadelphia Brand Cream Cheese)
    Kraft Foods Div., Kraftco Corp.
Naturally it's delicious. . .it's made by Bordens
    Borden, Inc.

Data Processing—*see* **Electronic Data Processing**

Deodorants—*see* **Personal Products**

Design
America's foremost leg specialists
    Plastic Industries, Inc.
Basic products and engineering for industry's basic work
    Link-Belt Co.
Better castings through advanced foundry technology
    Meehanite Metal Corp.
Designs them. . .builds them!
    Chicago Bridge and Iron Co.
Engineering know-how. . .by Blaw-Knox
    Blaw-Knox Co.
If it's conveyed, processed or mined, it's a job for Jeffrey
    The Jeffrey Mfg. Co.
Industry's partner in production
    E. F. Houghton and Co.
The leader in vibration/shock/noise control
    Lord Mfg. Co.
Leaders in thermal engineering design
    Struthers Thermo-Floor Corp.

Mastery of precision optics
    Varo Optical, Inc.
Originators and designers of ultrasonic sealing equipment
    Ultra Sonic Seal, Inc.
The products with the pluses
    Dodge Mfg. Corp.
Put Alliance in your appliance
    The Alliance Mfg. Co., Inc.
World leaders in the development of pulp and paper mills for the use of local fibers
    Parsons & Whittemore, Inc.
You can't afford to be without Swagelok
    Crawford Fitting Co.

Detergents—*see* **Cleaning Compounds**

Dictionaries
The leading name in dictionaries since 1847 (Merriam-Webster)
    G. and C. Merriam Co.
Since 1847, the trusted and authoritative name in dictionaries (Merriam-Webster)
    G. and C. Merriam Co.
There's a world of difference in Webster dictionaries
    G. and C. Merriam Co.
To be sure you're right. . .insist on Merriam-Webster
    G. and C. Merriam Co.
The trusted and authoritative name in dictionaries (Merriam-Webster)
    G. and C. Merriam Co.

Dietary Products—*see also* **Beverages**
The best friend your willpower ever had (Slim-Mint gum)
    Thompson Medical Co., Inc.
Consult your doctor about your weight problems (Sego)
    Milk Products Div., Pet, Inc.
Consult your physician on matters of weight control (Metrecal)
    Mead Johnson and Co.
The modern aid to appetite control (Slim-Mint Gum)
    Thompson Medical Co., Inc.

Domestic Appliances—*see also* **Electric Apparatus; and Appliances, Domestic**
Backed by a century-old tradition of fine craftsmanship
    Amana Refrigeration, Inc.

Better because it's gas. . .best because it's
    Caloric
    Caloric Corp.
Build-in satisfaction. . .build-in Frigidaire
    Frigidaire Div., General Motors Corp.
The dependable automatics
    Maytag Co.
The dependability people
    Maytag Co.
First with the features women want most
    Hotpoint Div., General Electric Co.
Jet action washers
    Frigidaire Div., General Motors Corp.
Sanitize your dishes sparkling clean!
    Frigidaire Div., General Motors Corp.
The very good washer (RCA Whirlpool)
    Whirlpool Corp.
Years from now you'll be glad it's Norge
    Norge Div., Borg-Warner Corp.
You cook better automatically with a
        Tappan
    Tappan Co.
You live better automatically with Tappan
    Tappan Co.

Doors
America's finest basement door
    Bilce Co.
Best way to close an opening
    Cookson Co.
Saving ways in doorways since 1895
    Kinnear Corp.

Drug Industry—see also Medicines, Proprie-
    tary
Another clinical-strength medication from
    Warner-Lambert
    Warner-Lambert Pharmaceutical Co.
Better medicines for a better world
    Parke, Davis and Co.
A leader in dental research
    Squibb Beech-Nut, Inc.
Making today's medicines with integrity...
        seeking tomorrow's with persistence
    A. H. Robins Co.
A name you can trust
    Squibb Beech-Nut, Inc.
Original research serving the physician
    Sandoz, Inc.
Prescription medicines around the world
    Eli Lilly and Co.
The priceless ingredient, Squibb quality
    Squibb Beech-Nut, Inc.

Research in the service of medicine
    G. D. Searle and Co.
Science for the world's well being (R)
    Chas. Pfizer and Co., Inc.
Service to medicine (R)
    Wyeth Laboratories Div., American Home
    Products Corp.
Sharing the responsibilities of modern
        medicine
    Stanlabs, Inc.
Where today's theory is tomorrow's remedy
    Merck, Sharp and Dohme Div., Merck and
    Co., Inc.

Dyes and Dyeing
Don't miss the magic of Rit
    Best Foods Div., CPC International, Inc.
Dyeing with Rit is fast, fun, almost fool-
        proof!
    Best Foods Div., CPC International, Inc.
Thinks ahead with textiles, Sandoz
    Sandoz, Inc.
When it comes to color, come to Cyanamid
    American Cyanamid Co.

Electric Apparatus and Appliances, Domes-
    tic—see also Domestic Appliances
Built with integrity, backed by service
    Sunbeam Corp.
A bright new world of electric housewares
        (Norelco)
    North American Philips Corp.
The complete line of electric cooking appa-
        ratus (Toastmaster)
    McGraw-Edison Co.
Live better electrically
    Edison Electric Institute
Originator and perfecter of the garbage dis-
        poser
    In-Sink-Erator Mfg. Co.
Progress is our most important product
    General Electric Co.
Quality you can trust. Value you can recog-
        nize
    Iona Mfg. Co.
World's oldest and largest manufacturer of
        electric blankets
    Northern Electric Co.
You can be sure it it's Westinghouse
    Westinghouse Electric Corp.

Electric Apparatus, Industrial
Power across land and sea
    ASEA Electric Systems

The power behind the leading products
  Bodine Electric Co.
Put quality first and everything follows
  Fuji Electric Co., Ltd.
Where the brightest ideas come to light
  General Electric Co.
"Who we serve proves how we serve" (con-
    tractors)
  Fishback and Moore, Inc.

Electric Batteries
Big name in batteries
  Ray-O-Vac Div., ESB, Inc.
Portable power for progress
  Battery Div., Sonotone Corp.
"Power to spare" (Eveready)
  Union Carbide Corp.

Electric Blankets—see Electric Apparatus; and Appliances, Domestic

Electric Shavers
The close electric shave (Norelco)
  North American Philips Corp.
The comfort shave (Norelco)
  North American Philips Corp.
The mark of quality
  Schick Electric, Inc.
You can't get any closer (Norelco)
  North American Philips Corp.

Electric Utilities—see Public Utilities

Electronic Data Processing
An American leader in advanced systems of
    photo-optics for information proc-
    essing
  Itek Corp.
The automated answer to the paper explo-
    sion
  Remington Office Systems Div., Sperry
  Rand Corp.
Automation is economical
  Fusion, Inc.
The computer with a future, System/360
  International Business Machines, Inc.
The first computer (Univac)
  Sperry Rand Corp.
Is saving a lot of people a lot of time, Univac
  Sperry Rand Corp.
Leader in computer graphics (Cal Comp)
  California Computer Products, Inc.
Leadership in low-cost/high-reliability digital
    magnetic tape handling
  Datamec Corp.

Leads in automatic log computation
  Schlumberger, Ltd.
Machines that make data move
  Teletype Corp.
The other computer company
  Honeywell, Inc.
Our business is the intelligent use of com-
    puters
  Electronic Data Systems
The problem solvers (G. E. Computers)
  General Electric Co.
Specialists in digital technology (Cal Comp)
  California Computer Products, Inc.
Standard of the plotting industry (Cal Comp)
  California Computer Products, Inc.
Where the data movement started and start-
    ling moves are made
  Teletype Corp.

Electronic Instruments
An extra measure of quality
  Hewlett-Packard Co.
Builders of the tools of automation
  Reliance Electric and Engineering Co.
Creating a new world with electronics
  Hughes Aircraft Co.
It's good business to do business with
    Mallory
  P. R. Mallory and Co., Inc.
The "light" touch in automation and control
  Clairex Corp.
Manning the frontiers of electronic progress
  Autonetics Div., North American Rock-
  well Corp.
The most trusted name in electronics
  R.C.A. Corp.
New ideas in automation control
  Photoswitch Div., Electronics Corp. of
  America
New leader in the lively art of electronics
  Motorola, Inc.
Quality electric components
  Allen-Bradley Co.
Total communications from a single source
    through Sylvania
  Sylvania Electric Products, Inc.
A world of experience
  Collins Radio Co.
The world's most broadly based electronics
    company
  R.C.A. Corp.
Worldwide electronics telecommunications
  International Telephone and Telegraph
  Co.

Elevators—see **Buildings**

Employees, Temporary
Can do, Kelly
    Kelly Services, Inc.
Good people
    Olsten Temporary Services
Office help—temporary or permanent
    American Girl Service
100% guaranteed temporary office help
    Kelly Services, Inc.
One source, one standard—nationwide
    Kelly Services, Inc.
The very best in temporary help
    Manpower, Inc.

Engines
Leadership through creative engineering
    McCulloch Corp.
Cummins means diesel
    Cummins Engine Co., Inc.
Most respected name in power
    Briggs and Stratton Corp.
One proven design throughout the line builds
    greater value into every engine
    Detroit Diesel Engine Div., General
    Motors Corp.
World's largest builder of heavy-duty air-
    cooled engines
    Wisconsin Motor Corp.
Your job is well powered when it's Ford
    powered
    Industrial Engine Dept., Ford Div., Ford
    Motor Co.

Eyeglasses
Don't say sunglasses—say C'Bon
    Polaroid Corp.
Since 1833...better vision for better living
    American Optical Co.

Fabrics—see **Textiles**

Farm Machinery—see **Agricultural Machinery**

Fastenings
The authority on fastening
    The Apex Machine and Tool Co.
Costs less than trouble, UNBRAKO
    Precision Fastener Div., Standard Pressed
    Steel Co.
Fasten it better and faster with Bostitch
    Bostitch, Inc.
In fast to hold fast
    Duo-Fastener Corp.

It's a snap with Dot
    Carr Fastener Co.
Look for the Tinnerman "T", the mark of
    total reliability
    Tinnerman Products, Inc.
The mark of total reliability
    Tinnerman Products, Inc.
Quality fastening products for industry
    Simmons Fastener Corp.

Feed and Feed Stuffs
Builders of tomorrow's feeds. . .today!
    (Wayne feeds)
    Allied Mills Corp.
Serving the businessman in the blue denim
    suit (Master Mix)
    Central Soya Co., Inc.

Fertilizer
Don't just fertilize. . .Spencerize
    Spencer Chemical Div., Gulf Oil Corp.
Since 1886. . .scientifically designed for prac-
    tical use
    John Blue Co., Inc.
You can depend on the integrity and quality
    of Smith-Douglass
    Smith-Douglass Div., Borden Chemical Co.

Files and Filing—see **Office Equipment**

Finance—see also **Investments**
. . .Helping people and business help them-
    selves
    Commercial Credit Co.
Instant news service (R)
    Dow Jones and Co.
The man from A. G. Becker is always worth
    listening to
    A. G. Becker & Co., Inc.
Over one billion dollars annually for indus-
    try
    Walter E. Heller and Co.
Since 1808, a tradition in factoring and
    financing
    William Iselin and Co., Inc.
Specialists in financing
    Associates Investment Co.
Working funds for industry
    Walter E. Heller and Co.

Firearms
The custom crafted shotgun
    Charles Daly
Expert's choice. . .since 1880
    Ithaca Gun Co., Inc.

First in sporting arms
Browning Arms Co.
For accuracy, Mossberg
O. F. Mossberg and Sons, Inc.
"On the range"
Williams Gun Sight Co.
Symbol of accuracy since 1870
Marlin Firearms Co.
World's largest producer of non-powder guns
and ammo
Daisy/Heddon Div., Victor Comptometer
Corp.
World's most complete line of sporting arms
and accessories
Savage Arms Div., Emhart Corp.

First Aid
The best aid is first aid
Johnson and Johnson
Products you can trust from people you
know (dressings)
Will Ross, Inc.
The tape that won't hurt coming off (Micro-
pore)
Minnesota Mining and Mfg. Co.

Fishing Tackle
Adds science to fisherman's luck
True Temper Corp.
America's finest fishing rods
Browning Arms Co.
"Bait of champions"
Fred Arbogast Co., Inc.
Creating world-famed fishing tackle since
1893
South Bend Tackle Co., Div. Gladding
Corp.
First choice in fishing tackle hardware
Allan Mfg. Co.
First in world records
Ashaway Line and Twine Mfg. Co.
First on famous waters
Johnson Reels, Inc.
The fish hook people
O. Mustad and Son
For the discriminating sportsman
O. Mustad and Son
Make your own luck with Heddon
James Heddon and Sons
The most respected name in fishing tackle
Zebco Div., Brunswick Corp.
Pick a Perrine today!
Aladdin Laboratories, Inc.

Precision fishing reels since 1883
Martin Reel Co.
Put a Burke where they lurk!
Flexo-Products Div., McCllelan Industries
The reels of champions
Penn Fishing Tackle Mfg. Co.
"Service guaranteed for life!"
The Garcia Corp.
Think system
Scientific Anglers, Inc.
"Weavers of the world's finest netting"
Victory Sports Net Div., The Fishnet and
Twine Co.
Where the action is!
Zebco Div., Brunswick Corp.
World's finest
Phillipson Rod Co.
World's largest exclusive fly line manufac-
turer
Scientific Anglers, Inc.
World's most wanted lure
Rapala Div., Nordic Enterprises, Inc.

Fleets, Motor Vehicle—see Motor Vehicle
Fleets

Flooring, Floor Covering
Distinctive floor coverings since 1917
Ernest Treganowan
Fine flooring
Ruberoid Co.
Fine floors (Congoleum-Nairn)
Congoleum Industries, Inc.
Finest in flooring since 1898
Harris Hardwood Co.
A generation of worldwide acceptance
Torginol of America, Inc.
More ideas from the Armstrong world of
interior design
Armstrong Cork Co.
Originators of prefinished hardwood flooring
The Cromar Co.
Wholesale floor coverings of distinction
Manuel Feldman Co., Inc.

Food and Food Ingredients
All fresh-fruit good! (jellies, preserves)
Kraft Foods Div., Kraftco Corp.
"Always an adventure in good eating." (Dun-
can Hines)
Procter and Gamble Co.
America's best-liked cereal assortment
Kellogg Co.

America's first, finest and favorite pork and beans
    Stokely-Van Camp, Inc.
Best cooks know foods fried in Crisco don't taste greasy!
    Procter and Gamble
The best to you each morning
    Kellogg Co.
Better buy Birds Eye
    Birds Eye Div., General Foods Corp.
Breakfast of Champions (Wheaties)
    General Foods Corp.
The catsup with the big tomato taste
    Hunt-Wesson Foods, Inc.
Color is nature's way of saying flavor. Stokely is your way of getting it
    Stokely-Van Camp, Inc.
Easy, delicious. . .versatile, nutritious
    Rice Council
Famous for candy flavors
    Fenn Bros., Inc.
The finest name in frozen foods
    Dunlany Foods, Inc.
For good food and good food ideas
    Kraft Foods Div., Kraftco Corp.
For the best, Hunt
For the best, Hunt
    Hunt-Wesson Foods, Inc.
The good kind to keep handy because they stay soft (marshmallows)
    Kraft Foods Div., Kraftco Corp.
Good things from the garden
    Green Giant Co.
Good things to eat come from 1 Mustard St.
    The R. T. French Co.
Helps build strong bodies 12 ways! (Wonder Bread)
    Continental Baking Co., Inc.
The house of flavor
    McCormick and Co., Inc.
If you could see inside oranges, you'd buy Sunkist every time
    Sunkist Growers, Inc.
It's no secret. . .Schilling flavor makes all the difference in the world!
    Schilling Div., McCormick and Co., Inc.
The kind you cook up fresh...and quick (home cooked dinners)
    Kraft Foods Div., Kraftco Corp.
Look-alikes aren't cook-alikes
    Idaho Potato Growers, Inc.
Make Sunsweet your daily good health habit
    Sunsweet Growers, Inc.

Measure of quality (rice)
    Uncle Ben's, Inc.
Moist as homemade (Duncan Hines cake mixes)
    Procter and Gamble Co.
The most experienced food processor in the world
    Libby, McNeill and Libby
The name for quality
    Planters Peanuts Div., Standard Brands, Inc.
Not just good...but wonderful (R)
    Johnston's Pie Co. Div., Ward Foods, Inc.
—Not only light but deliciously light (peanut oil)
    Planters Peanuts Div., Standard Brands, Inc.
Quality food products used with confidence (commercial)
    Procter and Gamble
Quality foods (commercial)
    John Sexton Co.
The quick kind you cook up fresh (home cooked dinners)
    Kraft Foods Div., Kraftco Corp.
The rice people, Uncle Ben's
    Uncle Ben's, Inc.
Shot from guns
    Quaker Oats Co.
Silent partners in famous foods (R) (coloring, flavoring)
    Stange Co.
Start with—stay with Knox
    Knox Gelatine, Inc.
Sugar's got what it takes
    Sugar Information, Inc.
Tastes so good and so good for you (Cream of Rice)
    Grocery Store Products Co.
The tender-textured gelatin (Royal)
    Standard Brands, Inc.
The tender tuna with the delicate taste
    Star-Kist Foods, Inc.
Thank goodness for Banquet cooking bag foods
    Banquet Canning Div., F. M. Stamper Co.
Thank goodness for Banquet frozen foods
    Banquet Canning Div., F. M. Stamper Co.
There are imitations—be sure the brand is Tabasco
    McIlhenny Co.
To get more that's good. . .trust Swanson (frozen dinners)

To serve something fancy start with something fancy (Flav-R-Pac)
  Stayton Canning Co.
The way the best lemons sign their name
  Sunkist Growers, Inc.
When it rains, it pours
  Morton Salt Co.
When it's Domino Sugar, your're sure it's pure!
  American Sugar Refining Co.
The world's largest and finest
  Lindsay Ripe Olive Co.

Food Ingredients—*see* **Food and Food Ingredients**

Forms and Blanks—*see* **Office Supplies**

Foundation Garments
The aristocrat of fine corsetry
  Corde de Parie, Inc.
Behind every Olga there really is an Olga
  Olga Co.
Every Bali has a bow
  Bali Brassiere Co.
For the girl who knows value by heart (brassieres)
  The Loveable Co.
Keep your eye on Maidenform
  Maidenform, Inc.
Nicest next to you
  H. W. Gossard Co.
Shapemakers to the world's most beautiful women
  Treo Co., Inc.
This is the dream you can be. . .with Maidenform
  Maidenform, Inc.

Fountain Pens
America's finest writing instruments since 1846
  A. T. Cross Co.
Engineering with imagination
  Scripto, Inc.
Creator of advanced writing instruments
  Micropoint, Inc.
Maker of the world's most wanted pens
  Parker Pen Co.
Originators of the world-famous Utility (TM) ball pen
  Lindy Pen Co., Inc.
Quality first. . .from America's first penmaker
  Esterbrook Pen Co.

Your assurance of the best (TM)
  W. A. Sheaffer Pen Co.

Freight—*see* **Railroads; Motor Truck Freight Service; Barge Lines; and Ocean Travel**

Frozen Foods—**Foods and Food Ingredients**

Fruit Juices—*see* **Beverages**

Furniture
America's largest manufacturer of custom day beds and sofa beds
  M. Mittman Co.
America's most distinguished source for fine English furniture
  Wood and Hogan
America's oldest and largest showroom distributor of fine decorative furniture
  Knapp and Tubbs, Inc.
Another fine creation by Krueger
  Krueger Metal Products Co.
At home with your young ideas
  Bassett Furniture Industries, Inc.
Built to take it. . .beautifully
  Daystrom Furniture Div., Daystrom, Inc.
By design. . .furniture distinguished for value since 1904
  Thomasville Furniture Industries, Inc.
Carefree furniture
  Viko Furniture
The costume jewelry of the home
  Mersman Tables
Craftsmen of fine solid wood furniture
  Davis Cabinet Co.
Creators of the world famous Stratolounger
  Futorian Mfg. Corp.
Definitive modern furniture
  Founders Furniture, Inc.
Fine cabinetmakers since 1886
  Karges Furniture Co.
Fine furniture
  Henredon Furniture Industries, Inc.
Fine furniture
  George J. Kempler Co.
For more than a century makers of fine furniture in traditional and modern idiom
  John Widdicomb Co.
Furniture of timeless beauty
  Romweber Industries
Furniture that's fun to live with
  H. T. Cushman Mfg. Corp.
If it folds. . .ask Howe
  Howe Folding Furniture, Inc.

Importers and makers of fine furniture
  Leopold Colombo, Inc.
In a word. . .it's Selig
  Selig Mfg. Co., Inc.
It's the very finest because it's Rubee
  Rubee Furniture Mfg. Corp.
. . .Keeping tradition alive
  Meldan Co., Inc.
A living tradition in furniture
  Heritage Furniture, Inc.
Master craftsmen since 1890
  Biggs Antique Co., Inc.
The more living you do, the more you need
    Samsonite
  Samsonite Corp.
The most famous name in rattan furniture
  Ficks Reed Co.
The most trusted name in furniture
  Drexel Enterprises, Inc.
. . .The name for fine rattan furniture
  Whitecraft, Inc.
The one bed frame people ask for by name
  Harvard Mfg. Co.
Preferred for America's most dintinguished
    homes
  Romweber Industries
Quality shows through
  Drew Furniture Co.
Solid comfort seating
  Hampden Specialty Products Co.
The South's oldest makers of fine furniture
  White Furniture Co.
Style authority in wrought iron
  Lee L. Woodward and Sons, Inc.
There's a quality about a home with Henre-
    don
  Henredon Furniture Industries, Inc.
Tomorrow is a friend of Dunbar (R)
  Dunbar Furniture Corp.
Where pride of craftsmanship comes first
  Empire Furniture Corp.
A world of furniture made in a way that
    makes a world of difference
  Kroehler Mfg. Co.

Gas as Fuel

America's fastest growing fuel
  Thermogas, Inc.
Do it tomorrow's way. . .with gas
  American Gas Assn., Inc.
For commercial cooking. . .gas is good busi-
    ness
  American Gas Assn., Inc.

For heating and cooling. . .gas is good business
  American Gas Assn., Inc.
Gas makes the big difference
  American Gas Assn., Inc.
Live modern for less with gas
  American Gas Assn., Inc.
Of America's great sources of energy, only
      National serves you in so many ways
  National LP-Gas Market Development
  Council

Gas Companies—see Public Utilities

Gasoline

The chevron—the sign of excellence
  Standard Oil Co. of California
Fire up with Firebird
  The Pure Oil Co.
For quality you can depend on. . .depend on
    Skelgas
  Skelly Oil Co.
Go first class. . .go Phillips 66
  Phillips Petroleum Co.
Happy Motoring! (R)
  Enco Div., Humble Oil and Refining Co.
Hottest brand going! (R) (Conoco)
  Continental Oil Co.
Localized for you (Texaco Sky Chief)
  Texaco, Inc.
Put a tiger in your tank (Enco)
  Humble Oil and Refining Co.
Quality. . .the best economy of all
  Sun Oil Co.
Worth changing brands to get
  Pure Oil Co.

Glass

Everyday good. . .glass with flair
  Anchor Hocking Glass Corp.
A famous brand in glass
  Latchford Glass Co.
Get it in glass
  Glass Containers Manufacturers Institute
The greatest line in glassware!
  Anchor Hocking Glass Corp.
Pioneers in colored glass technology
  Houze Glass Corp.
The quality mark to look for
  Libbey-Owens-Ford Co.
This is the open world of LOF glass
  Libbey-Owens-Ford Co.
Treasured American glass
  Viking Glass Co.

Unusual reliability and service. . .the usual at
    Kopp Glass
    Kopp Glass, Inc.
When you start with metal. . .finish with
    Duracron!
    PPG Industries, Inc.
Where there's a window. . .there's a place for
    Thermopane
    Libbey-Owens-Ford Co.
World's largest manufacturer of glass table-
    ware
    Anchor Hocking Glass Corp.

Glue—*see* **Adhesives**

Golf—*see* **Sporting Goods**

Goods and Services
Action people (Yellow Pages)
    American Telephone and Telegraph Co.
Advertise for action (Yellow Pages)
    American Telephone and Telegraph Co.
Find it faster in the Yellow Pages
    American Telephone and Telegraph Co.
Let your fingers do the walking (Yellow
    Pages)
    American Telephone and Telegraph Co.

Greeting Cards
If you care enough to send the very best
    Hallmark Cards, Inc.
When you care enough to send the very best
    Hallmark Cards, Inc.

Guns—*see* **Firearms**

Hair Preparations
Approved by professional hair colorists
    (Nestle Color Tint)
    Nestle—LeMur Co.
Does she. . .or doesn't she (R)
    Clairol, Inc.
Everyone knows, if it's Caryl Richards, it is
    just wonderful for your hair
    Caryl Richards, Inc.
For twenty-five years, first in professional
    hair care
    Rayette-Faberge, Inc.
Hair color so natural only her hairdresser
    knows for sure (TM)
    Clairol, Inc.
Makes your husband feel younger, too. . .just
    to look at you! (Loving Care)
    Clairol, Inc.
Only her hairdresser knows for sure (TM)
    Clairol, Inc.

Professional cosmetics for lovelier hair color
    Roux Labs, Inc.

Hardware
Ask for K-V. . .it's a known value!
    Knape & Vogt Mfg. Co.
America's largest selling residential locksets
    Kwikset Div., Emhart Corp.
Everything hinges on Hager
    Hager Hinge Co.
The finest name in locks and hardware (Yale
    and Towne)
    Eaton Yale and Town, Inc.
First family in drapery hardware since 1903
    Newell Mfg. Co.
Helps you do things right (Stanley hardware)
    The Stanley Works
It pays to make it Corbin—throughout!
    (door lockset)
    P and F Corbin Div., Emhart Corp.
Keeps you in the driver's seat, Genie!
    Alliance Mfg. Co., Inc.
Manufacturers of quality drapery hardware
    since 1903
    Silent Gliss, Inc.
More doors fold on Fold-Aside (R) than any
    other kind!
    Acme Appliance Mfg. Co.
No sash hardware installs faster than Grand
    Rapids Hardware
    Grand Rapids Hardware
The safe way out
    Von Duprin Div., Vonnegut Hardware
    Co., Inc.
The silent drapery track (R)
    Silent Gliss, Inc.
A trustworthy name in electrical protection
    (Buss fuses)
    Bussman Mfg. Div., McGraw-Edison Co.
"Unlocking new concepts in architectural
    hardware since 1839" (keys)
    Russwin-Emhart Corp.
World's strongest padlocks
    Master Lock Co.
You expect the best from Hanson. . .and you
    get it
    Henry L. Hanson Co.

Health Insurance—*see* **Insurance, Health**

Heating
It's matchless
    Hunter Div., Robbins and Meyers, Inc.
Specialists in solving unusual heating problems
    Glas-Col Apparatus Co.

Helicopters—*see* **Airplanes**

High Fidelity Sound Equipment—*see also*
Phonograph, High Fidelity Equipment
Ampex Corp.
Ask anyone who knows
Ampex Corp.
Known in millions of homes
Nutone, Inc.
Leadership through design
Mercury Record Corp.
The most trusted name in sound
RCA Corp.

Hoisting Machinery
In advance of progress
Euclid Crane and Hoist Co.
The right hoist for every application
Harnischfeger Corp.
A world of engineering experience
Globe Hoist Co.

Home Building—*see* **Houses**

Hose
The lifeline of your equipment
Aeroquip Corp.
The original reinforced plastic hose
Supplex Co.

Hosiery
Finer seamless stockings
Oleg Cassini, Inc.
Hosiery fashion on five continents
Berkshire International Corp.
Knows how to please him, Hanes
Hanes Corp.
Legsize stockings (Belle-Sharmeer)
Wayne Gossard Corp.
They fit (Round-the-Clock)
National Mills Div., U.S. Industries

Hotels
The friendly world of Hilton
Hilton Hotels Corp.
Go international. . .with all the comforts of
Hilton
Hilton Hotels Corp.

Household Appliances—*see* **Domestic Appliances, Electric**; and **Appliances, Domestic**

Household Products
Always first with the best (Polly-Flex housewares)
Republic Molding Corp.

The can opener people
Dazey Products
. . .Fashioned for those who enjoy extraordinary quality
Gerber Legendary Blades
50 years of brighter tasting meals (Corning Ware)
Corning Glass Works
First in home service
Watkins Products, Inc.
Home-care know-how. . .at your doorstep!
Amway Corp.
It makes a dust magnet of your dust mop or cloth (Endust)
Drackett Co.
It's fun to own a gift by Rival
Rival Mfg. Co.
Means better made, Rubbermaid
Rubbermaid, Inc.
New ideas for happier homemaking
The West Bend Co.
No-stick cooking with no-scour clean-up (Teflon)
E. I. duPont de Nemours and Co.
The original polyethylene coated freezer wrap
St. Regis Paper Co.
Oven-tempered for flexible strength! (Reynolds Wrap)
The pressure cooker people
National Presto Industries, Inc.
The trusted name in household products since 1917
Gem, Inc.
Useful products for family living
Hamilton Cosco, Inc.
Where the nicest people meet the nicest things
Stanley Home Products, Inc.
"Woman's best friend" (Polly Flex Housewares)
Republic Molding Corp.
World's largest producer of bath scales (Counselor)
The Brearley Co.
You'll find the woman's touch in every Purex product
Purex Corp., Ltd.
Your kitchen companion since 1899
Dazey Products Co.

Houses—*see also* **Building Materials**; and
Windows
The homes teamwork builds
Inland Homes Corp.

The name of the game is living. . .explore a
new home today (C)
National Association of Home Builders

Housewares—*see* **Household Products**

Industrial Design—*see* **Design**

Industrial Development Programs
America's most interesting state
Tennessee Dept. of Conservation
The big sky country
Montana Highway Commission
Birthplace of the nation
Virginia Dept. of Conservation and Eco-
nomic Development
Brainpower builds profits, Minnesota
Minnesota Dept. of Business Development
Builders in and of the South
Daniel Construction Co., Inc.
Come to Kentucky! It's a profitable move!
Kentucky Dept. of Commerce
Discover the new in New York State
New York State Dept. of Commerce
Friendly land of infinite variety
South Dakota Dept. of Highways
The hospitality state
Mississippi
Industrious Maine, New England's big stake
in the future
Maine Dept. of Economic Development
Industry is on the move to Iowa
Iowa Development Commission
Industry's friendliest climate
Public Services of Indiana, Inc.
Keep Missouri in the center of your thinking
Missouri Commerce and Industrial Devel-
opment Commission.
The land of elbow room and elbow grease
Omaha Public Power District
Look ahead. Look South
Southern Railway Co.
Make the capital choice
Port Authority of the City of St. Paul
Means profits for business
State of Louisiana Dept. of Commerce
and Industry
Mix fun and history in Virginia
Virginia Dept. of Conservation and Eco-
nomic Development
State of excitement
Oregon Highway Dept.
The surprising state
State of Washington

"We like it here"
Wisconsin Div. of Economic Development
When you make your move—make sure it's a
planned move
Central Illinois Light Co.
Where big things are happening
Commonwealth of Kentucky
Where free enterprise is still growing
Indiana Dept. of Commerce
Where good government is a habit
North Carolina Dept. of Conservation

Information Storage and Retrieval Systems—
see **Electronic Data Processing**

Insurance
The finest protection available for your fam-
ily, your property and your business
Fireman's Fund American Insurance
For all kinds of insurance in a single plan,
call your Travelers man
Travelers, Inc.
. . .For your family and business—your auto,
home, and everything youo
(casualty)
Aetna Insurance Co.
"Hot-Line" claim service
Imperial Auto Insurance
Leader in business insurance
New York Life Insurance Co.
P.S.—Personal Service (casualty)
Aetna Insurance Co.
You can get all types of insurance under the
Travelers umbrella
The Travelers Insurance Co.
You're in good hands with Allstate (R)
Allstate Insurance Co.

Insurance, Automobile—*see* **Insurance**

Insurance, Boiler
"Inspection is our middle name"
Hartford Steam Boiler Inspection and
Insurance Co.
Insurors of energy systems
Hartford Steam Boiler Inspection and
Insurance Co.

Insurance, Business—*see* **Insurance**

Insurance, Casualty—*see* **Insurance**

Insurance, Health
The greatest name in health insurance
Mutual of Omaha Insurance Co.
For doctor bills
Blue Shield

Insurance, Life

An idea whose time has come!
  Harlan Insurance Co.
Be sure, insure in INA
  Insurance Co. of North America
Call your Investors man—today!
  Investors Diversified Services, Inc.
The choice of businessmen lets you choose
    with confidence
  Aetna Insurance Co.
The company with the partnership philoso-
    phy
  American United Life Insurance Co.
"Dollar wise group insurance"
  Pan-American Life Insurance Co.
The fourth necessity
  Metropolitan Life Insurance Co.
The friendly
  Franklin Life Insurance Co.
The future belongs to those who prepare for
    it
  The Prudential Insurance Co. of America
The good things of life
  Bankers Life Insurance Co. of Nebraska
Has the strength of Gibraltar, The Prudential
  The Prudential Insurance Co. of America
Its name indicates its character
  The Lincoln National Life Insurance Co.
Lifelong security through programmed pro-
    tection
  Monarch Life Insurance Co.
Light that never fails
  The Metropolitan Life Insurance Co.
Living insurance
  Equitable Life Assurance Society of the
  United States
Look ahead with living insurance
  Equitable Life Assorance Society of the
  United States
Looks out for you
  Sentry Insurance Co.
More choose Metropolitan. Millions more
    than any other company.
  Metropolitan Life Insurance Co.
The name again. . .Nationwide Life
  Nationwide Life Insurance Co.
Our concern is people
  Aetna Insurance Co.
Procrastination is the highest cost of life
    insurance. It increases both your pre-
    mium and your risk
  The Union Central Life Insurance Co.
Protection in a new light
  Monumental Life Insurance Co.

Restituimus—"We restore". . .since 1854
  Phoenix of Hartford Insurance Co.
Security is our business
  United of Omaha
Serving you around the world. . .around the
    clock
  The St. Paul Insurance Co.
Six and a half billion dollars of protection
    for our policyholders
  Great-West Life Assurance Co.
The small business that got big serving small
    business
  Sentry Insurance Co.
The strength of Gibraltar
  The Prudential Insurance Co. of America
There's no obligation. . .except to those you
    love
  Metropolitan Life Insurance Co.
"Value" is a good word for Benefit Trust
    Life.
  Benefit Trust Life Insurance
Where people and ideas create security for
    millions
  Connecticut General Life Insurance Co.
Where you are always number one
  The Glen Falls Group
Will bring peace of mind to you and your
    family
  The Guardian Life Insurance Co. of
  America
Will enrich and safeguard your retirement
    years, Guardian
  The Guardian Life Insurance Co. of
  America
You can count on Kemper care under the
    Kemper flag
  Kemper Insurance Co.
Your guardian for life
  Guardian Life Insurance Co.

Insurance, Mutual

"Because there is a difference"
  The Northwestern Mutual Life Insurance
  Co.
The Blue Chip company
  Connecticut Mutual Life Insurance Co.
For a sure tomorrow—insure enough today!
  American Hardware Mutual Insurance Co.
"Good people to do business with"
  Employers Mutual Liability Insurance Co.
  of Wisconsin
Industry-owned to conserve property and
    profits
  Factory Mutual Insurance Co.

It pays to insure with the "Blue Chip" company
  Connecticut Mutual Life Insurance Co.
A leading writer of workmen's compensation, all forms of liability, crime, accident and health insurance
  American Mutual Liability Insurance Co.
Men care for people, MONY
  Mutual of New York
Protection in depth
  Liberty Mutual Insurance Co.

Insurance Agents
The New York Agent in your community is a good man to know
  New York Life Insurance Co.
Protecting the nation—through hometown agents
  Great American Insurance Co.
"Serves you first" (R)
  Independent Insurance Agent
Your Hartford agent does more than he really has to
  The Hartford Insurance Group

Insurance Brokers
Industry's leading insurance brokers
  Marsh and McLennan, Inc.
On the job wherever a client's interest is at stake
  Marsh and McLennan, Inc.
Sets the standard in world-wide insurance brokerage service, J and H
  Johnson and Higgins

Interior Decoration
America's foremost manufacturer of decorative accessories since 1890
  Syroco Div., Dart Industries, Inc.
Creators of 1001 products for home decorating
  Conso Products Co., Div. Consolidated Foods Corp.
"Custom of course"
  Lew Smith Beads
Designs that dreams are made of
  M/B Designs, Inc.
Everything for the fireplace since 1827
  Wm. H. Jackson Co.
Fireplace specialists for four generations
  Edwin Jackson, Inc.
For connoisseurs by connoisseurs (accessories)
  Mottahedeh and Sons

For the decorator touch (Best Pleat Nip-tite)
  Conso Products Co., Div. Consolidated Foods Corp.
The great name in American ceramics
  Haeger Potteries, Inc.
A heritage of quality, craftsmanship, service
  Virginia Mirror Co.
The look of quality
  La Barge Mirrors, Inc.
Quality-made by Illinois Shade
  Illinois Shade Div., Slick Industrial Co.
The surprise of Formica products
  Formica Corp.
Tops everything for lasting beauty (Nevamar)
  National Plastics Products Co.
Where beauty is material
  The Masland Duraleather Co.
The world's largest manufacturer and designer
  Bead Design Studio
World's largest manufacturer of mirrors
  Carolina Mirror Corp.
You can rely on America's oldest and most experienced custom finisher
  Synthetics Finishing Corp.

Investments
Help yourself as you help your country
  United States Savings Bonds
Own your share of American Business
  New York Stock Exchange Members
Promoting high standards in the public interest
  New York Stock Exchange
Safe as America
  United States Savings Bonds
Where you save does make a difference (R)
  The Savings and Loan Foundation, Inc.
Where your dollar works harder. . .grows bigger!
  Insured Savings and Loan Associations
A world of profits awaits the well informed
  Dow Theory Forecasts, Inc.
Your investment success is our business
  Francis I. duPont and Co.

Jelly and Jam—see Food and Food Ingredients

Jewelry
Could it be the real thing? (pearls)
  Marvella, Inc.
A diamond is forever
  De Beers Consolidated Mines, Ltd.
Dream carved rings (Art Carved)
  J. R. Wood and Sons, Inc.

Fine fashion jewelry
   Sarah Coventry, Inc.
For gifts of love (R) (jeweler)
   N. Pfeffer
Jewelry of tradition for the contemporary
      man
   Swank, Inc.
Leading direct sellers of fine fashion jewelry
   Sarah Coventry, Inc.
Master jeweler
   Monet Jewelers
The originator of cultured pearls
   K. Mikimoto, Inc.
The talked-about jewelry
   Castlecliff, Inc.
The world's most precious simulated pearls
   Majorica

Kitchens
The birch line
   Kitchen Kompact, Inc.
The kitchen people with different ideas
   I-X-L Co., Inc.
The most beautiful kitchens of them all
   H. J. Scheirich Co.
The world's largest manufacturer of fine
      kitchen cabinets
   Colonial Products Co.

Lamps
"Jewelry for the home"
   Greene Bros., Inc.
Lamps of elegance
   Frederick Cooper Lamps, Inc.
The royalty of lamps
   The Stiffel Co.

Landscaping
The grass people
   O. M. Scott and Co.
The lawn people
   O. M. Scott and Co.
Leaders in lawn research
   O. M. Scott and Co.
The oldest and largest tree saving service in
      the world
   The Davey Tree Expert Co.

Laundry Equipment, Domestic—see Domestic
   Appliances

Lawn and Garden Products
Famous for power mowers for over 50 years
      (Toro)
   Wheel Horse Products, Inc.

Lets you take weekends easy the year around
      (garden tractor)
   Deere and Co.
The modern way to grow (sprinkler)
   National Rain Bird Sales and Engineering
   Corp.
Reliables. . .the powerful performers, Reo
   Wheel Horse Products Co.
Sign of the leader in lawn/garden equipment
   Wheel Horse Products Co.
World's number one weed killers (Weedone)
   Amchem Products, Inc.

Leather Industry
Best for your money
   Buxton, Inc.
Distinctive designs in leather accessories
   Prince Gardner Co.
There's a need-keyed billfold for you
   Amity Leather Products Co.

Leather Substitutes
The finest in expanded vinyl fabric (Royal
      Naugahyde)
   Uniroyal, Inc.
The finest in vinyl upholstery (Royal Nauga-
      hyde)
   Uniroyal, Inc.

Life Insurance—see Insurance, Life

Light Airplanes—see Airplanes

Lighting Fixtures
America's first name in lighting
   Lightolier, Inc.
America's largest manufacturer of lighting
      productions
   Ruby Lighting Corp.
Beauty mark of fine lighting
   Champion Mfg. Co., Inc.
Guardian lighting (C)
   Guardian Light Co.
The "one stop" creative lighting source
   Petelco Div., Pyle-National Co.

Lingerie—see Underwear

Lipstick—see Cosmetics

Liqueurs—see Liquors

Liquors—see also Beer; Whiskey; and Wine
The aristocrat of liqueurs (Cherristock)
   Schenley Import Co.
Basic for better beer
   Froedtert Malt Co.

The drier liqueur (DOM B and B)
  Julius Wile Sons and Co., Inc.
Dutch name, world fame (Bols liqueurs)
  Brown-Forman Distillers Corp.
11 Kinds—better than most people make
    (Heublein cocktails)
  Heublein, Inc.
Enjoyable always and all ways (rum)
  Bacardi Imports, Inc.
Excellence doubly safeguarded (Beefeater
    gin)
  Kobrand Corp.
Fine coffee liqueur. . .from sunny Mexico
    (Kahlua)
  Jules Berman and Associates, Inc.
First name for the martini, Beefeater (gin)
  Kobrand Corp.
Fond of things Italiano? Try a sip of Galiano.
  Liquor Div., McKesson and Robbins, Inc.
La grande liqueur francaise (DOM Benedic-
    tine)
  Julius Wile Sons and Co., Inc.
Have the genius to chill it (Chartreuse)
  Schiefflin and Co.
The imported one (Beefeater gin)
  Kobrand Corp.
It leaves you breathless (R) (Smirnoff vodka)
  G. G. Heublein and Bro.
Jamaica's legendary liqueur (Tia Maria)
  W. A. Taylor and Co.
Leaves you breathless, Smirnoff vodka
  G. F. Heublein and Bro.
Let this seal be your guide to quality
  Julius Wile Sons and Co.
The original and largest-selling in the world
    (cocktail mixes)
  Holland House Brands, Inc.
A rainbow of distinctive flavors (Hiram
    Walker's cordials)
  Hiram Walker—Gooderham Worts, Ltd.
A rum to remember, Ronrico
  General Wine and Spirits Co., Inc.
Smart, smooth, sensibly priced (Gilbey's
    vodka)
  National Distillers and Chemical Corp.
12 kinds—better than most people make
    (Heublein cocktails)
  Heublein, Inc.
The world's best climate makes the world's
    best rum (Puerto Rican)
  Schiefflin and Co.
"Yes, I know. . .Marie Brizard"
  Schiefflin and Co.

Lubricating Oils
Engine life preserver
  Quaker State Oil Refining Corp.
It pays to be particular about your oil
  Wolf's Head Oil Refining Co., Inc.
Lubrication is a major factor in cost control
  Texaco, Inc.
Makes things run better, Gulf
  Gulf Oil Corp.
The superior brake fluid
  Wagner Electric Corp.
World's first—world's finest
  Valvoline Oil Co. Div. Ashland Oil and
    Refining Co.

Luggage
America's greatest luggage value (Lady
    Baltimore)
  Baltimore Luggage Co.
Business case that knows its way around the
    world
  Samsonite Corp.
Custom make luggage (Lark)
  Droutman Mfg. Co.
Fashion luggage (Lady Baltimore)
  Baltimore Luggage Co.
For people who travel. . .and expect to again
    and again (Stafflight)
  The Sardis Luggage Co.
If you have an instinct for quality (Amelia
    Earhart)
  Baltimore Luggage Co.
Known the world over as the world's best
  Karl Seeger
The luggage that knows its way around the
    world
  Samsonite Corp.
The luggage that sets the pace for luxury
  Samsonite Corp.
So high in fashion. . .so light in weight
  Ventura Travelware, Inc.

Machines and Machinery—see also Bearings
Always right on the job
  The Bowdil Co.
And away go troubles down the drain
  Roto-Rooter Corp.
Assurance of quality, dependability since
    1917
  Moorhead Machine and Boiler Co.
The best way to better yarns (R)
  Whitten Machine Works
Better by design
  Mesta Machine Co.

Better products at lower cost through better
  methods
    Standard Tool and Mfg. Co.
Commitment to quality
  Bucyrus-Erie Co.
Continuing research for lower cost drilling
  Hycalog, Inc.
Creators of dependability
  Geartronics Corp.
Engineers to the woodworking industry
  Wisconsin Knife Works, Inc.
The finest ice making unit ever made
  Henry Vogt Machine Co.
First in automation
  The Cross Co.
First in fabric forming equipment
  Textile Machinery Div., Crompton and
  Knowles
First in quality conveyors and driers for
  plastics industry
    Whitlock Associates, Inc.
First name in pneumatic protection
  C. A. Norgren Co.
The first name in textile machinery
  Platts Bros., Ltd.
For exacting service
  Whitey Research Tool Co.
A good name in industry (gears, drives)
  The Falk Corp.
In design and performance, always a year
  ahead
    Prodex Div., Koehring Co.
Industry's helping hand
  Rex Chainbelt, Inc.
Keeps you years ahead, Roberts
  Roberts Co.
The leader around the world
  Cocker Machine and Foundry Co.
Let's talk Maxitorq
  The Carlyle Johnson Co.
The long line of construction machinery
  Allis-Chalmers Mfg. Co.
Machines at work around the world
  Joy Mfg. Co.
Machines for total productivity
  Ghisholt Machine Co.
Machines that build for a growing America
  Caterpillar Tractor Co.
Manufacturers of equipment to make coal a
  better fuel
    McNally Pittsburgh Mfg. Corp.
Masterworkers in machinery for printing and
  converting
    Mecca Machinery Co.

Miles ahead (road machinery)
  The Galion Iron Works and Mfg. Co.
The muscles of automation, Sheffer cylinders
  The Sheffer Corp.
No one is in a better position to solve your
  lubrication problems
    Manzel Div., Houdaille Industries
Originators and pioneers of allsteel stamping
  press operation
    Verson Allsteel Press Co.
Outselling all others. . .by far (wrecking
  machinery)
    Ernest Holmes Co.
The performance line
  HPM Div., Koehring Co.
Pioneered the continuous extrusion process
  in 1880
    John Royle and Sons
Pioneers in pneumatic bar feeding
  Lipe-Rollway Corp.
Powered by Howard (R) (motors)
  Howard Industries, Inc.
The precision line
  Fellows Gear Shaper Co.
Precision machinery since 1880
  Warner and Swasey Co.
Progress begins with digging
  Marion Power Shovel Co.
Protecting the new in your pneumatics
  Wilkerson Corp.
Purposeful growth in power transmission
  Diamond Chain Co.
See what air can do for you (compressors)
  Gardner-Denver Co.
Shares the risk. . .to assure performance,
  Bodine
    Bodine Corp.
The sure test. . .Scott
  Scott Testers, Inc.
A team of specialists
  Cameron Machine Co.
There should be a Lee in your future
  Lee Machinery Corp.
Today's ideas. . .engineered for tomorrow
  Powermatic, Inc.
Used where performance counts
  Grant Oil Tool Co.
Value keeps you years ahead, Roberts
  Roberts Co.
Where progress is a daily practice
  Oil Center Tool Div., FMC Corp.
Wherever fruit grows, our machinery goes
  Elliott Mfg. Co., Inc.

Who changed it?
    H. K. Porter Co., Inc.
Works best under pressure (cylinders)
    Hydro-Line Mfg. Co.
The world's most distinctive digging machines
        are Davis
    Davis Mfg., Inc.
Your best bet for the best bits
    Rock Bit Div., Timken Roller Bearing Co.

Magnetic Tape—*see* Magnetic Tape Recorders

Magnetic Tape Recorders
Feature rich (Aiwa)
    Selectron International Co.
It speaks for itself (Audiotape)
    Audio Devices, Inc.
The pro line
    Roberts Div., Rheem Mfg. Co.
The tapeway to stereo (R)
    Sony Corp. of America
What you want is a Wollensack
    Revere-Wollensack Div., Minnesota Mining
        and Mfg. Co.
You never heard it so good (Sony Super-
        scope)
    Superscope, Inc.
Your assurance of quality in tape compo-
        nents
    Viking of Minneapolis, Inc.

Malt Liquor—*see* Beer

Margarine
America's largest selling corn oil margarines
        (Fleischmann's)
    Standard Brands, Inc.
Everything's better with Blue Bonnet on it
    Standard Brands, Inc.
Makes good eating sense, Mazola
    Best Foods Div., Corn Products Co.
The name you can trust in margarine
        (Mazola)
    Best Foods Div., Corn Products Co.
Be soft. . .it comes in a tub (Chiffon)
    Anderson, Clayton and Co.

Marking Processes and Equipment
Helping your product speak for itself
    Markem Machine Co.
"If someone makes it—we can mark it!"
    Carter's Ink Co.
Mark it for market. . .the Weber Way
    Weber Marking Systems, Inc.
Marks practically everything best, Peerless
    Peerless Roll Leaf Co.

Materials Handling
Be sure to get a quote (lift trucks)
    Allis-Chalmers Mfg. Co.
The big name in little wheels
    Cushman Motors Div., Outboard Marine
    Corp.
Finest quality on wheels—since 1885
    The Colson Corp.
First in automated materials handling
    Barrett Electronics Corp.
Giving industry a lift since 1878
    Shephard Niles Crane and Hoist Corp.
Idea leader in strapping
    Acme Steel Co.
Is material handling, Clark
    Clark Equipment Co.
Let's find better ways. . .we'll follow through
    Strapping Div., Signode Corp.
The one-man gang (R)
    Towmotor Corp.
Originator and world's largest builder of
        narrow aisle trucks
    Raymond Handling Equipment, Ltd.
Pioneer in the development and construction
        of electric industrial trucks
    Elwell-Parker Electric Co.
Products you can depend on. . .day in. . .day
        out
    NVF Co.
Since 1867. . .the first name in materials
        handling
    The Louden Machinery Co.
Takes a load off your mind, Big Joe
    Big Joe Mfg. Co.
World's largest exclusive manufacturer of
        electric industrial trucks
    Lewis-Shepard Co.
World's largest manufacturer of steel ship-
        ping containers
    Rheem Mfg. Co.

Mattresses
The finest name in sleep
    Englander Co., Inc.
The modern mattress (Koylon)
    Uniroyal, Inc.
Sleeping on a Sealy is like sleeping on a cloud
    Sealy Mattress Co.
Words to go to sleep by (Perfect Sleeper)
    Serta Associates, Inc.
World's largest mattress maker
    Simmons Co.
You sleep on it. . .not in it!
    Serta Mattress Co.

Your morning is as good as your mattress
  Sealy Mattress Co.

Measuring Devices
Measure up with the best
  The Lufkin Rule Co.
White is right
  The Lufkin Rule Co.
You're right with Lufkin
  The Lufkin Rule Co.

Meat
Big enough to serve you—small enough to
    know you
  E. Kahn's Sons Co.
Fine food products
  Geo. A. Hormel and Co.
Fresh ideas in meat. . .from Hormel
  Geo. A. Hormel and Co.
If this Gold Seal is on it—there's better meat
    in it
  Wilson and Co., Inc.
The Wilson label protects your table
  Wilson and Co., Inc.
The meats that wear the Armour star are the
    meats the butcher brings home
  Armour and Co.
Real farm sausage from a real Wisconsin farm
  Jones Dairy Farm
Smoked with hickory (ham)
  Rath Packing Co.
The two most trusted names in meat (Swift's
    Premium)
  Swift and Co.
You can trust the man who sells this brand
    (Swift's Premium)
  Swift and Co.

Medicines, Proprietary
The different antacid (Gelusil)
  Warner-Lambert Pharmaceutical Co.
For a good night's sleep (Nytol)
  Block Drug Co.
It's your guarantee of quality (Con-tac)
  Menley and James Labs
Largest selling pain reliever (Anacin)
  Whitehall Labs Div., American Home
  Products Co.
No water needed (Phillips' Milk of Magnesia
    tablets)
  Glenbrook Labs Div., Sterling Drug, Inc.
Pain is the test that Bayer meets best
  Glenbrook Labs Div., Sterling Drug, Inc.

Proprietary pharmaceuticals made to ethical
    standards (Con-tac)
  Menley and James Labs
Relief is just a swallow away (Alka Seltzer)
  Miles Laboratories, Inc.
Soothes. Cleanses. Refreshes.
  Murine Co., Inc.
Speedy is its middle name (Alka Seltzer)
  Miles Laboratories, Inc.
Stay fit for fun with Phillips (Milk of Mag-
    nesia)
  Glenbrook Labs Div., Sterling Drug, Inc.
Taste as good as they make you feel (Tums)
  Lewis-Howe Co.
The "Twin Formula" head cold tablet (Vicks
    Tri-Span)
  Vick Chemical Co.
Works wonders, Bayer
  Glenbrook Labs Div., Sterling Drug, Inc.
World's most widely used brand of colds
    medication (Vicks VapoRub)
  Vick Chemical Co.

Men's Clothing—*see also* Shirts; and Sportswear
The aristocrat of polyester neckwear
  Wembley Ties, Inc.
Because it might rain (TM)
  Harbor Master Ltd. Div., Jonathan Logan
The best name in all-weather coats and rain-
    wear
  The Alligator Co.
Born in America. Worn round the world.
  John B. Stetson Co.
Clothes that enhance your public appearance
  The House of Worsted-Tex
The "Color Guide" (TM) tie
  Wembley Ties, Inc.
For the man on the move
  McGregor-Doniger, Inc.
The greatest name in socks (Interwoven)
  Kayser-Roth Corp.
Guaranteed, the hardest working workwear
  H. D. Lee Co., Inc.
It's not Jockey brand if it doesn't have the
    Jockey boy
  Jockey Menswear Div., Coopers, Inc.
Official tailors to the West
  H. D. Lee Co., Inc.
Takes the guessing out of dressing (R)
  Wembley Ties, Inc.

Metals
America's foremost producer of custom steels
  Sharon Steel Corp.

America's pioneer manufacturer of pre-
    finished metals
    American Nickeloid Co.
Change for the better with Alcoa Aluminum
    Aluminum Co. of America
The company for precious metals
    Handy and Harman
Consistently better
    Apex Smelting Co.
Customer satisfaction—our no. 1 job
    Detroit Steel Corp.
Developers and producers of extraordinary
    materials
    The Beryllium Corp.
Die casting is the process. . .zinc, the metal
    St. Joseph Lead Co.
Exacting standards only
    Sommers Brass Co., Inc.
The finest aluminum
    Mirro Aluminum Co.
First and finest in copper and brass...Fully
    integrated in aluminum
    Revere Copper and Brass, Inc.
First name in cast steel!
    Farrell-Cheek Steel Co.
For almost any product, aluminum makes it
    better and Kaiser aluminum makes
    aluminum work best
    Kaiser Aluminum and Chemical Corp.
Growth leader of the aluminum industry
    Consolidated Aluminum Corp.
The house of experience
    Mirro Aluminum Co.
Imagination in steel for the needs of today's
    architecture
    Granco Steel Products Co.
In a word, confidence
    The Carpenter Steel Co.
In stainless, too, you can take the pulse of
    progress at Republic
    Republic Steel Corp.
It bends with the heat (thermostatic bimetal)
    W. M. Chace Co.
Keep a cupboard full of cans
    National Steel Corp.
Look ahead with lead
    Lead Industries Assn., Inc.
Metallurgy is our business
    Vanadium-Alloys Steel Co.
The most progressive name in steel
    Nippon Kokan
Nickel. . .its contribution is quality
    International Nickel Co.

Pioneer in powder and molten metallurgy
    Firth Sterling, Inc.
Pioneering in ideas for industry
    United States Gypsum Co.
Producers of quality steel for industry and
    construction
    Laclede Steel Co.
Producers of zinc for American industry
    St. Joseph Lead Co.
Service that never sleeps
    Reynolds Aluminum Supply Co.
The specialist in plate steels
    Lukens Steel Co.
The specialty steel company
    Latrobe Steel Co.
Think copper (Anaconda)
    American Brass Co.
Value engineering favors zinc
    American Zinc Institute
What next from Alcoa!
    Aluminum Corp. of America
Where big ideas turn into aluminum extru-
    sions
    Superior Industries, Inc.
Where new ideas take shape in aluminum
    Reynolds Metals Co.
Where the big idea is innovation
    United States Steel Corp.
You can count on Continental to take care
    of you
    Continental Steel Corp.
You can take the pulse of
    Republic Steel Corp.

Microfilm Records—*see* **Office Equipment**

Motels
"The fine old innkeeping tradition in a mod-
    ern setting" (R)
    Holiday Inns of America, Inc.
First choice in food, lodging and services
    nationwide!
    Holiday Inns of America, Inc.
"Luxury for less" (R)
    Ramada Inns, Inc.
The nation's innkeeper (R)
    Holiday Inns of America, Inc.
"Sign of happy travel"
    Downtowner Corp.
This is living. . .this is Marriott
    Marriott Motor Hotels, Inc.

Models and Modelmaking—*see* **Toys**

Motor Bus Travel
Leave the driving to us
    Greyhound Corp.
Easiest travel on earth
    Continental Trailways Bus System

Motor Truck
"Build a truck to do a job—change it only to
    do better"
    Motor Truck Div., International Harvester
    Co.
Builds tough trucks, Dodge
    Dodge Div., Chrysler Corp.
Built to last longer (Econoline van trucks)
    Ford Motor Co.
Buy today's best truck. Own tomorrow's
    best trade
    Hyster Co.
Is more truck. . .day in, day out, Chevrolet
    Chevrolet Div., General Motors Corp.
"The Money truck"
    Mack Trucks, Inc.
No. 1 heavy-duty sales leader
    Motor Truck Div., International Harvester
    Co.
The only truck bodies built like a trailer
    Fruehauf Corp.
Quality trucks always cost less!
    Chevrolet Div., General Motors Corp.
Total transportation
    Fruehauf Corp.
World leader in heavy-duty trucks
    White Motor Co.
World's finest
    Autocar Div., White Motor Co.

Motor Truck Freight Service
Leading name in truck transportation
    Consolidated Freightways, Inc.
More than a truck line—a transportation
    system
    Interstate Motor Freight System
"The motor carrier with more Go-How"
    (TM)
    Eastern Express, Inc.
"Speed with economy"
    Yale Express System, Inc.
Super service
    T.I.M.E. Freight, Inc.
Vital link in America's supply line
    Transamerican Freight Lines, Inc.
The wheels that go everywhere
    American Trucking Associations, Inc.

Your best bet over the long haul
    D.C. Trucking Co., Inc.

Motor Trucks—Parts
Delivers in the clutch, Lipe
    Lipe-Rollway Corp.
World's largest producer of commercial
    heavy-duty truck drive axles
    Axle Div., Eaton Mfg. Co.

Motor Vehicle Fleets
America's best fleet buy (Rambler)
    American Motors Corp.
Biggest name in fleet cars and trucks
    Chevrolet Div., General Motors Corp.

Moving and Storage
America's most recommended mover
    (Mayflower)
    Aero Mayflower Transit Co., Inc.
America's number 1 mover
    Allied Van Lines, Inc.
Dedicated to people on the move
    U.S. Van Lines, Inc.
Families that move the most call the world's
    largest mover
    Allied Van Lines, Inc.
The gentlemen of the moving industry
    North American Van Lines, Inc.
Leaving the moving to us
    Greyhound Corp.
Let Lyon guard your goods (R)
    Lyon Van Lines, Inc.
Moves the people that move the world,
    United
    United Van Lines, Inc.
Moving up
    U.S. Van Lines, Inc.
Moving with care. . .everywhere (R)
    United Van Lines, Inc.
The people who care about people who
    move
    Fernstrom Storage and Van Co.
The professionals
    Bekins Van and Storage Co.
We move families, not just furniture
    Allied Van Lines, Inc.

Motivation
Motivating men to sell your product is our
    business
    Maritz, Inc.
Since 1922, leader in motivating people
    E. F. MacDonald Co.

Musical Instruments

All ways look to Linton for leadership!
   Linton Mfg. Co.
The difference is quality (guitar)
   Epiphone, Inc.
For the home that enjoys home life
   Conn Organ Corp.
The foremost in drums
   Slingerland Drum Co.
Harp-maker to the world since 1889
   Lyon-Healy Co.
Heirloom quality pianos since 1896
   Kohler and Campbell, Inc.
Instruments worthy of the masters since
      1857 (pianos, organs)
   W. W. Kimball Co.
Made with the extra measure of care (Cor-
      dova guitars)
   David Wexler and Co.
Making music possible for everyone
      (Guitaro)
   Oscar Schmidt International, Inc.
Means music to millions, Wurlitzer
   Wurlitzer Co.
Most famous name on drums
   Ludwig Drum Co.
More music for the money
   Kay Musical Instrument Co.
Music's most glorious voice
   Hammond Organ Co.
The one and only
   Hammond Organ Co.
Since 1874 stringed instrument house of the
      masters
   William Lewis and Son
The sound investment
   D. H. Baldwin Co.
The tone heard 'round the world
   Wm. S. Haynes Co.
Total quality (pianos, organs)
   W. W. Kimball Co.
"The world's finest"
   Goya Guitars, Inc.
World's largest builder of organs and pianos
   Wurlitzer Co.
The world's most beautiful organs
   Story and Clark Piano Co.

Mutual Insurance—*see* Insurance, Mutual

Nylon—*see* Textile Fibers, Synthetic

Ocean Travel

African business is our business (shipping)
   Farrell Lines, Inc.
The "Champagne Touch"
   Moore-McCormack Lines, Inc.
Cruising everywhere under the sun
   American President Lines
The experience cruise line
   Furness, Withy and Co., Ltd.
. . .Just for the sun of it
   T. S. Hanseatic German Atlantic Line
Life at sea is like nothing on earth
   P and O Lines
Luxury and comfort with utmost safety
   United States Lines, Inc.
More fun per ton than any other line
   Italian Line
The people who invented a nicer way to
      cruise
   Holland-American Line
Run away to sea with P and O
   P and O Lines
Sail a happy ship
   Holland-American Line
Sunlane (R) cruises to Europe
   American Export Isbrandtsen Lines, Inc.
Unwind your way to Europe
   Italian Line
The vacation way to Hawaii
   Matson Navigation Co.
The white Viking fleet
   Swedish American Line

Office Equipment—*see* Typewriters; and
      Copying Processes

Built like a skyscraper (R)
   Shaw-Walker Co.
The company of specialists (filing equip-
      ment)
   Watson Mfg. Co., Inc.
Cutting costs is our business
   Addressograph-Multigraph Corp.
Electrics give more people more time for
      more important jobs, Boston
   Hunt Mfg. Co.
First and foremost in microfilming since
      1928
   Recordak Corp.
First name in filing
   Oxford Filing Supply Co.
Interested personal service—always—when
      you buy from Eastman
   Eastman Chemical Products, Inc.
Machines should work. People should think.
   Office Products Div., International Busi-
      ness Machines Corp.

Make no mistake about figurework: call
    Friden
    Friden Div., Singer Co.
Put errors out of business
    Victor Computer Corp.
Puts you ahead in offset duplicating (Kodak
    Ektalith)
    Eastman Kodak Co.
Specialists in filing supplies and equipment
    since 1894
    The Weis Mfg. Co.
Speed. Simplicity. Versatility. (business
    machines
    Dura Corp.
The touch of tomorrow in office living
    The Globe-Wernicke Co.
World's easiest-to-use dictating machines
    Stenocord Dictation Systems

Office Furniture—*see also* **Chairs**
The accepted name for value
    Haskell, Inc.
The choice when you want quality, too
    All-Steel Equipment, Inc.
The coat rack people
    Vogel-Peterson Co.
The company with the "know-how"
    Metropolitan Furniture Adjusters
A complete source for fine office furniture
    Desks, Inc.
Design/plus
    Steelcase, Inc.
Distinguished furniture for distinguished
    offices
    Stow and Davis Furniture Co.

Office Machines- *see* **Office Equipment**

Office Supplies
Correct mistakes in any language (erasers)
    Weldon Roberts Rubber Co.
"The finest pads have purple bindings"
    The Universal Pad and Tablet Corp.
First name in paper punches
    Mutual Products Co., Inc.
Look to Eberhard Faber for the finest. . .first!
    Eberhard Faber, Inc.
The name indicates the quality
    Keener Rubber, Inc.
The nation's largest-selling drawing pencils
    and leads
    Eagle Pencil Co.
Puts its quality in writing
    Eberhard Faber, Inc.

The retailer's line
    National Blank Book Co.
"The right business form for every form of
    business"
    Moore Business Forms, Inc.
The world leaders in duplicating supplies
    since 1906
    Frankel Mfg. Co.
World's largest manufacturer of staplers for
    home and office
    Swingline, Inc.
World-wide suppliers of the finest ball pen
    inks
    Formulabs, Inc.
Your one-source solution to every filing
    problem
    The Smead Mfg. Co.
You're better off with Bostitch
    Bostitch Div., Textron, Inc.

Oil Fuel—*see* **Petroleum Products**

Optical Instruments
Birthplace and centre of modern optics
    Carl Zeiss, Inc.
Symbol of excellence in West German optics
    (Zeiss Ikon)
    Carl Zeiss, Inc.

Organs—*see* **Musical Instruments**

Ovens, Baking
Backed by a century-old tradition of fine
    craftsmanship
    Amana Refrigeration, Inc.
Everybody appreciates the finest (Radi-
    Oven)
    Knapp-Monarch Co.
The name known in millions of American
    homes
    Nutone, Inc.
Seven leagues ahead (R)
    Thermador Electrical Mfg. Co. Div.,
    Norris Industries, Inc.
So beautifully practical
    Jenn-Air Corp.

Packaging
Containers of distinction
    J. L. Clark Mfg. Co.
Corrugated packaging specialists
    Hoerner Boxes, Inc.
Don't say it can't be done. . .talk to Olin
    Olin Mathieson Chemical Corp.

Every day, Bemis develops a new packaging idea to serve you better
Bemis Co., Inc.
Full circle packaging
Alton Box Board Co.
If it's a bag. . .we make it
KOBI Polyethylene Bag Mfg. Co., Inc.
It gets there right in wirebounds
Wirebound Box Manufacturers Assn.
Look to Eastman to look your best!
Plastic Sheeting Div., Eastman Chemical Products, Inc.
Packaging materials for American industry
Cellu-Craft Products Co.
Packaging that builds and holds sales
Alton Box Board Co.
Plus packaging
Ekco Containers, Inc.
Spanning the spectrum of packaging (Reynolds aluminum)
Reynolds Metals Co.
Specialists in frozen food packaging
Iceland Products, Inc.
Takes many shapes to serve you, O-I Plastechnics
Owens-Illinois Glass Co.
Tri-sure the world over
American Flange and Mfg. Co., Inc.
Where new ideas bring you better packaging
Reynolds Metals Co.
Where the newest in packaging is happening today
Milprint, Inc.
Your packaging deserves Crown quality
Crown Cork and Seal Co., Inc.
Your partner in packaging progress
Ball Brothers Co., Inc.

Packaging Machinery
Call the man from Cozzoli
Cozzoli Machine Co.
Continuous flow packaging (R)
Battle Creek Packaging Machines, Inc.
Creates new dimensions in automatic packaging machinery!
Favorite of the nation's bakers
National Bakery Div., Package Machinery Co.
Means craftsmanship, Scandia
Scandia Packaging Machinery Co.
New concepts in corrugated packaging machinery
Huntingdon Industries, Inc.

Pacemakers in flexible package-makers
Mira-Pak, Inc.
Packages better...for a wide range of industries, Doughboy
Doughboy Industries, Inc.
Superior performance through design simplicity
Triangle Package Machinery Co.
Tops them all, 'Cap' Resina
Resina Automatic Machinery Co., Inc.
The world's largest manufacturer of blister packaging machinery
Packaging Industries Ltd., Inc.

Packaging Materials—see Packaging

Paint
Coatings, colors and chemicals for industry
Sherwin-Williams Co.
Cover the earth
Sherwin-Williams Co.
If you prize it. . .Krylon-ize it
Krylon Dept., Borden Chemical Co.
Master of color finishes since 1858
Martin Senour Co.
Master of color since 1858
Martin Senour Co.
More years to the gallon (Dutch Boy)
Pigments and Chemicals Div., National Lead Co.

Paper and Paper Products
America's cities are Bergstrom's forests
Bergstrom Paper Co.
America's most used products away from home
Fort Howard Paper Co.
Consider paper
Champion Papers, Inc.
Consider the power of paper used with imagination
Champion Papers, Inc.
A dynamic force with paper
Kimberly-Clark Corp.
Fine letter papers
Eaton Paper Corp.
Fine papers
Crane and Co., Inc.
First in carbonless papers
National Cash Register Co.
First in cellulose
Buckeye Cellulose Corp.
For every business need
Nekoosa-Edwards Paper Co.

For many converting purposes
  Nekoosa-Edwards Paper Co.
For quality paper products you can't beat,
    Marathon
  Marathon Div., American Can Co.
For serving. . .it's Erving
  Erving Paper Mills
For special industrial requirements
  Nekoosa-Edwards Paper Co.
Functional papers
  Thilmany Pulp and Paper Co.
A good business letter is always better. . .
    written on a Gilbert paper
  Gilbert Paper Co.
If it's paper
  Dillard Paper Co.
Important name in the box business
  Forest Products Div., Owens-Illinois, Inc.
Inspirations lead to new value in paper and
    packaging, Westvaco
  Westvaco Corp.
Lasting impressions begin with Oxford
    papers
  Oxford Paper Co.
The line with the carbon gripper
  Codo Mfg. Co.
Makes it better for you, Scott
  Scott Paper Co.
The merchant-minded mill with variety and
    reliability
  Riegel Paper Corp.
Multiple copies without carbons (NCR
    paper)
  National Cash Register Co.
The nation's printing papers
  Howard Paper Mills Div., St. Regis Paper
  Co.
No. 1 source of gummed papers
  Dennison Mfg. Co.
The paper people
  Brown Co.
Papers for the printer who puts quality first
  S. D. Warren Co., Div. Scott Paper Co.
Pioneers in polycoatings
  H. P. Smith Paper Co.
Quality papers for industry since 1889
  Sonoco Products Co.
The roll specialists
  Eastern Specialties Co., Inc.
Specialist in enamel papers/printing paper
  Consolidated Paper Co.
Specialists in the application of adhesives
  The Brown-Bridge Mills, Inc.

Whenever good impressions count, rely on
    carbonizing papers by Schweitzer
  Peter J. Schweitzer Div., Kimberly-Clark
  Corp.
Where quality is traditional
  Old Colony Envelope Co.
A world of paper products—from frozen
    food cartons to printing paper
  International Paper Co.
World's largest manufacturer of fine carbon-
    izing papers
  Peter J. Schweitzer Div., Kimberly-Clark
  Corp.
Writing papers that create an impression
  Montag, Inc., Div. Westab, Inc.
Your paper problems are in good hands with
    Marathon
  Marathon Div., American Can Co.
Your printer's performance starts with fine
    papers
  Crocker Hamilton Papers, Inc.
Value-engineered papers from the mills of
    Mosinee
  Mosinee Paper Mills Co.

Paper and Pulp Mills—*see* **Paper**

Paper Boxes—*see* **Paper**

Paper Coating—*see* **Paper**

Part-Time Employment—*see* **Employees,
  Temporary**

Patterns—*see* **Women's Apparel**

Pencils—*see* **Office Supplies**

Pens—*see* **Fountain Pens**

Perfumers
Anything can happen when you wear Fame
  Parfums Corday, Inc.
Cherished as one of the world's seven great
    fragrances (Intimate)
  Revlon, Inc.
Every woman alive wants Chanel No. 5
  Chanel, Inc.
For the woman who dares to be different
    (Emraude)
  Coty Div., Chas. Pfizer and Co., Inc.
The 'forbidden' fragrance (Tabu)
  Dana Perfumes, Inc.
High fashion in fragrance from France
  Carven Parfums
The most treasured name in perfume
  Chanel, Inc.

The perfume of romance (Chanel No. 22)
Chanel, Inc.
Promise her anything but give her Arpege
Lanvin-Charles of the Ritz, Inc.
Really cares about the sorcery, Tussy
Lehn and Fink Products Co.

Periodicals
America's biggest selling weekly magazine
T. V. Guide
The business management magazine
Dun's Review and Modern Industry
A business paper for the farm chemical
industry
Crop Life
Capitalist tool
Forbes
The complete authority of packaging
Modern Packaging
"Dedicated to serving the families of the
West and Hawaii. . .no one else"
Sunset
Each week the facts add up to success
Sports Illustrated
Editorial excellence in action
Pit and Quarry
First magazine for women
McCalls
For oil marketing
National Petroleum News
For the men in charge
Fortune
For the smart young woman
Mademoiselle
Getting results in rural America is *Farm
Journal's* business
Farm Journal
Important to important people
Advertising Age
Industry spokesman to CPI management
Chemical Week
The industry's marketplace
Electronics
The international authority on visual mer-
chandising
Display World
It pays to be in the news
Architectural and Engineering News
The magazine farm families depend on
Farm Journal
The magazine for all manufacturing
Factory
The magazine for professional builders
NAHB Journal of Homebuilding

The magazine of architectural technology
Building Construction
The magazine of broadcast advertising
Sponsor
The magazine of business leaders around the
world
Fortune
The magazine of business leadership
Fortune
Magazine of mass feeding, mass housing
Institutions
The magazine of methods, personnel and
equipment
Administrative Management
The magazine of the American market
Look
The magazine of Western living
Sunset
The magazine of world business
International Management
A magazine only a homemaker could love
Family Circle
The magazine that moves the men who move
the merchandise
Progressive Farmer
Management publication of the housing
industry
House and Home
The massive men's market in print
True
The most important magazine to the world's
most important people
Time
The most useful magazine in metalworking
American Machinist
News of consequence for people of conse-
quence
U.S. News and World Report
The newsweekly that separates fact from
opinion
Newsweek
The no. 1 buy in the design field
Product Engineering
The no. 1 men's service magazine
Argosy
On rearing children from crib to college
Parents
One of America's great weeklies
Railway Age
Our readers manage the country
Successful Farming
People have faith in *Reader's Digest*
Reader's Digest

Put your money where the market is
  Modern Machine Shop
Reach her when home is on her mind
  American Home
Read and preferred by construction men
  Construction Methods and Equipment
Sell at the decision level
  Business Week
Sell the man who talks to the farmer just
  before the sale
  Farm Store Merchandising
Selling and advertising to business and
  industry
  Industrial Marketing
Sells hard wherever hardware sells
  Hardware Age
The service shop authority
  Motor Service
So long as the rig is on the location
  Drilling
Sports isn't just fun and games
  Sports Illustrated
Talk to the right people in the right places
  Time
The taste that sets the trend
  Harper's Bazaar
Thundering power in the eye of the market
  Metalworking News
To energize your sales curve, put *Power*
  behind it
  Power
The traveler's world
  Venture
The weekly news magazine
  Time
What's happening. In business. To business.
  Nation's Business
Where quality makes sense
  House Beautiful
Where telling the world means selling the
  world
  Life International
World's best seller
  Reader's Digest

Personal Products
Because. . .(Modess)
  Personal Products Co.
Invented by a doctor—now used by millions
  of women
  Tampax, Inc.
Really cares about people who care, Tussy
  (deodorant)
  Lehn and Fink Products Corp.

You feel so cool, so clean, so fresh. . .
  Tampax, Inc.

Pet Food—*see* Pet Products

Pet Products
Better products for man's best friend
  (Sergeant's)
  Polk Miller Products Co.
The canned dog food without the can, Gaines-
  burgers
  General Foods Corp.
The complete family of dog and cat foods
  from the world leader in nutrition
  (Friskies)
  Carnation Co.
Dog food of champions (Ken-L-Biskit)
  Ken-L-Products Div., Quaker Oats Co.
From world leaders in nutrition (Friskies)
  Carnation Co.
Help make him all the dog he's meant to be
  (Ken-L-Biskit)
  Ken-L-Products Div., Quaker Oats Co.
Maker of America's number 1 cat food (Puss
  'n Boots)
  Quaker Oats Co.
Makes its own gravy (Gravy Train dog food)
  General Foods Corp.
When it comes to cooking for dogs—Rival
  has no rival
  Rival Pet Foods Div., Associated Products,
  Inc.

Petrochemicals—*see* Petroleum Products

Petroleum Products
America's leading energy company
  Enco Div., Humble Oil and Refining Co.
America's most customer-minded oil com-
  pany!
  Sunray DX Oil Co.
Anticipating tomorrow's needs today. . .
  Enjay Chemical Co. Div., Humble Oil and
  Refining Co.
Be sure with Pure
  The Pure Oil Co.
Call the man who puts the farmer first—your
  Standard Oil Farm Man
  Standard Oil Div., American Oil Co.
First in resources/first in capability
  Enco Div., Humble Oil and Refining Co.
A great name in oil
  Sinclair Oil Corp.
The independent supplier for independents
  Ashland Oil and Refining Co.

The industrial resources company
Ashland Oil and Refining Co.
Making petroleum do more things for more
people
Atlantic Richfield Refining Co.
Making things happen with petroleum energy
Atlantic Richfield Co.
Quality you can trust
Crown Central Petroleum Corp.
See what happens when you start using
American ingenuity
Standard Oil Div., American Oil Co.
Where research is planned with progress in
mind (R)
Universal Oil Products Co.
World leader in filtration
Great Lakes Carbon Corp.
World's finest petrochemical products
Gulf Oil Corp.
You can depend on it
National Oil Fuel Institute, Inc.

Petroleum Products—Pipe Lines

From natural gas and oil. . .heat, power,
petrochemicals that mean ever wider
service to man
Tenneco, Inc.
Pipeliners of energy
Texas Eastern Transmission Corp.
Serving the big river region
Texas Gas Transmission Corp.

Petroleum Refineries—see Petroleum Products

Pharmaceuticals—see Drug Industry

Phonograph Records
"Angels of the highest order" (Seraphim)
Capitol Records, Inc.
His master's voice
RCA Corp.
Of the world, "Capitol"
Capitol Records, Inc.
Recordings for the connoisseur
Vanguard Recording Society, Inc.
World leader in recorded sound (Command)
ABC Records, Inc.

Phonographs—High Fidelity Equipment
Discover what sound is all about
James B. Lansing Sound, Inc.
The finest. . .the record proves it since 1900,
Dual's
United Audio Products, Inc.
For those who can hear the difference
Pickering and Co., Inc.

High fidelity phono cartridges. . .world stan-
dard wherever sound quality is para-
mount
Shure Brothers, Inc.
The leader in solid-state high-fidelity compo-
nents
Harmon Kardon, Inc.
Setting new standards in sound
Electro-Voice, Inc.
The sound approach to quality
Kenwood Electronics, Inc.
We want you to hear more music
Harmon Kardon, Inc.
World renowned for perfection in sound
James B. Lansing Sound, Inc.
World's finest (Garrard)
British Industries Corp.
The world's "first family" of changers and
tape decks
BSR (USA), Ltd.
The world's largest and most experienced
manufacturer of magnetic pickups
Pickering and Co., Inc.
World's most perfect high fidelity compo-
nents
Empire Scientific Corp.

Physical Fitness
The leadership line
Battle Creek Manufacturers, Inc.
A trusted name. . .proved by medical research
and the experience of millions (Niagra
Cyclo-Massage)
Niagra Therapy Mfg. Corp.
"Works with you—works for you"
Battle Creek Manufacturers, Inc.

Pianos—see Musical Instruments

Plastics
First in engineered plastics (C)
Hareg Industries, Inc.
In plastics, it's Spencer. . .for action
Spencer Chemical Div., Gulf Oil Corp.
Marketing methods since 1850
Industrial Marketing Div., Jas. H.
Matthews and Co.
Newest look in laminates (Enjay Nevamar)
Enjay Chemical Co. Div., Humble Oil and
Refining Co.
Pioneers in plastics
Hopp Plastics Div., Hopp Press, Inc.
Pioneers in plastics
Flex-O-Film, Inc.

Plastics make a material difference, Celanese
Celanese Plastics Co. Div., Celanese Corp.
The registered symbol of quality since 1908
(R) (molding)
Garfield Mfg. Co.
Where everything is done in plastics
American Insulator Corp.
World's broadest line of thermoplastic sheet
materials, Seilon
Plastics Div., Seiberling Rubber Co.
World's leading manufacturer of plastic prod-
ucts for 35 diversified industries
Colorite Plastics, Inc.
You furnish the print. . .we'll furnish the part
Synthane Corp.

Plumbing Fixtures
Be seated by. . .Bemis
Bemis Mfg. Co.
The best seat in the house
C. F. Church Div., American Standard,
Inc.
The first name in seats—the last name in
quality
Beneke Corp.
Leader in bathroom fashion
Showerfold Dor Corp.
Master crafted
Eljer Plumbingware Div., Wallace-Murray
Corp.
The seat of the in house
Magnolia Products, Inc.
Since 1904 fine plumbing fixtures
Eljer Plumbingware Div., Wallace-Murray
Corp.
Where quality is produced in quantity
Sterling Faucet Co.

Printing Industry
Pioneers in automated lithography
H. S. Crocker Co., Inc.
Where engraving is still an art
Roehlen Engraving Works

Proprietary Medicines—*see* Medicines, Proprietary

Public Service
College is America's best friend
Council for Financial Aid to Education
Give so more will live
Heart Fund
It takes a man to help a boy
Big Brother

Please! Only you can prevent forest fires
The Advertising Council

Public Utilities
Ask the man from Northern Plains
Northern Natural Gas Co.
The heart of the market
Pennsylvania Power and Light Co.
People you can depend on to power
America's progress
Investor-Owned Electric Light and Power
Cos.
Power for progress
Consolidated Edison Co.
Power for progress
The Southern Co.
The power to please!
Florida Power Corp.
Service first
Houston Lighting and Power Co.
SERVICE, in the broadest sense, is the dif-
ference
Century Electric Co.
Service is the difference
Century Electric Co.
Taxpaying servant of a great state
New Jersey Public Service Electric and
Gas Co.
This is the center of industrial America
Ohio Edison—Pennsylvania Power
You've got good things going for you with
service by Investor-Owned Electric
Light and Power Companies
Investor-Owned Electric Light and Power
Cos.

Publishers and Publishing
Buy us like advertising. . .use us like salesmen
Home State Farm Publications
For the climate of excellence
Cahners Publishing Co., Inc.
A good society is good business
McGraw-Hill Publications Div., McGraw-
Hill, Inc.
The live ones!
Cahners Publishing Co., Inc.
"Market-directed"
McGraw-Hill Publications Div., McGraw-
Hill, Inc.
Serving America's schools, homes, commerce
and industry
Rand McNally and Co.
Serving industry constructively since 1902
Miller Freeman Publications

Serving man's need for knowledge. . .in many
    ways
    McGraw-Hill, Inc.
World's largest specialized publisher
    Gulf Publishing Co.
Your world of ideas and products
    MPA Magazines

Pumps
The best pump—the best buy
    Reda Pump Co.
Best pumps in the oil patch
    Harbison-Fischer Mfg. Co.
The finest name in pumps, Myers
    F. E. Myers and Bro., Inc.
Leader in the field. Choice of the leaders
    Gilbarco, Inc.
Master designers of modern centrifugal
    pumps
    Morris Machine Works
The only name for both fuel and water
    pumps
    Airtex Products Co.
The pumportation people (Graco)
    Gray Co., Inc.
Symbol of excellence (gasoline)
    Tokheim Corp.
The tough pumping problems go to Aldrich
    Aldrich Pump Co.
World's largest manufacturer of gasoline
    pumps and service station equipment
    Wayne Pump Co.

Radio Receiving Apparatus
From the space age laboratories of Olympic
    Olympic Radio and Television Div., Lear
    Siegler, Inc.
Quality through craftsmanship
    The Hallicrafters Co.
"There is nothing finer than a Stromberg-
    Carlson"
    Stromberg-Carlson Corp.
Today's leader in tomorrow's look
    Panasonic
Unquestionably the world's finest stereo-
    phonic console
    Pilot Radio Corp.

Railroads
"Accent is on you, Southern's"
    Southern Railway Co.
America's resourceful railroad
    Milwaukee Road
Be specific, route Union Pacific
    Union Pacific Railroad

Be specific. . .say "Union Pacific"
    Union Pacific Railroad
Everywhere west
    Chicago, Burlington and Quincy Railroad
Gateway to and from the booming west
    Union Pacific Railroad
Gateway to and from your world markets
    Union Pacific Railroad
Grow, grow by the rail way
    Association of American Railroads
Holiday all the way with. . .
    Canadian Pacific Railway
Innovations that squeeze the waste out of
    distribution
    Southern Railway Co.
Knows the territory, Chessie
    Chesapeake and Ohio Railway
The nation's going-est railroad
    Norfolk and Western Railway
On-time-delivery is our #1 concern
    Reading Railroad
The railroad of "creative crews"
    Milwaukee Road
The railroad of planned progress. . .geared to
    the nation's future
    Rock Island Lines
"The railroad that runs by the customer's
    clock"
    Nickel Plate Railroad
The railroad that's always on the move
    toward a better way
    Santa Fe System Lines
"The railway is the right way"
    French National Railroads
Rely on us
    Louisville and Nashville Railroad
Road to the future
    New York Central System
Route of the incomparable empire builder
    Great Northern Railway
Route of the vista-dome North coast limited
    Northern Pacific Railway
Serves the South, Southern
    Southern Railroad Co.
Serving the Golden Empire
    Southern Pacific Co.
Thanks for using coast line
    Atlantic Coast Line Railroad
This is the way to run a railroad
    Northern Pacific Railway
The wheels of transportation help turn the
    wheels of industry
    Union Pacific Railroad

World's most complete transportation system
    Canadian Pacific Railway

Rainwear—*see* Men's Clothing

Recreation
America's finest campers
    Highway Cruisers, Inc.
America's finest camping tents (Hoosier)
    Hoosier Tarpaulin and Canvas Goods Co.
America's largest builder of camping trailers
    Nimrod Ward Mfg. Co.
America's largest selling camping trailer
    Nimrod Ward Mfg. Co.
"Developing products for recreation through
    electronic research" (C)
    Byrd Industries, Inc.
Foremost brand in outdoor living
    American Thermos Products Co.
Foremost name in indoor comfort
    Coleman Co., Inc.
Greatest name in the great outdoors. Fore-
    most name in indoor comfort.
    Coleman Co., Inc.
Wide world of recreation, the Starcraft
    (boats, camping trailers)
    Starcraft Co.
World's biggest seller! (motorcycles)
    American Honda Motor Co., Inc.

Refrigeration and Refrigeration Machinery
Builders of better refrigerator bodies
    Hackney Bros. Body Co.
It's the contacts that count
    Amerio Contact Plate Freezers, Inc.
Leader in the manufacture of custom built-in
    refrigeration
    Revco, Inc.
Maximum refrigeration efficiency
    Dole Refrigeration Co.
Refrigeration is our business. . .our only
    business
    Norcold, Inc.
Total environmental control
    Tectrol Div., Whirlpool Corp.
"Where inches count"
    Acme National Refrigeration Co.
World leader in commercial refrigeration
    Tyler Refrigeration Div., Clark Equip-
    ment Co.
World leader in transport refrigeration
    Thermo King Corp.
The world's largest manufacturer of reach-in
    refrigerators and freezers
    Victory Metal Mfg. Co.

Refrigerators—*see* Domestic Appliances

Reprography—*see* Copying Processes

Research
Probing deeper to serve you better
    Ford Motor Co. Research Laboratories
Trust in Phillips is world-wide
    Phillips Research Laboratories

Restaurant Equipment and Supplies
America's finest cooking centers
    Jenn-Air Corp.
Beautiful on the table. Carefree in the
    kitchen. (Weavewood-Ware)
    Weavewood, Inc.
Better pans for better baking
    Chicago Metallic Mfg. Co.
Better continuous production through con-
    tinuous research!
    J. W. Greer Co.
Complete line of mobile food service equip-
    ment
    Crescent Metal Products, Inc.
The good food service
    Prophet Co.
Headquarters for steam-cookers
    The Cleveland Range Co.
Leadership through quality (utensil handling
    equipment)
    The Steril-Sil Co.
Make the seasons come to you (Crystal Tips
    ice machine)
    McQuay, Inc.
The most complete line of electronic ovens
    Raytheon Co.
The name that means quality (Trade Wind
    ventilating hood)
    Robbins and Myers, Inc.
Pioneers of disposers dedicated to quality
    National Commercial Disposers
Quality all the way
    The Hobart Mfg. Co.
Quality products known throughout the
    world for engineered quality
    Bastian-Blessing Co.
There is no equal
    Lowerator Div., American Machine and
    Foundry Co.
World's first and largest manufacturer of
    deep fat frying equipment
    J. C. Pitman and Sons, Inc.
The world's finest the world over
    Vulcan-Hart Corp.

World's largest commercial oven manufacturer since 1888
Middleby-Marshall Oven Co.

Restaurants
Host of the Highways
Howard Johnson Co.
Landmark for hungry Americans
Howard Johnson Co.

Retail Stores
Always first quality
J. C. Penney and Co.
For that certain kind of woman
Peck and Peck
A store a woman should look into
Hoffritz for Cutlery
You can't do better than Sears
Sears Roebuck and Co.

Rifles—*see* **Firearms**

Road Machinery—*see* **Machines and
Machinery**

Rubber Industry
Known 'round the world for quality in
sporting goods and tires
Dunlop Tire and Rubber Corp.
No. 1 in V-belts and hose
Gates Rubber Co.
Pioneer and pacemaker in essential fields of
industry
Firestone Tire and Rubber Co.
World's largest manufacturer of industrial
rubber products
Uniroyal, Inc.

Rugs—*see* **Carpets**

Rust—*see* **Corrosion and Anti-corrosives**

Safes
For a big difference in your profits. . .the line
with the big difference
Meilink Steel Safe Co.
Our products are your protection
Schwab Safe Co., Inc.
Quality is standard equipment
Mosler Safe Co.

Salad Dressings
America's favorite mayonnaise (Best Foods)
Best Foods Div., CPC International, Inc.
America's favorite mayonnaise (Hellmann's)
Best Foods Div., CPC International, Inc.

Flavor so delicious only your figure knows
they're low calorie (Wish Bone)
Thos. J. Lipton, Inc.
This is no place for "second best" (Hell-
mann's mayonnaise)
Best Foods Div., CPC International, Inc.

Savings and Loan—*see* **Investments**

Securities—*see* **Investments**

Service Stations—*see* **Automobile Service
Stations**

Shampoos
Beautiful hair
John H. Breck, Inc.
The colorfast shampoo
Clairol, Inc.

Shipping—*see* **Ocean Travel**

Shirts
Expensive shirts ought to look it (Excello)
Kayser-Roth Corp.
Internationally known mark of quality
Manhattan Industries, Inc.
"Never wear a white shirt before sundown,"
says Hathaway (R)
C. F. Hathaway Co.
Wherever you go you look better in Arrow
Cluett, Peabody and Co.
Younger by design (Van Heusen)
Phillips—Van Heusen Corp.

Shoes
Always a step ahead in style
Connolly Shoe Co.
Ankle-fashioned shoes
Nunn-Bush Shoe Co.
Any Palizzio is better than no Palizzio
Palizzio, Inc.
Breathin' brushed pigskin (R) (Hush Puppies)
Wolverine World Wide, Inc.
Every pair shows the care of the shoemaker's
hand (Bostonian)
The Commonwealth Shoe and Leather Co.
The fashion shoe (Mademoiselle)
Genesco, Inc.
Fine bootmakers since 1876
Charles A. Eaton Co.
First in quality!
Nunn-Bush Shoe Co.
Look for the red ball
Mishawaka Rubber Co., Inc.
Look risqué from the ankles down
Risqué Shoes Div., Brown Shoe Co.

Makers of fine shoes for men and women
Florsheim Shoe Co.
Quality at your feet (R)
Brown Shoe Co.
The shoe with a memory (Johnston and
Murphy)
Genesco, Inc.
The shoe with the beautiful fit (Naturalizer)
Brown Shoe Co., Inc.
Since 1857...the standard of excellence in
men's footwear (Foot-Joy)
Brockton Footwear, Inc.
Wear tested for your comfort (Jarman)
Genesco, Inc.
When you're out to beat the world (tennis
shoes)
Converse Rubber Co.
The young point of view in shoes (Life Stride)
Brown Shoe Co.

Shortening—*see* **Food and Food Products**

Shrinkage of Textiles—*see* **Textile Fabrics**

Silverware
America's leading silversmiths since 1831
Gorham Div., Textron, Inc.
Grows more beautiful with use
Wallace Silversmiths Div., The Hamilton
Watch Co.
Mark of excellence
Oneida, Ltd.

Soaps
Aren't you glad you use Dial? Don't you
wish everybody did?
Armour and Co.
Cares for more complexions than any other
soap in the world, Palmolive
Colgate-Palmolive Co.
Creams your skin while you wash, Dove
Personal Products Div., Lever Bros. Co.
It floats (Ivory)
Procter and Gamble Co.
99 44/100% pure (R) (Ivory)
Procter and Gamble Co.
No wonder more women rely on Ivory
Liquid to help them keep their hands
soft, young-looking
Procter and Gamble Co.
World's worst beauty soap. World's best
hand soap (Lava)
Procter and Gamble Co.

Soups
It's uncanny (Knorr)
Best Foods Div., CPC International, Inc.
Reach for the Campbell's. It's right on your
shelf.
Campbell Soup Co.
They always eat better when you remember
the soup
Campbell Soup Co.

Spark Plugs
Best for all engines, Champion
Champion Spark Plug Co.
Dependable spark plugs
Champion Spark Plug Co.
The heart of a tune-up
Champion Spark Plug Co.
To feel new power, instantly, install new
Champions now and every 10,000
miles
Champion Spark Plug Co.

Sporting Goods
And who makes great skis? Head, of course.
Head Ski Co.
Authentically ski (R)
Ski Industries America
The best with the most on the ball
Adirondack Bats, Inc.
Bowl where you see the Magic Triangle
American Machine and Foundry Co.
The brightest star in golf (Burke-Worthing-
ton)
Victor Golf Co.
Covers a world of sports
Slazengers, Inc.
"The finest in the field" (R)
Rawlings Corp.
First to develop the latest in bat develop-
ments
Hanna Mfg. Co.
For the finest, Golfcraft
Golfcraft, Inc.
The greatest name in golf (MacGregor)
Brunswick Sports Co.
Hand made to fit you (golf clubs)
Kenneth Smith
Hottest name in golf
Kroydon Golf Corp.
The name for quality athletic goods
Nacona Athletic Goods Co.
The name to look for
Golfcraft, Inc.

Named for the original American professionals
  Indian Archery Corp.
The nation's big name in archery
  Ben Pearson, Inc.
The no. 1 name in billiards
  Brunswick Corp.
No. 1 name in bowling
  Brunswick Corp.
Often imitated, never duplicated (Davis tennis rackets)
  Victor Sports, Inc.
Play to win with Wilson
  Wilson Sporting Goods Co.
"Power without powder"
  Crosman Arms Co., Inc.
A progressive past. A golden future.
  Wilson Sporting Goods Co.
Remember: no one is paid to play Titleist (golf balls)
  Acushnet Co.
World's finest golf clubs and accessories
  Bristol Pro-Golf, Inc.
World's largest exclusive manufacturer of golf balls
  Plymouth Golf Ball Co.
World's largest ski maker
  Northland Ski Mfg. Co.
World's most experienced ski maker
  Northland Ski Mfg. Co.
"You don't have to be a millionaire to play like one"
  Walter Hagen Golf Equipment Co.

Sportswear
The brand with loyalty to quality (Billy the Kid slacks)
  Hortex Mfg. Co.
Not the biggest—but the best! (Seven Seas slacks)
  Anthony Gesture
The skier's tailor since 1929
  White Stag Mfg. Co.
Sportswear for sportsmen
  Jantzen, Inc.

Stationery—*see* **Paper**

Steamship Lines—*see* **Ocean Travel**

Stereo—*see* **High Fidelity Sound Equipment**; and **Phonographs, High Fidelity Sound Equipment**

Stock Exchange—*see* **Investments**

Storage and Storage Systems
Idea leader in storage systems
  Acme Steel Co.
Our integrity is your security
  American Warehousemen's Assn.
Store more. . .better. . .at less cost (systems)
  Vidmar, Inc.

Storage Batteries
More power from more research
  Gould-National Batteries, Inc.
Stampede of power (Exide)
  ESB, Inc.
World leader in packaged power
  ESB, Inc.

Store Equipment
Leadership built on the research and experience of over 48,000 store installations
  Bulman Corp.
More and more the complete source for your store
  The H.O.N. Co.

Sun Glasses—*see* **Eye Glasses**

Surgical Dressing—*see* **First Aid**

Synthetic Fabrics—*see also* **Textile Fibers, Synthetic**
The fabric with reflex action (Expandra)
  Burlington Industries
The fiber glass for finer fabrics
  PPG Industries, Inc.
Keeps the shape
  Pellon Corp.
One of the oldest names in textiles...for the newest development in synthetics
  Conmark Plastics Div., Cohn-Hall-Marx Co.
Rhymes with increase (Cantrece)
  E. I. duPont de Nemours and Co.
Your assurance that this fabric has been pre-tested for performance by Celanese (Arnel)
  Celanese Corp.

Synthetic Textile Fibers—*see* **Textile Fibers, Synthetic**

Tableware
The beginning of taste
  Syracuse China Corp.
Don't wait to inherit Spode
  Spode, Inc.
Fine dinnerware (Vernonware)
  Vernon Div., Metlox Mfg. Co.

Finest in china since 1735 (Richard Ginori)
Pasmantier, Inc.
Know the best by this mark
Jackson China Co.
The world's most beautiful china
Minton, Inc.

Tan Lotions—*see* **Cosmetics**

Tape, Magnetic—*see* **Magnetic Tape Recorders**

Tape Recorders—*see* **Magnetic Tape Recorders**

Tea—*see* **Beverages**

Telephone—*see* **Communications**

Television
Built better because it's handcrafted
Zenith Radio Corp.
Famous for quality the world over (R)
Philco Corp.
A flair for elegance
Sylvania Electric Products, Inc.
The handcrafted T.V.
Zenith Radio Corp.
The international one
Toshiba America, Inc.
The magnificent
Magnavox Co.
Mark of quality throughout the world
Admiral Corp.
The most trusted name in television
RCA Corp.
The quality goes in before the name goes on
Zenith Radio Corp.

Temporary Employees—*see* **Employees, Temporary**

Textile Fabrics
"America's leading producer of quality canvas products"
Fulton Cotton Mills Div., Allied Products Corp.
Be suspicious! (Sanforized)
Cluett, Peabody Co., Inc.
Comfortable, carefree cotton
Cotton Producers Institute
Cotton, you can feel how good it looks
National Cotton Council
Fabrics used in the most wanted women's and children's sportswear (Clan Crest)
Glen Raven Mills
Fabrics with the character of quality
Greenwood Mills, Inc.

The fiber you can trust
Cotton Producers Institute
Fine fabrics made in America since 1813
J. P. Stevens and Co., Inc.
First in fabrics for industry
Industrial Fabrics Div., West Point-Pepperell, Inc.
Gateway to the world of fabrics (Westgate)
Reese B. Davis and Co., Inc.
A man you can lean on, that's Klopman
Klopman Mills, Inc.
100% cotton. The fiber you can trust.
National Cotton Council
The search ends at Wellington Sears
West Point-Pepperell, Inc.
There are imitations, of course
Viyella International, Inc.
"Well dressed/wool dressed"
American Wool Council
World's finest cottons
Supima Association of America

Textile Fibers, Synthetic
Add a fiber from Celanese and good things get better
Celanese Corp.
America lives in Dacron
E. I. duPont de Nemours and Co.
The more colorful nylon (Caprolan)
Allied Chemical Corp.
Contemporary fibers
Celanese Corp.
Continuous filament textured nylon (Tycora)
Textured Yarn Co., Inc.
The creating fiber, Source
Allied Chemical Corp.
The extraordinary fiber (Trevira)
Hystron Fibers, Inc.
The home furnishings fiber (Herculon)
Hercules, Inc.
Luxury acrylic fiber (Creslan)
American Cyanamid Co.
The luxury of velvet with the worry left out (Islon)
Textiles Div., Monsanto Co.
Nothing but nylon makes you feel so female
Textiles Div., Monsanto Co.
Nothing but Spandex makes you look so female
Textiles Div., Monsanto Co.

Tires, Automobile
America's fastest-growing tire company
Cooper Tire and Rubber Co.

The greatest tire name in racing
   Firestone Tire and Rubber Co.
High-performance tirepower
   Firestone Tire and Rubber Co.
More people ride on Goodyear tires than on
      any other brand
   Goodyear Tire and Rubber Co.
The name that's known is Firestone—all over
      the world
   Firestone Tire and Rubber Co.
New dimensions in driving on the safer Kelly
      road
   The Kelly-Springfield Tire Co.
The round tire that rolls 3,000 miles further
      (Atlas Plycron)
   General Tire and Rubber Co.
The sign of tomorrow. . .today
   General Tire and Rubber Co.
The straight-talk tire people
   B. F. Goodrich Tire Co.
Top quality for 50 years
   General Tire and Rubber Co.
The tough breed of tire
   B. F. Goodrich Tire Co.
Where research and development make excit-
      ing ideas
   General Tire and Rubber Co.
Your symbol of quality and service
   Firestone Tire and Rubber Co.
You're miles ahead with General Tire
   General Tire and Rubber Co.

Toilet Goods

The body cosmetic (Cashmere Bouquet
      talcum)
   Colgate-Palmolive Co.
For the private world of the bath
   House of Wrisley, Inc.
The light moisturizing bath oil for dry skin
      (Tender Touch)
   Helene Curtis Industries, Inc.
P.S. And it's especially great as a hand lotion
      (Dermassage)
   S. M. Edison Chemical Co.
Super-moisturizes dry skin zones instantly!
      (Dermassage)
   S. M. Edison Chemical Co.

Toilet Goods For Men

Spirited new scent of the sixties (Richard
      Hudnut Sportsman)
   Cosmetics and Toiletries Div., Warner-
   Lambert Pharmaceutical Co.
What Scandinavian men have (Teak)
   Shulton, Inc.

Toilet Paper

Softness is Northern
   Marathon Div., American Can Co.
Two layers of softness. . .and one is purest
      white (Aurora)
   Marathon Div., American Can Co.

Tools

Bonded for life. . .because they're built that
      way
   Ingersoll-Rand Co.
Choice of better mechanics
   Snap-On Tools Corp.
For all industry
   Snap-On Tools Corp.
Go with the pick of the pros
   Skil Corp.
Keep your eye on Elliott
   Elliott Div., Carrier Corp.
Make hard jobs easy
   K-D Manufacturing Co.
Maker of the world's first cordless electric
      tools
   The Black and Decker Mfg. Co.
Makes it easy, Skil
   Skil Corp.
Matched tools for unmatched performance
   Baash-Ross Div., Joy Mfg. Co.
The ones professionals reach for, Ingersoll-
      Rand power tools
   Ingersoll-Rand Co.
Re-equip/equip and profit
   Ammco Tools, Inc.
The right tool for the right job
   True Temper Corp.
Service-backed shop equipment
   Snap-On Tools Corp.
The tool box of the world
   Stanley Tool Div., Stanley Works
World's largest manufacturer of painters' and
      glaziers' tools—since 1872
   Red Devil, Inc.

Tourist Trade—see Travel

Towels

Just everyday things for the home made
      beautiful by Stevens
   J. P. Stevens and Co., Inc.
King of the kitchen
   Startex Mills, Inc.
Royal family of home fashions
   Cannon Mills, Inc.

Twin names in quality towels (Martex and
    Fairfax)
  West Point-Pepperell, Inc.

Toys
Most trusted name in modelling
  Hawk Model Co.
The name for quality hobby kits
  Monogram Models, Inc.
"Our work is child's play"
  Fisher-Price Toys, Inc.
Quality toys with a purpose (Tinkertoys)
  Toy Tinkers Div., A. G. Spalding and
  Bros., Inc.
Sane toys for healthy kids
  Lionel Toy Corp.
World's largest creator of preschool toys
  Fisher-Price Toys, Inc.

Tractors—see Agricultural Machinery

Trailer Transportation
Border to border. . .coast to coast!
  Trailer Train Co.
Builds better bodies, Batavia
  Batavia Body Co.
"Engineered transportation"
  Fruehauf Corp.
The "kid glove treatment" (R)
  Evans Transportation Equipment Div.,
  Evans Products Co.

Travel—see also Motor Bus Travel; and Ocean Travel
"Better than money" (R) (Travelers Checks)
  First National City Bank
The company for people who travel
  American Express Co.
Friendly, familiar, foreign and near
  Ontario, Canada, Department of Tourism
  and Information
Land of enchantment
  Department of Development, New
  Mexico
The land that was made for vacations
  Wisconsin Vacation and Travel Service
Now's the time to get away to it all!
  Southwest Sun Country Association
The place to go
  Spanish National Tourist Office
See America best by car
  American Petroleum Institute
Vacationing in San Antonio is a family affair
  San Antonio Municipal Information
  Bureau

Where your "resort dollar" buys more
  Stardust Hotel and Golf Club
You can't get the whole picture in just a day
  or two
  San Francisco Convention and Visitors
  Bureau
You haven't seen your country if you
  haven't seen Alaska
  Alaska Travel Div., Department of Eco-
  nomic Development and Planning

Traveler's Checks—see Travel

Truck Campers—see Recreation

Truck Coaches—see Recreation

Trucks—see Motor Trucks

Trust Companies—see Banks and Banking

Typewriters
Every year, more Royal typewriters are
  bought in America than any other brand
  Royal Typewriter Co., Inc., Div. Litton
  Industries
Means Swissmanship, Hermes...a step beyond
  craftsmanship
  Paillard, Inc.
Precision typewriters
  Olympia Div., Inter-Continental Trading
  Corp.
The quick brown fox
  SCM Corp.
Think ahead—think SCM
  SCM Corp.

Underwear
All is vanity. . .all is Vanity Fair
  Vanity Fair Mills, Inc.
Because you love nice things
  Van Raalte Co., Inc.
It's worth the difference
  Munsingwear, Inc.

Vacuum Cleaners
Matchless quality. . .superior service. . .endur-
  ing excellence
  Electrolux Corp.
The very best in floor care products
  Eureka Williams Co.

Valves
The air valve people
  Numatics, Inc.
Creative aerosol valve engineering
  Newman-Green, Inc.

Headquarters for hand valves
    Barksdale Valves
Leaders by design
    Precision Valve Corp.
Matchless valves for exacting service
    Whitey Research Tool Co.
Men who know valves know Powell
    The Wm. Powell Co.
Most trusted trademark in the valve world
    Jenkins Bros.
The one great name in valves
    The Lunkheimer Co.
World leader of the valve industry since 1846
    The Wm. Powell Co.

Ventilation
Better air is our business
    American Air Filter Co., Inc.
Far sighted planners choose Herman Nelson
    American Air Filter Co., Inc.
Gives you more to work with, Janitrol
    Janitrol Div., Midland-Ross Corp.
World's largest manufacturer of ventilating
    louvers
    Louver Mfg. Co., Inc.

Vitamins
Look for the label with the Big Red "1"
    (One-a-Day)
    Miles Laboratories, Inc.
World's leading direct-by-mail vitamin and
    drug company
    Hudson National, Inc.

Wall Coverings
First with the finest in wallcoverings. . .
    always!
    Timbertone Decorative Co., Inc.
Oldest in permanent type wall coverings
    Frederic Blank and Co., Inc.

Watches
America's "wake-up" voice
    Westclox Div., General Time Corp.
Le couturier de la monte
    Universal Geneve
Fine watchmakers since 1791 (Girard
    Perregaux)
    Jean R. Graef, Inc.
For a lifetime of proud possession
    Omega Watch Co.
Get time from a timepiece, but if you want a
    watch get a Hamilton
    Hamilton Watch Co.
If you want more than time, get a Hamilton
    Hamilton Watch Co.

If you want to give more than time, give
    Hamilton
    Hamilton Watch Co.
The jeweler's quality watch
    Vantage Products, Inc.
Leading maker of watches of the highest
    character for almost a century
    Longines-Wittnauer Watch Co.
One of the great watches of our time
    Waltham Watch Co.
Modern masters of time
    Seiko Time Corp.
The peak of Swiss watchmaking perfection
    Rado Watch Co.
Progress in the world of time
    Westclox Div., General Time Corp.
Sign of the right time
    Zodiac Watch Co.
Since 1867 maker of watches of the highest
    character
    Longines-Wittnauer Watch Co.
When something happy happens, it's Bulova
    time
    Bulova Watch Co., Inc.
The world's most honored watch (R)
    Longines-Wittnauer Watch Co.

Water Conditioning
Only Elgin gives you Elgineering
    Elgin Softener, Inc.
The only nicer water comes from clouds
    Servisoft Div., Water Treatment Corp.
Sure has a way with water, Calgon Corpora-
    tion
    Calgon Corp.
The world-wide water conditioning people
    Culligan, Inc.

Water Softening—*see* Water Conditioning

Whiskey
Aged for 8 (Bell's Blended scotch)
    Heublein, Inc.
Always smoother because it's slow-distilled
    (Early Times bourbon)
    Brown-Forman Distillers Corp.
"An inch of Pinch, please." (scotch)
    Renfield Importer, Ltd.
As long as you're up get me a Grants (R)
    (scotch)
    Austin, Nichols and Co., Inc.
"The best in the house" (R) in 87 lands
    (Canadian Club)
    Hiram Walker, Inc.

Born in 1820. . .still going strong! (Johnnie
  Walker Red Label scotch)
  Canada Dry Corp.
Charcoal mellowed drop by drop
  Jack Daniels Distillery
Don't be vague. . .ask for Haig and Haig
  Renfield Importers, Ltd.
Famous. Smooth. Mellow. (Old Crow)
  National Distillers and Chemical Corp.
Fine whiskey on the mild side (Corby's)
  Jas. Barclay and Co., Ltd.
The first taste will tell you why! (Fleisch-
  mann)
  Fleischmann Distilling Corp.
The gold medal Kentucky bourbon since
  1872 (I. W. Harper)
  Schenley Industries, Inc.
The greatest name in bourbon (Old Crow)
  National Distillers and Chemical Corp.
Head of the bourbon family (Old Grand-
  Dad)
  National Distillers and Chemical Corp.
The incomparable (Imperial)
  Hiram Walker, Inc.
It's always a pleasure (I. W. Harper bourbon)
  Schenley Industries, Inc.
"It's smart to buy right" (Highland Scotch
  Mist)
  Heublein, Inc.
Just smooth, very smooth (Johnnie Walker
  Red Label scotch)
  Canada Dry Corp.
Knowledgeable people buy Imperial
  Hiram Walker, Inc.
Known by the company it keeps (Seagram's
  Canadian VO)
  Seagram Distillers Co.
No scotch improves the flavour of water like
  Teacher's
  Schieffelin and Co.
Nothing else quite measures up (Walker's
  DeLuxe bourbon)
  Hiram Walker, Inc.
Pennies more in cost. . .worlds apart in quality
  (J and B scotch)
  James Moroney, Inc.
The responsibility of being the best (Wild
  Turkey bourbon)
  Austin, Nichols and Co., Inc.
Say Seagrams and be sure (7 Crown)
  Seagram Distillers Co.
Soft whiskey (Calvert Extra)
  Calvert Distillers Co. Div., The House of
  Seagram, Inc.

"There is nothing better in the market" (Old
  Forester bourbon)
  Brown-Forman Distillers Corp.
The true old-style Kentucky bourbon (Early
  Times)
  Brown-Forman Distillers Corp.
Two scotches of exceptional character (Black
  and White)
  Fleischmann Distilling Corp.
We'll wait. Grant's 8 (R) (scotch)
  Austin, Nichols and Co., Inc.
Wherever you go, there it is (Hiram Walker
  bourbon)
  Hiram Walker, Inc.
The world's finest bourbon since 1795
  James B. Beam Distilling Co.
Your key to hospitality (Old Fitzgerald)
  Stitzel-Walker Distillery, Inc.

Windows
For the beautiful point of view (R)
  Woodco Corp.
The line and design for creative window
  planning
  Malta Mfg. Co.
Only the rich can afford poor windows
  Andersen Corp.
Window beauty is Andersen
  Andersen Corp.

Wines
The brandy of Napoleon (Courvoisier
  cognac)
  W. A. Taylor and Co.
California's premier wines
  Almaden Vineyards, Inc.
The centaur. . .your symbol of quality (Remy-
  Martin cognac)
  Renfield Importers, Ltd.
Don't stir without Noilly Prat
  Browne-Vintners Co.
The finest wines of France
  Barton and Guestier
From the largest cellars in the world (Moët
  champagne)
  Schieffelin and Co.
Imported from Spain, of course. True sherry
  is. (Duff Gordon)
  Munson G. Shaw Co. Div., National Dis-
  tillers and Chemical Corp.
Mountain grown
  Almaden Vineyards, Inc.
The nobility of Italian wines
  Marchesi L and P Antinori

Pop goes the Piper (Piper-Heidsieck champagne)
Renfield Importers, Ltd.
Pride of cognac since 1724 (Remy Martin)
Renfield Importers, Ltd.
When you mix with CinZano, you mix with the best
Schieffelin and Co.
Wines of California. Since 1882. (Christian Brothers)
Fromm and Sichel, Inc.
The word for champagne, Mumm's
G. H. Mumm and Co.
World-famous Spanish sherries (Williams and Humbert dry sack)
Julius Wile Sons and Co., Inc.

Wire
The source for answers to wire problems
Page Steel and Wire Div., American Chain and Cable Co.
Wire for Industry
Keystone Steel and Wire Co.
Working wonders with wire
E. H. Titchener Co.
You fence for keeps with Red Brand
Keystone Steel and Wire Co.

Women's Apparel
Always virgin wool
Pendleton Woolen Mills
America lives in R and K Originals
R and K Originals, Inc.
Are not just for dancing, Danskins
Danskin, Inc.
Definitely Glenoit for happy persons
Glenoit Mills, Inc.
"Designs for the world's best dressed"
Mr. John
Everything to wear
Genesco, Inc.
For the elegant petite (coats, suits)
Lilli-Ann Corp.
For the typical American size (R)
Leslie Fay, Inc.
"Important occasion dresses" (R)
Lorrie Deb Corp.
Just wear a smile and a Jantzen
Jantzen, Inc.
The label to ask for
Davidow Suits, Inc.
Lead the Ship 'n Shore life (blouses)
Ship 'n Shore, Inc.
The pattern people
Simplicity Patterns Co., Inc.

World's finest mink
United Mink Producers Assn.

Woolen and Worsted Fabrics—see Textile Fabrics

Work Clothes—see Men's Clothing

Wrecking Machinery—see Machines and Machinery

Miscellaneous (Not Classified Elsewhere)
The finest tribute. . .the most trusted protection
Clark Metal Grave Vault Co.
First name in power transmission equipment
Lovejoy Flexible Coupling Co.
For languages, Berlitz
The Berlitz Schools of Languages of America
Greatest name in color (movie film)
Technicolor Corp.
The green cleans in-between. . .the white polishes bright
Pro-phy-lac-tic Brush Co.
Hey man!. . .say Heyman
Heyman Mfg. Co.
Innovators of research-engineered products
Bostrom Corp.
Instruments mean accuracy first, Taylor (compasses, navigational aids)
Taylor Instrument Cos.
It's a National (R)
National Tank Co.
It's what's inside that counts
Explosives Div., Atlas Chemical Industries, Inc.
Leads the industry in quality and dependability (cabinets, vending machine parts)
Universal Metal Products Div., UMC Industries, Inc.
Master navigators through time and space (spacecraft equipment parts)
A C Sparkplug Div., General Motors Corp.
The men who make it make the difference
Steel and Tube Div., Timkin Roller Bearing Co.
More dentists use Lavoris than any other mouthwash. Shouldn't you?
Vick Chemical Co.
Moving ahead fast...to keep you competitive
National Castings Co.

The original self-adhesive pin-fed labels
   Avery Label Co., Div. Avery Products
   Corp.
Pool products from a name you know—
      Purex (Guardex)
   Purex Corp., Ltd.
Prime source for weighing equipment and
      technology
   Toledo Scale Co.
The pursuit of excellence
   International Flavors and Fragrances, Inc.
Recommended by dentists surveyed 9 to 1
      over all toothpastes combined
      (Polident)
   Block Drug Co., Inc.
The right hand of production
   Industrial Distributors, Ltd.
Safety on the road. Security in space (para-
      chutes, seat belts)
   Irving Air Chute Co.

The successful ones (agricultural hybrids)
   P-A-G Div., W. R. Grace and Co.
There's no place like this showplace!
   Chicago Merchandise Mart
Total capability in fire protection (alarm
      system)
   Grinnell Corp.
We mass produce quality! (tubing)
   Atlas Bradford Co.
Where outstanding performance is standard
   New York Shipbuilding Corp.
Worldwide in heat and fluid processing
   Selas Corp. of America
World's largest citrus plant
   Pasco Packing Co.
World's largest manufacturer of school sup-
      plies and stationery
   Westab, Inc.
World's leading supplier of diamonds for
      industry
   De Beers Consolidated Mines, Ltd.

In this section, slogans are alphabetized by source, whether this be a service, a periodical or, in the majority of cases, a company. Products or services, if necessary, are indicated in parentheses at the end of the phrase. If a company has generated a number of slogans, these are further alphabetized under the originating source.

A

ABC Records, Inc.
World leader in recorded sound (Command)

A.C. Spark Plug Div., General Motors Corp.
Master navigators through time and space (spacecraft equipment, parts)

A. P. Parts Corp.
Sold by more dealers than any other brand (mufflers)

ASEA Electric, Inc.
Power across land and sea

Abex Corp.
Means controls, Abex

Abbott Laboratories
Basic provider of chemicals in volume

Acme Appliance Mfg. Co.
More doors fold on Fold-Aside (R) than any other kind!

Acme Life Products Co.
Feather touch control

Acme National Refrigeration Co.
"Where inches count"

Acme Steel Co.
Idea leader in storage systems
Idea leader in strapping

Acushnet Co.
Remember: no one is paid to play Titleist (golf balls)

Addressograph-Multigraph Corp.
Cutting costs is our business
Helping people communicate

Adirondack Bats, Inc.
The bat with the most on the ball

Administrative Management
The magazine of methods, personnel and equipment

Admiral Corp.
Mark of quality throughout the world (television)

Advertising Age
Important to important people

The Advertising Council
Please! Only you can prevent forest fires

Aero Mayflower Transit Co., Inc.
America's most recommended mover (Mayflower)

Aeroquip Corp.
The lifeline of your equipment (industrial hose)

Aetna Insurance Co.
The choice of business men lets you choose with confidence
. . .For your family and business—your auto, home, and everything you own
Our concern is people
P.S.—Personal service

Agfa-Gevaert, Inc.
World's second largest manufacturer of cameras and films

Air Canada
A friend of the family

Air France
À votre service
We know where you're going
The world's largest airline

Air-India
The airline that treats you like a maharajah

Air New Zealand
The airline that knows the South Pacific best

Airborne Freight Corp.
World's most dependable air freight service

Airtex Products, Inc.
  Number 1 in acceptance (automobile
    parts)
  The only name for both fuel and water
    pumps
Aladdin Laboratories, Inc.
  Pick a Perrine today! (fishing tackle)
Alaska Airlines, Inc.
  Golden nugget jet service
  Golden nugget jets
Alaska Travel Div., Dept. of Economic
Development and Planning
  You haven't seen your country if you
    haven't seen Alaska
Aldrich Pump Co.
  The tough pumping problems go to
    Aldrich
Allan Mfg. Co.
  First choice in fishing tackle hardware
Allegheny Airlines, Inc.
  Your air commuter service in 12 busy
    states
Allegheny Industrial Chemical Co.
  The bright new silicates for industry
Allen-Bradley Co.
  Quality electronic components
  Quality motor control
The Alliance Mfg. Co., Inc.
  Keeps you in the driver's seat, Genie
    (garage door opener)
  Put Alliance in your appliance (motors)
Allied Chemical Corp.
  Ask Allied Chemical
  Basic to America's progress
  The creating fiber, Source
  The more colorful nylon (Caprolan)
  Producers of all basic urethane chemicals
  Putting the "push" in America's finest
    aerosols (Genetron)
Allied Mills Corp.
  Builders of tomorrow's feeds. . .today!
    (Wayne feeds)
Allied Van Lines, Inc.
  America's number 1 mover
  Families that move the most call the
    world's largest mover
  We move families, not just furniture
The Alligator Co.
  The best name in all-weather coats and
    rainwear
The Louis Allis Co.
  Pace setting engineered systems to con-
    trol materials in motion

Allis-Chalmers Mfg. Co.
  Be sure to get a quote (lift trucks)
  Does its share to help you share in a bet-
    ter future, Allis-Chalmers
  From the tractor people who make the
    big ones
  The long line of construction machinery
  The tractor people, Allis-Chalmers
Allstate Insurance Co.
  You're in good hands with Allstate (R)
All-Steel Equipment, Inc.
  The choice when you want quality, too
    (office furniture)
Almaden Vineyards, Inc.
  California's premier wines
  Mountain grown
Alton Box Board Co.
  Full circle packaging
  Packaging that builds and holds sales
Aluminum Co. of America
  Change for the better with Alcoa
    Aluminum
  What next from Alcoa!
Amana Refrigeration, Inc.
  Backed by a century-old tradition of fine
    craftsmanship (domestic appliances)
Amchem Products, Inc.
  First name in herbicide research
  World's number one weed killers
    (Weedone)
American Air Filter Co., Inc.
  Better air is our business
  Far sighted planners choose Herman
    Nelson
American Airlines, Inc.
  Airline of the professionals
  America's leading airline
American Nickeloid Co.
  America's pioneer manufacturer of pre-
    finished metals
American Brands, Inc.
  The cigar that never lasts long enough
    (Antonio y Cleopatra)
  For those who want every puff to taste as
    fresh as the first puff! (Montclair
    cigarettes)
  I'm particular (Pall Mall cigarettes)
  Just enough! (Montclair cigarettes)
  Lightest smoke of all (Carlton cigarettes)
  New taste enjoyment, new smoking con-
    venience. . .anywhere, anytime
    (Roi-Tan Little Cigars)

Outstanding—and they are mild! (Pall
    Mall cigarettes)
"Tobacco is our middle name" (C)
"Us Tareyton smokers would rather fight
    than switch!"
American Brass Co.
    Think copper (Anaconda)
American Broadcasting Co.
    Wide world of entertainment
American Cyanamid Co.
    Basic in catalyst chemistry
    In home, health, farm and industry,
        science in action for you
    Luxury acrylic fiber (Creslan)
    Serves the man who makes a business of
        agriculture, Cyanamid
    When it comes to color, come to
        Cyanamid
American Enka Corp.
    The yarn with the "crepe" built in (Enka
        Crepeset)
American Export Isbrandtsen Lines, Inc.
    Sunlane (R) cruises to Europe
American Express Co.
    The company for people who travel
American Flange and Mfg. Co., Inc.
    Tri-sure the world over (packaging)
American Gas Assn., Inc.
    Do it tomorrow's way. . .with gas
    For commercial cooking. . .gas is good
        business
    For heating and cooling. . .gas is good
        business
    Gas makes the big difference
    Live modern for less with gas
American Girl Service
    Office help—temporary or permanent
American Hardware Mutual Insurance Co.
    For a sure tomorrow—insure enough
        today!
American Home
    Reach her when home is on her mind
American Honda Motor Co., Inc.
    World's biggest seller! (motorcycles)
American Insulator Corp.
    Where everything is done in plastics
        (molds)
American Latex Products Corp.
    Enjoy the rest of your life (Koolfoam
        pillows)
American Laundry Machinery Industries
    You get more from American

American Machine and Foundry Co.
    Bowl where you see the Magic Triangle
American Machinist
    The most useful magazine in metalwork-
        ing
American Motors Corp.
    America's best fleet buy (Rambler)
    Dedicated to excellence
    The sensible spectaculars
    Where quality is built in, not added on
American Mutual Liability Insurance Co.
    A leading writer of workmen's compensa-
        tion, all forms of liability, crime,
        accident and health insurance
American Optical Co.
    Products that extend and protect man's
        physical senses
    Since 1833. . .better vision for better living
American Petroleum Institute
    See America best by car
American Photocopy Equipment Co.
    Copies for communication throughout
        the world
American President Lines
    Cruising everywhere under the sun
American Saint Gobain Corp.
    Creative ideas in glass
American Sugar Refining Co.
    When it's Domino sugar, you're sure it's
        pure!
American Telephone and Telegraph Co.
    Action people (Yellow Pages)
    Advertise for action (Yellow Pages)
    Find it faster in the Yellow Pages
    Let your fingers do the walking (Yellow
        Pages)
    Long distance is the next best thing to
        being there (Bell System)
    Phone power in action (Bell System)
    Serving you (Bell System)
    Talk things over, get things done. . .by
        long distance!
    Your anywhere anything anytime net-
        work
American Thermos Products Co.
    Foremost brand in outdoor living
American Trucking Associations, Inc.
    The wheels that go everywhere
American United Life Insurance Co.
    The company with the partnership
        philosophy
American Warehousemen's Association
    Our integrity is your security

American Wool Council
  "Well dressed/wool dressed" (fabrics)
American Zinc Institute
  Value engineering favors zinc
Amerio Contact Plate Freezers, Inc.
  It's the contacts that count (commercial
    refrigeration)
Amerock Corp.
  Makes it authentic, Amerock (lumber,
    building materials)
Amity Leather Products Co.
  There's a need-keyed billfold for you
Ammco Tools, Inc.
  Re-equip/equip and profit
Amoco Chemicals Corp.
  Where what's happening gets its start
Ampex Corp.
  Ask anyone who knows (high fidelity
    sound equipment)
Amway Corp.
  Home-care know-how. . .at your doorstep!
Anchor Hocking Glass Co.
  Everyday good. . .glass with flair
  The greatest line in glassware!
  World's largest manufacturer of glass
    tableware
Andersen Corp.
  Only the rich can afford poor windows
  Window beauty is Andersen
Anderson Chemical Co., Inc.
  Specialists in making water behave
Anderson, Clayton and Co.
  So soft. . .it comes in a tub (Chiffon mar-
    garine)
Anheuser-Busch, Inc.
  It's worth it. . .it's Bud (Budweiser beer)
  That Bud. . .that's beer!
  Where there's life. . .there's Bud (R) (beer)
Marchesi L and P Antinori
  The nobility of Italian wines
The Apex Machine and Tool Co.
  The authority on fastening
Apex Smelting Co.
  Consistently better
Fred Arbogast Co., Inc.
  "Bait of champions"
Architectural and Engineering News
  It pays to be in the news
Ar-ex Products, Inc.
  The lipstick without the dye
Argosy
  The no. 1 men's service magazine

Armco Steel Corp.
  New steels are born at Armco
Armour and Co.
  Aren't you glad you use Dial? Don't you
    wish everybody did?
  Get better yields from your fields with
    Armour
  Let us help put Armour Idea chemicals to
    work for you
  The meats that wear the Armour Star are
    the meats the butcher brings home
Armstrong Cork Co.
  More ideas from the Armstrong world of
    interior design
Arno Adhesive Tapes, Inc.
  The best in tapes has "Able" on the label
Arvin Industries, Inc.
  Where great ideas are meant to happen
Ashaway Line and Twine Mfg. Co.
  First in world records
Ashland Oil and Refining Co.
  The independent supplier for independents
  The industrial resources company
Associates Investment Co.
  Specialists in financing
Association of American Railroads
  Grow, grow by the rail way
Atlantic Coast Line Railroad
  Thanks for using Coast Line
Atlantic Richfield Co.
  Making petroleum do more things for
    more people
  Making things happy with petroleum
    energy
Atlas Bradford Co.
  We mass produce quality! (tubing)
Audio Devices, Inc.
  It speaks for itself (Audiotape)
Austin, Nichols and Co., Inc.
  As long as you're up get me a Grant's (R)
    (Scotch whiskey)
  The responsibility of being the best (Wild
    Turkey bourbon)
  We'll wait. Grant's 8 (R) (Scotch whiskey)
Autocar Div., White Motor Co.
  World's finest
Autonetics Div., North American Rockwell
Corp.
  Manning the frontiers of electronic prog-
    ress
Avery Label Co., Div. Avery Products Corp.
  The original self-adhesive pin-feed labels

Avianca
　First airline in the Americas
Avis, Inc.
　We try harder (automobile leasing)
Axle Div., Eaton Mfg. Co.
　World's largest producer of commercial
　　heavy-duty truck drive axles

B

B. B. Chemical Div., United Shoe Machinery
Corp.
　Join with Bostik for better bonding
BSR (USA), Ltd.
　The world's "first family" of changers
　　and tape decks
Baash-Ross Div., Joy Mfg. Co.
　Matched tools for unmatched perform-
　　ance
Bacardi Imports, Inc.
　Enjoyable always and all ways (rum)
D. H. Baldwin Co.
　The sound investment (pianos)
J. A. Baldwin Mfg. Co.
　World's finest (automobile filters)
Bali Brassiere Co.
　Every Bali has a bow
Ball Brothers Co., Inc.
　Your partner in packaging progress
Ing. Mario Ballestra and Co.
　World's most experienced detergent
　　engineers
Baltimore Luggage Co.
　America's greatest luggage value (Lady
　　Baltimore)
　Fashion luggage (Lady Baltimore)
　If you have an instinct for quality. . .
　　(Amelia Earhart luggage)
Bank of America
　First in banking
Bank of the Southwest
　The bank with the international point of
　　view
Bankers Life Insurance Co. of Nebraska
　The good things of life
Banquet Canning Div., F. M. Stamper Co.
　Thank goodness for Banquet cooking bag
　　foods
　Thank goodness for Banquet frozen foods
Jas. Barclay and Co., Ltd.
　Fine whiskey on the mild side (Corby's)
Barksdale Valves
　Headquarters for hand valves

Barrett Electronics Corp.
　First in automated materials handling
Barton and Guestier
　The finest wines of France
E. T. Barwick Industries, Inc.
　World's largest maker of tufted carpets
　　and rugs
Bassett Furniture Industries, Inc.
　At home with your young ideas
Bastian-Blessing Co.
　Quality products known throughout the
　　world for engineered quality (res-
　　taurant equipment, supplies)
Batavia Body Co.
　Builds better bodies, Batavia (refrigera-
　　tion transportation)
Battery Div., Sonotone Corp.
　Portable power for progress
Battle Creek Manufacturers, Inc.
　The leadership line (physical fitness
　　equipment)
　"Works with you—works for you" (physi-
　　cal fitness equipment)
Battle Creek Packaging Machines, Inc.
　Continuous flow packaging (R)
Bavarian Motor Works
　The sportsman's car (BMW)
Bead Design Studio
　The world's largest manufacturer and
　　designer
James B. Beam Distilling Co.
　The world's finest bourbon since 1795
Bear Mfg. Co.
　Re-equip/equip and profit with (auto-
　　mobile service equipment)
A. G. Becker and Co., Inc.
　The man from A. G. Becker is always
　　worth listening to (financial)
Beech Aircraft Corp.
　Accustomed to the finest. . .you'll find it
　　in a Beechcraft
　The world is small when you fly a Beech-
　　craft
Bekins Van and Storage Co.
　The professionals
Bell Helicopter Co.
　World standard
Bell and Howell Co.
　Brings out the expert in you (automati-
　　cally!), Bell and Howell
　Builds photographic instruments a little
　　better than they really have to be,
　　Bell and Howell

Bellows-Valvair Div., International Basic
Economy Corp.
  These names assure you the best in pneu-
    matic, hydraulic and electronic
    components
Bemis Co., Inc.
  Everyday, Bemis develops a new packag-
    ing idea to serve you better
Bemis Mfg. Co.
  Be seated by. . .Bemis
Bendix Corp.
  Where ideas unlock the future
Benefit Trust Life Insurance Co.
  "Value" is a good word for Benefit Trust
    Life
Beneke Corp.
  The first name in seats. The last word in
    quality (bathroom fixtures)
Bergstrom Paper Co.
  America's cities are Bergstrom's forests
Berkshire International Corp.
  Hosiery fashion on five continents
The Berlitz Schools of Language of America
  For languages, Berlitz
Jules Berman and Associates, Inc.
  Fine coffee liqueur. . .from sunny Mexico
    (Kahlúa)
The Beryllium Corp.
  Developers and producers of extraordi-
    nary materials
Charles Beseler Co.
  Today's finest-designed for tomorrow's
    needs (camera equipment)
Best Foods Div., CPC International, Inc.
  America's favorite mayonnaise (Best
    Foods)
  America's favorite mayonnaise (Hell-
    mann's)
  Don't miss the magic of Rit (dyes)
  Dyeing with Rit is fast, fun, almost fool-
    proof!
  It's uncanny (Knorr soups)
  Makes good eating sense, Mazola (mar-
    garine)
  The name you can trust in margarine
    (Mazola)
  This is no place for "second best" (Hell-
    mann's mayonnaise)
Big Brother
  It takes a man to help a boy
Big Joe Mfg. Co.
  Takes a load off your mind, Big Joe
    (materials handling)

Bigelow-Sanford, Inc.
  People who know buy Bigelow (carpets)
  Rugs, carpets since 1825
  A title on the door rates a Bigelow on the
    floor
Biggs Antique Co., Inc.
  Master craftsmen since 1890
Bilco Co.
  America's finest basement door
Bird and Son, Inc.
  The classic name in the building field
    (materials)
  Takes the burden out of keeping up your
    home, Bird (building materials)
Birds Eye Div., General Foods Corp.
  Better buy Birds Eye
Bishman Mfg. Co.
  The quality equipment line (automobile
    parts)
Bishop Industries, Inc.
  For the women who can afford the best.
    Even though it costs less. (Hazel
    Bishop cosmetics)
The Black and Decker Mfg. Co.
  Maker of the world's finest cordless elec-
    tric tools
Blair-Knox Co.
  Engineering know-how. . .by Blair-Knox
Frederic Blank and Co., Inc.
  Oldest in permanent type wall coverings
Block Drug Co.
  For a good night's sleep (Nytol)
  Recommended by dentists surveyed 9 to
    1 over all toothpastes combined
    (Polident)
John Blue Co., Inc.
  Since 1886. . .scientifically designed for
    practical use (fertilizer, agricultural
    equipment)
Blue Shield
  For doctor bills
Bodine Corp.
  Shares the risk. . .to assure performance,
    Bodine (machines)
Bodine Electric Co.
  Power behind the leading products (motors)
Boeing Co.
  Capability has many faces at Boeing
  World's first family of jets
Bolens Div., FMC Corp.
  First in powered equipment since 1918
    (compact tractor)

Boling Chair Co.
   Best buy Boling
   Chairs for all business
Bonne Bell, Inc.
   Your face never had it so clean! (1006
      lotion)
Borden Chemical Div., Borden, Inc.
   Best glue in the joint (Elmer's)
Borden, Inc.
   If it's Borden's it's got to be good (dairy
      products)
   Just has to be good, Borden's (dairy
      products)
   Naturally it's delicious. . .It's made by
      Bordens (dairy products)
Borg-Warner Corp.
   The great engineers
   Your best single source for quality drive
      train replacement parts
Bostitch Div., Textron, Inc.
   You're better off with Bostitch (office
      supplies)
Bostitch, Inc.
   Fasten it better and faster with Bostitch
Bostrom Corp.
   Innovators of research-engineered prod-
      ucts
The Bowdil Co.
   Always right on the job (mining machin-
      ery)
Braniff Airways, Inc.
   Specialists in international jet service to
      Texas or South America
John H. Breck, Inc.
   Beautiful hair (shampoo)
Breon Laboratories, Inc.
   If babies were born trained, they wouldn't
      need Diaparene baby powder
The Brearley Co.
   World's largest producer of bath scales
      (Counselor)
Briggs and Stratton Corp.
   Most respected name in power (engines)
Brillion Iron Works, Inc.
   Farm implements with a future—yours!
The Bristol Co.
   For improved production through meas-
      urement and control
Bristol Pro-Golf, Inc.
   World's finest golf clubs and accessories
British European Airways
   Europe's foremost airline

British Industries Corp.
   World's finest (Garrard) (phonograph
      high fidelity equipment)
British Overseas Airway Corp.
   All over the world BOAC takes good care
      of you
   Takes good care of you, BOAC
Brockton Footwear, Inc.
   Since 1857. . .the standard of excellence in
      men's footwear (Foot-Joy)
Brown and Williamson Tobacco Corp.
   Come up to the Kool taste
   Discover extra coolness (Kool cigarettes)
   The filter for the taste that's right!
      (Viceroy cigarettes)
   For the taste that's right (Viceroy ciga-
      rettes)
   Got the deepweave filter and the taste
      that's right, Viceroy's
   The mark of quality in tobacco products
   Smoke all 7 (Viceroy cigarettes)
   The taste that's right (Viceroy cigarettes)
The Brown-Bridge Mills, Inc.
   Specialists in the application of adhesives
      (paper)
Brown Co.
   The paper people
Brown-Forman Distillers Corp.
   Always smoother because it's slow-
      distilled (Early Times bourbon)
   Dutch name, world fame (Bols liqueurs)
   "There is nothing better in the market"
      (Old Forester bourbon)
   The true old-style Kentucky bourbon
      (Early Times)
Brown Shoe Co.
   Quality at your feet (R)
   The shoe with the beautiful fit (Natural-
      izer)
   The young point of view in shoes (Life
      Stride)
Browne-Vintners Co.
   Don't stir without Noilly Prat (vermouth)
Browning Arms Co.
   America's finest fishing rods
   Finest in sporting arms
E. L. Bruce Co.
   Leader in prefinished hardwoods
Chas. Bruning Co.
   The most beautiful copies of all
Brunswick Corp.
   The No. 1 name in billiards
   No. 1 name in bowling

Brunswick Rubber Co.
Famous for quality (automobile accessories)
Brunswick Sports Co.
The greatest name in golf (MacGregor)
Buckeye Cellulose Corp.
First in cellulose
Bucyrus-Eve Co.
Commitment to quality (machinery)
Budd Co.
In metals, plastics and paper Budd works to make tomorrow. . .today
The people movers
Wherever you look. . .you see Budd
Buick Motor Div., General Motors Corp.
The mini-brutes (Opel Kadett)
The tuned car
Wouldn't you really rather have a Buick?
Building Construction
The magazine of architectural technology
Bulman Corp.
Leadership built on the research and experience of over 48,000 store installations (store equipment)
Bulova Watch Co., Inc.
When something happy happens—it's Bulova time
Burleigh Brooks, Inc.
Classics of optical precision (Schneider lenses)
Burlington Industries
The fabric with reflex action (Expandra)
Business Jets Div., Pan American World Airways, Inc.
The business jet that's backed by an airline (Fan Jet Falcon)
Business Week
Sell at the decision level
Bussman Mfg. Div., McGraw-Edison Co.
Be profit wise. . .(sell only Buss) (fuses)
A trustworthy name in electrical protection (Buss fuses)
Buxton, Inc.
Best for your money (luggage, leather goods)
Byrd Industries, Inc.
"Developing products for recreation through electronic research" (C)

C

CIBA Products Co.
First in epoxies. . .in the age of ideas

C-P Fittings Div., Essex Wire Corp.
In products, performance, purpose. . . Essex measures up! (automobile parts)
Cadillac Motor Car Div., General Motors Corp.
So new! So right! So obviously Cadillac!
Standard of the world
Cahners Publishing Co., Inc.
For the climate of excellence (periodicals)
The live ones! (periodicals)
Calgon Corp.
Sure has a way with water, Calgon Corporation
California Computer Products, Inc.
Leader in computer graphics (Cal Comp)
Specialists in digital technology (Cal Comp)
Standard of the plotting industry (Cal Comp)
California Packing Corp.
The prune juice with the fruit juice appeal (Del Monte)
Caloric Corp.
Better because it's gas. . .best because it's Caloric (domestic appliances)
Calvert Distillers Co. Div., The House of of Seagram, Inc.
Soft whiskey (Calvert Extra)
Cameron Machine Co.
A team of specialists
Campbell Soup Co.
Reach for the Campbell's. It's right on your shelf.
They always eat better when you remember the soup
To get more that's good. . .trust Swanson (frozen dinners)
Canada Dry Corp.
Born 1820. . .still going strong! (Johnnie Walker Red Label scotch)
Just smooth, very smooth (Johnnie Walker Red Label scotch)
Canadian Pacific Railway
Holiday all the way with. . .
World's most complete transportation system
Canon, Inc.
Meets tomorrow's challenges today, Canon (cameras)
Cannon Mills, Inc.
Royal family of home fashions (linens)

122

Capitol Records, Inc.
  "Angels of the highest order" (Seraphim)
  Of the world, 'Capitol'
Caradco, Inc.
  Manufacturers of creative building prod-
      ucts
Carlisle Chemical Works, Inc.
  Special chemicals for industry
  Specialty chemicals for industry
Carnation Co.
  The complete family of dog and cat foods
      from the world leader in nutrition
      (Friskies)
  From contented cows
  From world leaders in nutrition (Friskies
      pet food)
Carnes Corp.
  Leaders go to Carnes for the newest in air
      distribution equipment
Carolina Mirror Corp.
  World's largest manufacturer of mirrors
The Carpenter Steel Co.
  In a word, confidence
Carr Fastener Co.
  It's a snap with Dot
Carrier Corp.
  More people put their confidence in
      Carrier air conditioning than in any
      other make
Carter's Ink Co.
  "If someone makes it—we can mark it"
Carven Parfums
  High fashion in fragrance from France
Oleg Cassini, Inc.
  Finer seamless stockings
Castlecliff, Inc.
  The talked-about jewelry
Caterpillar Tractor Co.
  Machines that build for a growing
      America
Cedar Rapids Block Co.
  The original masonry wall reinforcement
      with the truss design (Dur-O-Wal)
Cedar Rapids Engineering Co.
  Engineered for the ultimate in precision
      (Kwik-Way Brake Service Centers)
Celanese Corp.
  Add a fiber from Celanese and good
      things get better
  Contemporary fibers
  Your assurance that this fabric has been
      pretested for performance by
      Celanese (Arnel)

Celanese Plastics Co. Div., Celanese Corp.
  Plastics make a material difference,
      Celanese
Cellu-Craft Products Co.
  Packaging materials for American industry
Central Illinois Light Co.
  When you make your move—make sure
      it's a planned move (industrial de-
      velopment)
Central Soya Co., Inc.
  The foodpower (R) people
  Serving the businessman in the blue denim
      suit (Master Mix)
Century Electric Co.
  SERVICE, in the broadest sense, is the
      difference (public utility)
  Service is the difference (public utility)
Cessna Aircraft Co.
  More people buy Cessna twins than any
      other make
  More people fly Cessna airplanes than any
      other make
W. M. Chace Co.
  It bends with the heat (thermostatic bi-
      metal)
Champ-Items, Inc.
  The problem solver people (TM) (auto-
      mobile service equipment)
Champion Mfg. Co., Inc.
  Beauty mark of fine lighting
Champion Papers, Inc.
  Consider paper
  Consider the power of paper used with
      imagination
Champion Spark Plug Co.
  Best for all engines, Champion
  Dependable spark plugs
  The heart of a tune-up
  To feel new power, instantly, install new
      Champions now and every 10,000
      miles
Chanel, Inc.
  Every woman alive wants Chanel No. 5
      (perfume)
  The most treasured name in perfume
  The perfume of romance (Chanel No. 22)
Chap Stick Co.
  Specialists in skin care
Chase Manhattan Bank
  First in loans to business and industry
  You have a friend at Chase Manhattan
Chemical Bank New York Trust Co.
  The bank that works hardest for you

123

Chemical Div., General Mills, Inc.
  Plus values
Chemical Div., PPG Industries, Inc.
  Basic chemicals and cost-cutting ideas
Chemical Week
  Industry spokesman to CPI management
Chesapeake and Ohio Railway
  Knows the territory, Chessie
Chevrolet Motor Div., General Motors Corp.
  Biggest name in fleet cars and trucks
  The great highway performers (Corvair,
    Monza)
  Is more truck. . .day in, day out, Chevrolet
  Putting you first, keeps us first
  Quality trucks always cost less!
Chicago Bridge and Iron Co.
  Designs them. . .builds them!
Chicago, Burlington and Quincy Railroad
  Everywhere west
Chicago Merchandise Mart
  There's no place like this showplace!
Chicago Metallic Mfg. Co.
  Better pans for better baking
Chicago Rawhide Mfg. Co.
  Quality seals build the reputation of pro-
    fessional mechanics
  The seal mechanics see most, use most
C. F. Church Div., American Standard, Inc.
  The best seat in the house (bathroom
    fixtures)
Circle Design and Mfg. Corp.
  Creates new dimensions in automatic
    packaging machinery!
Cities Service Co.
  Energy chemicals
  A natural resource company
Clairex Corp.
  The "light" touch in automation and
    control (electronic instruments)
Clairol, Inc.
  The colorfast shampoo
  Does she. . .or doesn't she (R) (hair color)
  The girl with the beautiful face (TM)
  The girl with the beautiful mouth (TM)
    (lipstick)
  Hair color so natural only her hairdresser
    knows for sure (TM)
  Makes your husband feel younger, too. . .
    just to look at you! (Loving Care
    hair color)
  Only her hairdresser knows for sure (TM)
    (hair color)
  She has it made (TM) (lipstick

Clark Equipment Co.
  Is material handling, Clark
J. L. Clark Mfg. Co.
  Containers of distinction
Clark Metal Grave Vault Co.
  The finest tribute. . .the most trusted pro
    tection
The Cleveland Range Co.
  Headquarters for steam-cookers
The Climalene Co.
  Thoughtfully designed with a woman in
    in mind (Bowlene cleaner)
Cluett, Peabody Co., Inc.
  Be suspicious! (Sanforized)
  Wherever you go you look better in
    Arrow (shirts)
The Coca-Cola Co.
  How can just 1 calorie taste so good!
    (Tab)
  The pause that refreshes
  Things go better with Coke
Cocker Machine and Foundry Co.
  The leader around the world
Codo Mfg. Co.
  The line with the carbon gripper (paper)
Coleman Co., Inc.
  Greatest name in the great outdoors.
    Foremost name in indoor comfort
    (camping lanterns, stoves, etc.)
  Foremost name in indoor comfort (camp-
    ing lanterns, stoves, etc.)
Colgate-Palmolive Co.
  The body cosmetic (Cashmere Bouquet
    talcum)
  Cares for more complexions than any
    other soap in the world, Palmolive
  Cleans like a white tornado! (TM) (Ajax)
  The country garden soap for the "country
    complexion" (Cashmere Bouquet)
Collins Radio Co.
  A world of experience (electronic instru-
    ments)
Leopold Colombo, Inc.
  Importers and makers of fine furniture
Colonial Products Co.
  The world's largest manufacturer of fine
    kitchen cabinets
Colorite Plastics, Inc.
  World's leading manufacturer of plastic
    products for 35 diversified indus-
    tries
The Colson Corp.
  Finest quality on wheels—since 1885
    (materials handling)

Columbia Broadcasting System, Inc.
  The star's address, CBS
  Where what you want to know comes
    first
Combustion Engineering, Inc.
  Progress for industry worldwide
Commercial Carpet Corp.
  The remarkable new carpet that's flooring
    the country! (Densylon)
Commercial Credit Co.
  . . .Helping people and businesses help
    themselves
Commonwealth of Kentucky
  Where big things are happening
The Commonwealth Shoe and Leather Co.
  Every pair shows the care of the shoe-
    maker's hand (Bostonian)
Congoleum Industries, Inc.
  Fine floors (Congoleum-Nairn)
Conmark Plastics Div., Cohn-Hall-Marx Co.
  One of the oldest names in textiles. . .for
    the newest development in syn-
    thetics
Conn Organ Corp.
  For the home that enjoys home life
Connecticut General Life Insurance Co.
  Where people and ideas create security
    for millions
Connecticut Mutual Life Insurance Co.
  The Blue Chip company
  It pays to insure with the "Blue Chip"
    company
Connolly Shoe Co.
  Always a step ahead in style
Connor Lumber and Land Co.
  Manufacturers of quality hardwood prod-
    ucts since 1872
Conoflow Corp.
  Foremost in final control elements
Conso Products Co. Div., Consolidated
Foods Corp.
  Creators of 1,001 products for home
    decorating
  For the decorator touch (Best Pleat Nip-
    Tite)
Consolidated Aluminum Corp.
  Growth leader of the aluminum industry
Consolidated Edison Co.
  Power for progress
Consolidated Freightways, Inc.
  Leading name in truck transportation

Consolidated Paper Co.
  Specialist in enamel papers/printing
    paper
Construction Methods and Equipment
  Read and preferred by construction men
Container Corp. of America
  Means distinction, convenience, innovation,
    protection, inventory control, ser-
    vice, C.C.A.
Continental Air Lines, Inc.
  "A most remarkable airline"
  Proud bird with the golden tail
Continental Baking Co., Inc.
  Helps build strong bodies 12 ways! (R)
    (Wonder bread)
Continental Oil Co.
  Hottest brand going! (R) (Conoco gaso-
    line)
Continental Steel Corp.
  You can count on Continental to take
    care of you
Continental Trailways Bus System
  Easiest travel on earth
Converse Rubber Co.
  When you're out to beat the world
    (tennis shoes)
Cookson Co.
  Best way to close an opening (fire doors)
Frederick Cooper Lamps, Inc.
  Lamps of elegance
Cooper Tire and Rubber Co.
  America's fastest-growing tire company
The Coppertone Corp.
  Don't be a pale face (sun tan lotion)
P and F Corbin Div., Emhart Corp.
  It pays to make it Corbin—throughout!
    (door lockset)
Cordé de Parie, Inc.
  The aristocrat of fine corsetry
Corning Glass Works
  50 Years of brighter tasting meals (Corn-
    ing Ware)
Cosmetics and Toiletries Div., Warner-
    Lambert Pharmaceutical Co.
  Spirited new scent of the sixties (Richard
    Hudnut Sportsman)
Cotton Producers Institute
  Comfortable, carefree cotton
  The fiber you can trust
Coty Div., Chas. Pfizer and Co., Inc.
  For the woman who dares to be different
    (Emraude perfume)

Stays on till you take it off (Coty 24
Hour lipstick)
Tomorrow's skin care—today
Council for Financial Aid to Education
College is America's best friend
Sarah Coventry, Inc.
Fine fashion jewelry
Leading direct sellers of fine fashion
jewelry
Cozzoli Machine Co.
Call the man from Cozzoli
Crane Co.
The name is Crane
Crane and Co., Inc.
Fine papers
Crawford Fitting Co.
You can't afford to be without Swagelok
Crescent Metal Products, Inc.
Complete line of mobile food service
equipment
H. S. Crocker Co., Inc.
Pioneers in automated lithography
Crocker-Citizens National Bank
The bank that means business in California
Crocker Hamilton Papers, Inc.
Your printer's performance starts with
fine papers
The Cromar Co.
Originators of prefinished hardwood
flooring
Crop Life
A business paper for the farm chemical
industry
Crosman Arms Co., Inc.
"Power without powder"
A. T. Cross Co.
America's finest writing instruments
since 1846
The Cross Co.
First in automation (machinery)
Crown Central Petroleum Corp.
Quality you can trust
Crown Cork and Seal Co., Inc.
Your packaging deserves Crown quality
Culligan, Inc.
The world-wide water conditioning
people
Cullman Products Corp.
Keeps you in trim, John Lees (frames,
mouldings)
Cummins Engine Co., Inc.
Means diesel, Cummins

Helene Curtis Industries, Inc.
The light moisturizing bath oil for dry
skin (Tender Touch)
When a Studio Girl enters your home a
new kind of beauty brightens your
life (cosmetics)
Where beautiful young ideas begin (cosmetics)
H. T. Cushman Mfg. Corp.
Furniture that's fun to live with
Cushman Motors Div., Outboard Marine
Corp.
The big name in little wheels (materials
handling)
Cutler-Hammer, Inc.
Engineered for value (control systems)
What's new? Ask. . .Cutler (control systems)

D

Daisy/Heddon Div., Victor Comptometer
Corp.
World's largest producer of non-powder
guns and ammo
Da-Lite Screen Co., Inc.
Perfection in projection since 1909
Charles Daly
The custom crafted shotgun
Dana Perfumes, Inc.
The 'forbidden' fragrance (Tabu)
Daniel Construction Co., Inc.
Builders in and of the South
Jack Daniel Distillery
Charcoal mellowed drop by drop
Daniel Orifice Fitting Co.
Products made to measure
Danish Blue Cheese
A cut above the commonplace
Danskin, Inc.
Are not just for dancing, Danskins
(women's apparel)
Datamec Corp.
Leadership in low-cost/high reliability
digital magnetic tape handling
The Davey Tree Expert Co.
The oldest and largest tree saving service
in the world
Davidow Suits, Inc.
The label to ask for
Reese B. Davis and Co., Inc.
Gateway to the world of fabrics (Westgate)

Davis Cabinet Co.
  Craftsmen of fine solid wood furniture
Davis Mfg., Inc.
  The world's most distinctive digging
    machines are Davis
Daystrom Furniture Div., Daystrom, Inc.
  Built to take it. . .beautifully
Dazey Products Co.
  The can opener people
  Your kitchen companion since 1899
    (household products)
Dean Foods Co.
  Country charm quality (dairy products)
Lorrie Deb Corp.
  "Important occasion dresses" (R)
DeBeers Consolidated Mines, Ltd.
  A diamond is forever
  World's leading supplier of diamonds for
    industry
Deere and Co.
  Lets you take weekends easy the year
    around! (garden tractor)
Dellinger, Inc.
  Think original, think Dellinger (carpets)
  Where every carpet is custom made
Delta Air Lines, Inc.
  The airline with the big jets
Dennison Mfg. Co.
  No. 1 source of gummed papers
Desks, Inc.
  A complete source for fine office furni-
    ture
Detroit Aluminum and Brass Corp.
  America's leading bearing specialists since
    1925
Detroit Diesel Engine Div., General Motors
Corp.
  One proven design throughout the line
    builds greater value into every
    engine
Detroit Steel Corp.
  Customer satisfaction—our no. 1 job
Diamond Chain Co.
  Purposeful growth in power transmission
    (machinery)
Dierks Forests, Inc.
  Where quality is a tradition (building
    products)
Dillard Paper Co.
  If it's paper
Display World
  The international authority on visual
    merchandising

Dodge Div., Chrysler Corp.
  Builds tough trucks, Dodge
Dodge Mfg. Corp.
  The products with the pluses
Dole Refrigeration Co.
  Maximum refrigeration efficiency
Dole Valve Co.
  Control with Dole (R)
N. Dorman and Co.
  The cheese with the paper between the
    slices
Dorman Products, Inc.
  The quality line that's easy to find (auto-
    mobile parts)
Dorr-Oliver, Inc.
  World-wide engineering, manufacturing
    and construction
Doughboy Industries, Inc.
  Does it better. . .for a wide range of indus-
    tries, Doughboy
  Packages better. . .for a wide range of in-
    dustries, Doughboy
Douglas Aircraft Co., Inc. (now McDonnell-
  Douglas Corp.)
  In the air or outer space Douglas gets
    things done
Dow Corning Corp.
  Where experience guides exploration
    (industrial chemicals)
Dow Jones and Co.
  Instant news service (R)
Dow Theory Forecasts, Inc.
  A world of profits awaits the well in-
    formed
Downtowner Corp.
  "Sign of happy travel" (motels)
Drackett Co.
  It makes a dust magnet of your dust mop
    or cloth (Endust)
Dravo Corp.
  Combines experience and innovation to
    solve its customers' problems,
    Dravo. A company of uncommon
    enterprise
  A company of uncommon enterprise.
Drew Furniture Co.
  Quality shows through
Drexel Enterprises, Inc.
  The most trusted name in furniture
Drilling
  So long as the rig is on the location
Droutman Mfg. Co.
  Custom made luggage (Lark)

DuBois Chemical Div., W. R. Grace and Co.
  Use-engineered for cleaning, protecting
    and processing
Dunbar Furniture Corp.
  Tomorrow is a friend of Dunbar (R)
Dunlany Foods, Inc.
  The finest name in frozen foods
Dunlop Tire and Rubber Corp.
  Known 'round the world for quality in
    sporting goods and tires
Dun's Review and Modern Industry
  The business management magazine
Duo-Fastener Corp.
  In fast to hold fast
Duplicating Products Div., Minnesota Mining
and Mfg. Co.
  Look to 3M for imagination in image-
    making
E. I. duPont de Nemours and Co.
  America lives in Dacron
  The best anti-freeze since mink (Zerex)
  Better things for better living. . .through
    chemistry
  No-stick cooking with no-scour clean-up
    (Teflon)
  Rhymes with increase (Cantrece)
  Your investment success is our business
Dura Corp.
  Speed. Simplicity. Versatility. (business
    machines)
Duraflake Co.
  Makes only particleboard and only the
    best, Duraflake

E

ESB, Inc.
  Stampede of power (Exide storage bat-
    teries)
  World leader in packaged power (storage
    batteries)
Eagle Pencil Co.
  The nation's largest-selling drawing pen-
    cils and leads
Eastern Air Lines, Inc.
  Determined to serve you best
  See how much better an airline can be
Eastern Express, Inc.
  "The motor carrier with more go-how"
    (TM)
Eastern Specialties Co., Inc.
  The roll specialists (paper, paper prod-
    ucts)

Eastman Chemical Products, Inc.
  Interested personal service—always—when
    you buy from Eastman (office
    equipment)
Eastman Kodak Co.
  The easy ones (cameras)
  The more you learn about photography,
    the more you count on Kodak
  New advances in office copying keep
    coming from Kodak
  Puts you ahead in offset duplicating
    (Kodak Ektalith)
Charles A. Eaton Co.
  Fine bootmakers since 1876
Eaton Paper Corp.
  Fine letter papers
Eaton Yale and Towne, Inc.
  Applying advanced technology to bring
    you exciting new products
  The finest name in locks and hardware
    (Yale and Towne)
Economics Laboratories, Inc.
  By the world's largest maker of dish-
    washer detergents
E. Edelmann and Co.
  Precisioneered by Edelmann (automobile
    testing equipment)
S. M. Edison Chemical Co.
  P.S. And it's especially great as a hand
    lotion (Dermassage)
  Super-moisturizes dry skin zones in-
    stantly! (Dermassage)
Edison Electric Institute
  Live better electrically
Ekco Containers, Inc.
  Plus packaging
Elastic Stop Nut Corp. of America
  The red nylon ring of reliability
Electrolux Corp.
  Matchless quality. . .superior service. . .en-
    during excellence (vacuum cleaners)
Electronic Data Systems
  Our business is the intelligent use of
    computers
Electronics
  The industry's marketplace
Electro-Voice, Inc.
  Setting new standards in sound (phono-
    graph high fidelity systems)
Elgin Softener, Inc.
  Only Elgin gives you Elgineering (water
    conditioning)

Eljer Plumbingware Div., Wallace-Murray
Corp.
  Master crafted
  Since 1904 fine plumbing fixtures
Elliott Co. Div., Carrier Corp.
  Keep your eye on Elliott (tools)
Elliott Mfg. Co., Inc.
  Wherever fruit grows, our machinery goes
Elwell-Parker Electric Co.
  Pioneer in the development and construc-
    tion of electric industrial trucks
Emkay, Inc.
  A pioneer in the leasing field (automobile)
Empire Furniture Corp.
  Where pride of craftsmanship comes first
Empire Scientific Corp.
  World's most perfect high fidelity compo-
    nents
Employers Mutual Insurance Co. of Wiscon-
sin
  "Good people to do business with"
Enco Div., Humble Oil and Refining Co.
  America's leading energy company
  First in resources/first in capability
Englander Co., Inc.
  The finest name in sleep (mattress)
Enjay Chemical Co. Div., Humble Oil and
Refining Co.
  Anticipating tomorrow's needs today. . .
  Newest look in laminates (Enjay Nevamar)
Epiphone, Inc.
  The difference is quality (guitar)
Equitable Life Assurance Society of the
    United States
  Living insurance. . .
  Look ahead with living insurance
Erving Paper Mills
  For serving. . .it's Erving
Esterbrook Pen Co.
  Quality first. . .from America's first pen-
    maker
Euclid Crane and Hoist Co.
  In advance of progress
Eureka Williams Co.
  The very best in floor care products
    (vacuum cleaners)
Evans Products Co.
  The action line (building materials)
Evans Transportation Equipment Div., Evans
Products Co.
  The "Kid Glove Treatment" (R)
Evinrude Motors Div., Outboard Marine Co.
  First in outboards

Explosives Div., Atlas Chemical Industries,
Inc.
  It's what's inside that counts

F

FMC
  Putting ideas to work. . .in machinery,
    chemicals, defense, fibers and films
Eberhard Faber, Inc.
  Look to Eberhard Faber for the finest. . .
    first! (pencils)
  Puts its quality in writing
Max Factor and Co.
  The authority in the exciting world of
    beauty (cosmetics)
Factory
  The magazine for all manufacturing
Factory Mutual Insurance Co.
  Industry-owned to conserve property and
    profits
The Falk Corp.
  A good name in industry (gears, drives)
Falstaff Brewing Corp.
  America's premium quality beer
  Unmistakably. . .America's premium qual-
    ity beer
Family Circle
  A magazine only a homemaker could love
Farm Journal
  Getting results in rural America is *Farm
    Journal's* business
  The magazine farm families depend on
Farm Store Merchandising
  Sell the man who talks to the farmer just
    before the sale
Farrell-Cheek Steel Co.
  First name in cast steel!
Farrell Lines, Inc.
  African business is our business
Leslie Fay, Inc.
  For the typical American size (R)
    (women's apparel)
Fedders Corp.
  World's largest selling air conditioners
Federal-Mogul Corp.
  First for fast service (automobile parts)
Manuel Feldman Co., Inc.
  Wholesale floor coverings of distinction
Fellows Gear Shaper Co.
  The precision line
Felt Products Mfg. Co., Inc.
  Sets the standards for the gasketing in-
    dustry, FEL-PRO

Fenn Bros., Inc.
   Famous for candy flavors
Fenwal, Inc.
   Controls temperature. . .precisely
Fernstrom Storage and Van Co.
   The people who care about people who
      move
Fiber Glass Div., PPG Industries, Inc.
   Makes products better, safer, stronger,
      lighter
Ficks Reed Co.
   The most famous name in rattan furniture
Fieldcrest Mills, Inc.
   Coordinated fashions for bed and bath
Filko Ignition
   The crown jewels of ignition (R)
   The crown jewels of ignition and carbure-
      tion
Fireman's Fund American Insurance
   The finest protection available for your
      family, your property and your
      business
Firestone Tire and Rubber Co.
   The greatest tire name in racing
   High-performance tire power
   The name that's known is Firestone—all
      over the world
   Pioneer and pacemaker in essential fields
      of industry
   Your symbol of quality and service
First National Bank of Chicago
   Building with Chicago and the nation
      since 1863
First National City Bank
   "Better than money" (R) (travelers checks)
   Partners in progress around the world
First Penn Banking and Trust Co.
   First Pennsylvania means business
Firth Sterling, Inc.
   Pioneer in powder and molten metallurgy
Fishback and Moore, Inc.
   "Who we serve proves how we serve"
      (electrical contractors)
Fisher Governor Co.
   If it flows through pipe, chances are it's
      controlled by Fisher (valves, con-
      trols)
Fisher-Price Toys, Inc.
   "Our work is child's play"
   World's largest creator of preschool toys
Fleischmann Distilling Corp.
   The first taste will tell you why! (Fleisch-
      mann whiskey)

Two scotches of exceptional character
   ("Black and White")
Flex-O-Film, Inc.
   Pioneers in plastics
Flexo-Products Div., McClellan Industries
   Put a Burke where they lurk! (fishing
      lures)
Florida Citrus Commission
   The real thing from Florida (orange juice)
Florida Power Corp.
   The power to please! (public utility)
Florsheim Shoe Co.
   Makers of fine shoes for men and women
Flying Tiger Line, Inc.
   Air-freight specialists
   First in airfreight with airfreight first
Forbes
   Capitalist tool
Ford Authorized Leasing System
   America's largest leasing system (auto-
      mobile)
Ford Motor Co.
   America's favorite fun car (Mustang)
   America's most distinguished motorcar
      (Lincoln Continental)
   Best year yet to go Ford
   The bold engineering comes from. . .
   —built means better built, Ford
   Built to last longer (Econoline van
      trucks)
   Has a better idea, Ford
   It's the going thing
   Probing deeper to serve you better (re-
      search laboratories)
   Test drive total performance '65
   Total performance
   Unique in all the world (Thunderbird)
   The world's 100,000 mile durability
      champion (Mercury Comet)
Ford Tractor Div., Ford Motor Co.
   World's first mass produced tractor
Forest Products Div., Owens-Illinois, Inc.
   Important name in the box business
Formica Corp.
   The surprise of Formica products (inte-
      rior decoration)
Formulabs, Inc.
   World-wide suppliers of the finest ball
      pen inks
Fort Howard Paper Co.
   America's most used products away from
      home

Fortune
For the men in charge of change
The magazine of business leaders around the world
The magazine of business leadership
Foundation for Commercial Banks
Full service bank
"The place where you keep your checking account"
Founders Furniture, Inc.
Definitive modern furniture
The Foxboro Co.
Specialists in process and energy control
Frankel Mfg. Co.
The world leaders in duplicating supplies since 1906
Franklin Life Insurance Co.
The friendly
Fraser and Johnston Co.
Since 1928—industry leadership in heating and air conditioning
Miller Freeman Publications
Serving industry constructively since 1902
The R. T. French Co.
Good things to eat come from 1 Mustard St.
French National Railroads
"The railway is the right way"
Freon Products Div., E. I. duPont de Nemours and Co.
Best-selling aerosols are powered with Freon propellents
Friden Div., Singer Co.
Make no mistake about figurework: call Friden (office machines)
Make no mistake about paperwork automation. Call Friden (office machines)
Frigidaire Div., General Motors Corp.
Build-in satisfaction. . .build-in Frigidaire (domestic appliances)
Jet action washers
Sanitize your dishes sparkling clean! (dishmobiles)
Froedtert Malt Corp.
Basic for better beer
Fromm and Sichel, Inc.
Wines of California since 1882 (Christian Brothers)
Fruehauf Corp.
"Engineered transportation" (motor truck bodies)
The only truck bodies built like a trailer
Total transportation (motor truck bodies)
Fuji Electric Co., Ltd.
Put quality first and everything follows
H. B. Fuller Co.
Holds the world together (adhesives)
Leader in adhesive technology
Fulton Cotton Mills, Div. Allied Products Corp.
"America's leading producer of quality canvas products"
Furness, Withy and Co., Ltd.
The experienced cruise line
Fusion, Inc.
Automation is economical (electronic data processing)
Futorian Mfg. Corp.
Creaters of the world famous Stratolounger (furniture)

G

The Galion Iron Works and Mfg. Co.
Miles ahead (road machinery)
The Garcia Corp.
"Service guaranteed for life!" (fishing tackle)
Gardner-Denver Co.
See what air can do for you (compressors)
See what air-conditioning is doing now. . .
Garfield Mfg. Co.
The registered symbol of quality since 1908 (R) (plastics molding)
Garrett AiResearch, The Garrett Corp.
The future is building now at Garrett
Is experience, Garrett
Gates Rubber Co.
No. 1 in V-belts and hose
World's largest maker of V-belts
Geartronics Corp.
Creators of dependability (gears, gear drives)
Gehl Bros. Mfg. Co.
Where quality is a family tradition (agricultural machinery)
Geigy Chemical Corp.
Creators of chemicals for modern agriculture
Gem, Inc.
The trusted name in household products since 1917
General Chemical Div., Allied Chemical Corp.
Fine chemicals (Baker and Adamson)

General Electric Co.
  The problem solvers (G. E. Computers)
  Progress is our most important product
  Where the brightest ideas come to light
General Foods Corp.
  The canned dog food without the can,
    Gaines-burgers
  Makes its own gravy (Gravy Train dog
    food)
  The natural lift (Instant Postum)
General Mills, Inc.
  Breakfast of champions (Wheaties)
General Motors Corp.
  Mark of excellence
  Simply say Delco (storage batteries)
General Telephone and Electronics Corp.
  Sharing greatly in America's growth
General Tire and Rubber Co.
  The round tire that rolls 3,000 miles fur-
    ther (Atlas Plycron)
  The sign of tomorrow. . .today
  Top quality for 50 years
  Where research and development make
    exciting ideas
  You're miles ahead with General Tire
General Wine and Spirits Co., Inc.
  A rum to remember, Ronrico
Genesco, Inc.
  Everything to wear
  The fashion shoe (Mademoiselle)
  The shoe with a memory (Johnson and
    Murphy)
  Wear tested for your comfort (Jarman
    shoes)
Georgia-Pacific Corp.
  The growth company
Gerber Legendary Blades
  . . .Fashioned for those who enjoy extra-
    ordinary quality
Gerber Products Co.
  "Babies are our business. . .our only busi-
    ness" (R)
Anthony Gesture
  Not the biggest—but the best! (Seven
    Seas slacks)
Gilbarco, Inc.
  Leader in the field. Choice of the leaders.
    (pumps)
Gilbert Paper Co.
  A good business letter is always better. . .
    written on a Gilbert paper.
Gisholt Machine Co.
  Machines for total productivity

Glamorene Products Corp.
  Famous for products that really work
    (cleaning compounds)
Glas-Col Apparatus Co.
  Specialists in solving unusual heating
    problems
Glass Container's Manufacturers Institute
  Get it in glass
The Glen Falls Group
  Where you are always number one (insur-
    ance)
Glen Raven Mills
  Fabrics used in the most wanted women's
    and children's sportswear (Clan
    Crest)
Glenbrook Labs Div., Sterling Drug, Inc.
  No water needed (Phillips' Milk of Mag-
    nesia tablets)
  Pain is the test that Bayer meets best
  Stay fit for fun with Phillips (Milk of
    Magnesia)
  Works wonders, Bayer (aspirin)
Glenoit Mills, Inc.
  Definitely Glenoit for happy persons
    (apparel)
Globe Hoist Co.
  A world of engineering experience
Globe Steel Products Corp.
  Only when the finest is good enough
    (building materials)
The Globe-Wernicke Co.
  The touch of tomorrow in office living
    (office equipment)
Golfcraft, Inc.
  For the finest, Golfcraft
  The name to look for
B. F. Goodrich Co.
  The tough breed of tire
B. F. Goodrich Chemical Co.
  The material difference in building (Geon
    vinyls)
Goodrich-Gulf Chemicals, Inc.
  Leading innovators in polymer chemistry
  The one to watch for new developments
B. F. Goodrich Tire Co.
  The straight-talk tire people
Goodyear Tire and Rubber Co.
  More people ride on Goodyear tires than
    on any other brand
Gorham Div., Textron, Inc.
  America's leading silversmiths since 1831
H. W. Gossard Co.
  Nicest next to you (undergarments)

Wayne Gossard Corp.
　Legsize stockings (Belle-Sharmeer)
Gould-National Batteries, Inc.
　More power from more research
Goya Guitars, Inc.
　"The world's finest"
Gradiaz, Annis Div., General Cigar Co.
　World leader in luxury cigars (Gold Label)
Jean R. Graef, Inc.
　Fine watchmakers since 1791 (Girard
　　Perregaux)
Graflex, Inc.
　With Graflex the payoff is in the picture
Granco Steel Products Co.
　Imagination in steel for the needs of
　　today's architecture
Grand Rapids Hardware Co.
　No sash hardware installs faster than
　　Grand Rapids hardware
Grant Oil Tool Co.
　Used where performance counts
Gray Co., Inc.
　Get going great—with Graco (automobile
　　service equipment)
　The pumportation people (Graco)
Great American Insurance Cos.
　Protecting the nation—through hometown
　　agents
Great Lakes Carbon Corp.
　World leader in filtration
Great Northern Railway
　Route of the incomparable empire builder
Great-West Life Assurance Co.
　Six and a half billion dollars of protection
　　for our policyholders
Green Giant Co.
　Good things from the garden (canned,
　　frozen vegetables)
Greene Bros., Inc.
　"Jewelry for the home" (lamps)
Greenwood Mills, Inc.
　Fabrics with the character of quality
J. W. Greer Co.
　Betters continuous production through
　　continuous research! (institutional
　　food equipment)
Greyhound Corp.
　Leave the driving to us
　Leave the moving to us
Grey-Rock Div., Raybestos-Manhattan, Inc.
　Three steps to safety (brake lining)
　You can't buy a better brake lining to
　　save your life!

Grinnell Corp.
　Total capability in fire protection (alarm
　　system)
Grocery Store Products Co.
　Tastes so good and so good for you
　　(Cream of Rice)
The Guardian Life Insurance Co. of America
　Will bring peace of mind to you and your
　　family
　Will enrich and safeguard your retirement
　　years, Guardian
　Your Guardian for life
Guardian Light Co.
　Guardian lighting (C)
Gulf and Western Industries, Inc.
　The 21st century company
Gulf Oil Corp.
　Makes things run better, Gulf
　World's finest petrochemical products
Gulf Publishing Co.
　World's largest specialized publisher
Gunk Laboratories, Inc.
　First and foremost line of cleaning prod-
　　ucts (automobile service)

H

The H.O.N. Co.
　More and more the complete source for
　　your store (furniture, equipment)
HPM Div., Kolhring Co.
　The performance line (machinery)
Hackney Bros. Body Co.
　Builders of better refrigerator bodies
　　(refrigeration transportation)
Haeger Potteries, Inc.
　The great name in American ceramics
Walter Hagen Golf Equipment Co.
　"You don't have to be a millionaire to
　　play like one"
Hager Hinge Co.
　Everything hinges on Hager
W. J. Hagerty and Sons, Ltd., Inc.
　The world's finest name in silver care
Turner Hall Corp.
　Beauty designers (Dermetics cosmetics)
The Hallicrafters Co.
　Quality through craftsmanship (radio
　　receiving apparatus)
Hallmark Cards, Inc.
　If you care enough to send the very best
　When you care enough to send the very
　　best

Hamilton Cosco, Inc.
Useful products for family living
Hamilton Watch Co.
Get time from a timepiece, but if you
want a watch get a Hamilton
If you want more than time, get a Hamil-
ton
If you want to give more than time, give
Hamilton
Theo. Hamm Brewing Co.
From the land of sky blue waters
(Hamm's beer)
Hammer Blow Tool Co.
Never lets go (automobile parts)
Hammond Organ Co.
Music's most glorious voice
The one and only
Hampden Specialty Products Co.
Solid comfort seating
Handy and Harman
The company for precious metals
Hanes Corp.
Knows how to please him, Hanes
(hosiery)
Hanna Mfg. Co.
First to develop the latest in bat develop-
ments
T.S. Hanseatic German Atlantic Line
. . .Just for the sun of it
Harbor Master, Ltd., Div. Jonathan Logan
Because it might rain (TM) (raincoats)
Wm. S. Haynes Co.
The tone heard 'round the world (musical
instruments)
Henry L. Hanson Co.
You expect the best from Hanson. . .and
you get it (hardware)
Harbison-Fischer Mfg. Co.
Best pumps in the oil patch
Hardware Age
Sells hard wherever hardware sells
Hareg Industries, Inc.
First in engineered plastics (C)
Harlan Insurance Co.
An idea whose time has come!
Harnischfeger Corp.
The right hoist for every application. . .
Harper's Bazaar
The taste that sets the trend
The Hartford Insurance Group
Your Hartford agent does more than he
really has to

Hartford Steam Boiler Inspection and Insur-
ance Co.
"Inspection is our middle name"
Insurors of energy systems
Harris Hardwood Co.
Finest in flooring since 1898
Harrison Radiator Div., General Motors
Corp.
Temperature made to order
Harter Corp.
Specialists in seating—and seating only—
since 1927
Harvard Mfg. Co.
The one bed frame people ask for by
name
Haskell, Inc.
The accepted name for value (office
furniture)
C. F. Hathaway Co.
"Never wear a white short before sun-
down," says Hathaway (R)
Hawk Model Co.
Most trusted name in modeling
Hawker Siddeley Group, Ltd.
This one means business (DH 125 air-
plane)
Head Ski Co.
And who makes great skis? Head, of
course.
Heart Fund
Give so more will live
James Heddon and Sons
Make your own luck with Heddon (fish-
ing tackle)
Hein and Kopins, Inc.
The first name in custom bedding
Walter E. Heller and Co.
Over one billion dollars annually for
industry (financial)
Working funds for industry
Henredon Furniture Industries, Inc.
Fine furniture
There's a quality about a home with Hen-
redon
Hercules, Inc.
The home furnishings fiber (Herculon)
Heritage Furniture, Inc.
A living tradition in furniture
Hertz Corp.
Anywhere in the wide world (automobile
leasing)
The biggest should do more. It's only
right (automobile leasing)

Let Hertz put you in the driver's seat
Puts you in the driver's seat, Hertz
Hesston Corp., Inc.
　　World champions of worth! (agricultural
　　　　machinery)
G. F. Heublein and Bro.
　　It leaves you breathless (R) (Smirnoff
　　　　vodka)
　　Leaves you breathless, Smirnoff vodka
Heublein, Inc.
　　Aged for 8 (Bell's Blended scotch whis-
　　　　key)
　　11 kinds—better than most people make
　　　　(Heublein cocktails)
　　"It's smart to buy right" (Highland Scotch
　　　　Mist)
　　12 kinds—better than most people make
　　　　(Heublein cocktails)
Hewlett-Packard Co.
　　An extra measure of quality (electronic
　　　　instruments)
Heyman Mfg. Co.
　　Hey man!. . .say Heyman
Highway Cruisers, Inc.
　　America's finest campers
Hilton Hotels Corp.
　　The friendly world of Hilton
　　Go international. . .with all the comforts
　　　　of Hilton
The Hobart Mfg. Co.
　　Quality all the way (commercial kitchen
　　　　equipment)
Hoerner Boxes, Inc.
　　Corrugated packaging specialists
Hoffritz for Cutlery
　　A store a woman should look into
Holiday Inns of America, Inc.
　　"The fine old innkeeping tradition in a
　　　　modern setting" (R)
　　First choice in food, lodging and service
　　　　nationwide!
　　The nation's innkeeper (R)
Holland-American Line
　　The people who invented a nicer way to
　　　　cruise
　　Sail a happy ship
Holland House Brands, Inc.
　　The original and largest-selling in the
　　　　world (Holland House cocktail
　　　　mixes)
Holley Carburetor Co.
　　"Quality parts for auto makers and
　　　　owners"

Ernest Holmes Co.
　　Outselling all others. . .by far (wrecking
　　　　machinery)
Home State Farm Publications
　　Buy us like advertising. . .use us like sales-
　　　　men
Honeywell, Inc.
　　The other computer company
Hoosier Tarpaulin and Canvas Goods Co.
　　America's finest camping tents (Hoosier)
Hoover Bearing Div., Hoover Ball and Bear-
ing Co.
　　Leads in quiet bearings that last longer,
　　　　Hoover
Hopp Plastics Div., Hopp Press, Inc.
　　Pioneers in plastics
Geo. A. Hormel and Co.
　　Fine food products
　　Fresh ideas in meat. . .from Hormel
Horrocks-Ibbotson Co.
　　World's most complete fishing tackle line
Hortex Mfg. Co.
　　The brand with loyalty to quality (Billy
　　　　the Kid slacks)
Hotpoint Div., General Electric Co.
　　First with the features women want most
　　　　(domestic appliances)
Houdry Process and Chemical Co.
　　Means progress. . .through catalysis,
　　　　Houdry
E. F. Houghton and Co.
　　Industry's partner in production
House and Home
　　Management publication of the housing
　　　　industry
House Beautiful
　　Where quality makes sense
The House of Worsted-Tex
　　Clothes that enhance your public appear-
　　　　ance
Houston Lighting and Power Co.
　　Service first
Houze Glass Corp.
　　Pioneers in colored glass technology
Howard Industries, Inc.
　　Powered by Howard (R) (motors)
Howard Paper Mills Div., St. Regis Paper Co.
　　The nation's printing papers
Howe Folding Furniture, Inc.
　　If it folds. . .ask Howe
Hudson National, Inc.
　　World's leading direct-by-mail vitamin
　　　　and drug company

Hughes Aircraft Co.
  Creating a new world with electronics
Hughson Chemical Co., Div. Lord Corp.
  Watch Hughson...for progress through creative research
Humble Oil and Refining Co., Enco Div.
  Happy motoring! (R)
  Put a tiger in your tank (Enco)
Hunt Mfg. Co.
  Electrics give more people more time for more important jobs, Boston (office equipment)
Hunt Wesson Foods, Inc.
  The catsup with the big tomato taste
  For the best, Hunt
Hunter Div., Robbins and Meyers, Inc.
  It's matchless (heating)
Huntingdon Industries, Inc.
  New concepts in corrugated packaging machinery
Hycalog, Inc.
  Continuing research for lower cost drilling
Hydro-Line Mfg. Co.
  Works best under pressure (cylinders)
Hysol Div., Dexter Corp.
  Progressive products thru chemical research
Hyster Co.
  Buy today's best truck. Own tomorrow's best trade.
Hystron Fibers, Inc.
  The extraordinary fiber (Trevira)

I

I-X-L Co., Inc.
  The kitchen people with different ideas
Iberia Air Lines of Spain
  The way to get there
  Where only the plane gets more attention than you
Iceland Products, Inc.
  Specialists in frozen food packaging
Icelandic Airlines
  The pioneer of low fares to Europe
Idaho Potato Growers, Inc.
  Look-alikes aren't cook-alikes
Illinois Shade Div., Slick Industrial Co.
  Quality-made by Illinois Shade
Imperial Auto Insurance
  "Hot-Line" claims service
Imperial-Eastman Corp.
  To "test with the best" (automobile parts service)

Independent Insurance Agent
  "Serves you first" (R)
Indian Archery Corp.
  Named for the original American professionals
Indiana Dept. of Commerce
  Where free enterprise is still growing
Industrial Chemicals Marketing Div., Tennessee Corp.
  Basic producers from mine to finished product
Industrial Distributors, Ltd.
  The right hand of production
Industrial Engine Dept., Ford Div., Ford Motor Co.
  Your job is well powered when it's Ford powered
Industrial Fabrics Div., West Point-Pepperell, Inc.
  First in fabrics for industry
Industrial Marketing
  Selling and advertising to business and industry
Industrial Marketing Div., Jas. H. Matthews and Co.
  Marketing methods since 1850 (plastics)
Ingersoll-Rand Co.
  Bonded for life. . .because they're built that way (power tools)
  The ones professionals reach for, Ingersoll-Rand power tools
Inland Homes Corp.
  The homes teamwork builds
In-Sink-Erator Mfg. Co.
  Originator and perfecter of the garbage disposer
Institutions
  Magazine of mass feeding, mass housing
Insulite Div., Minnesota and Ontario Paper Co.
  Sells easy. . .sells fast. . .makes resales (building materials)
Insurance Co. of North America
  Be sure, insure with INA
Insured Savings and Loan Associations
  Where your dollar works harder. . .grows bigger!
International Business Machines Corp.
  The computer with a future, System/360
International Flavors and Fragrances, Inc.
  The pursuit of excellence

International Harvester Co.
   The courage to change. The strength to
      grow.
   First so serve the farmer (agricultural
      machinery)
   The people who bring you the machines
      that work (agricultural machinery)
International Management
   The magazine of world business
International Nickel Co.
   Nickel. . .its contribution is quality
International Paper Co.
   "Send me a man who reads!" (C)
   A world of paper products—from frozen
      food cartons to printing paper
International Telephone and Telegraph Corp.
   Worldwide electronics telecommunica-
      tions
Interstate Motor Freight System
   More than a truck line—a transportation
      system
Investor-Owned Electric Light and Power
Cos.
   People you can depend on to power
      America's progress
   You've got good things going for you
      with service by Investor-Owned
      Electric Light and Power Cos.
Investors Diversified Services, Inc.
   Call your Investors man—today! (insur-
      ance)
Iona Mfg. Co.
   Quality you can trust. Value you can
      recognize. (electric appliances,
      household products)
Iowa Development Commission
   Industry is on the move to Iowa
Irving Air Chute Co.
   Safety on the road. Security in space
      (parachutes, seat belts)
Irving Trust Co.
   The bank for bankers and businessmen
William Iselin and Co., Inc.
   Since 1808, a tradition in factoring and
      financing
Italian Line
   More fun per ton than any other line
   Unwind your way to Europe
Itek Corp.
   An American leader in advanced systems
      of photo-optics for information
      processing

Ithaca Gun Co., Inc.
   Expert's choice. . .since 1880

J

Edwin Jackson, Inc.
   Fireplace specialists for four generations
Wm. H. Jackson Co.
   Everything for the fireplace since 1827
Jackson China Co.
   Know the best by this mark
Janitrol Div., Midland-Ross Corp.
   Gives you more to work with, Janitrol
      (heating, air conditioning)
Jantzen, Inc.
   Just wear a smile and a Jantzen (bathing
      suits)
   Sportswear for sportsmen
Japan Air Lines
   The calm beauty of Japan at almost the
      speed of sound
The Jeffrey Mfg. Co.
   If it's conveyed, processed or mined, it's a
      job for Jeffrey
Jenkins Bros.
   Most trusted trademark in the valve
      world
Jenn-Air Corp.
   America's finest cooking centers
   So beautifully practical (ranges, ovens)
Jockey Menswear Div., Cooper's, Inc.
   It's not Jockey brand if it doesn't have
      the Jockey boy
The Carlyle Johnson Co.
   Let's talk Maxitorq (machinery)
E. F. Johnson Co.
   Manufacturers of world's most widely
      used personal communications
      transmitters
Howard Johnson Co.
   Host of the highways
   Landmark for hungry Americans
Mead Johnson and Co.
   Consult your physician on matters of
      weight control (Metrecal)
Johnson and Higgins
   Sets the standard in world-wide insurance
      brokerage service, J and H
Johnson and Johnson
   The best aid is first aid
Johnson Motors Div., Outboard Marine Co.
   Another carefree Johnson (boats, boating)
   First in dependability

Johnson Reels, Inc.
First on famous waters
Johnston's Pie Co. Div., Ward Foods, Inc.
Not just good. . .but wonderful (R)
Jones Dairy Farm
Real farm sausage from a real Wisconsin
farm
Joy Mfg. Co.
Machines at work around the world

K

K-D Manufacturing Co.
Make hard jobs easy (tools)
KOBI Polyethylene Bag Mfg. Co., Inc.
If it's a bag. . .we make it!
E. Kahn's Sons Co.
Big enough to serve you—small enough
to know you (meat packer)
Kaiser Aluminum and Chemical Corp.
For almost any product, aluminum makes
it better and Kaiser Aluminum
makes aluminum work best
Kaiser Jeep Corp.
The "unstoppables"
Karastan Rug Mills Div., Field Crest Mills,
Inc.
America's finest power-loomed rug
Harmon Kardon, Inc.
The leader in solid-state high-fidelity
components
We want you to hear more music (high
fidelity equipment)
Karges Furniture Co.
Fine cabinetmakers since 1886
Kay Musical Instrument Co.
More music for the money
Kayser-Roth Corp.
Expensive shirts ought to look it (Excello)
The greatest name in socks (Interwoven)
Keene Corp.
We've just begun to grow
Keener Rubber, Inc.
The name indicates the quality (office
supplies)
Keikhaefer Mercury Div., Brunswick Corp.
First a marine propulsion
Kellogg Co.
America's best-liked cereal assortment
The best to you each morning (breakfast
cereals)
Kelly Services, Inc.
Can do, Kelly (temporary employees)

100% guaranteed temporary office help
One source, one standard—nationwide
The Kelly-Springfield Tire Co.
New dimensions in driving on the safer
Kelly road
Kelsey-Hayes Co.
World's largest producer of automotive
wheels, hubs and drums
Kemper Insurance Co.
You can count on Kemper care under the
Kemper flag
George J. Kempler Co.
Fine furniture
Ken-L-Products Div., Quaker Oats Co.
Dog food of champions (Ken-L-Biskit)
Help make him all the dog he's meant to
be (Ken-L-Biskit)
Kentucky Dept. of Commerce
Come to Kentucky! It's a profitable move!
Kenwood Electronics, Inc.
The sound approach to quality (phono-
graph high fidelity equipment)
Keystone Steel and Wire Co.
Wire for industry
You fence for keeps with Red Brand
W. W. Kimball Co.
Instruments worthy of the masters since
1857 (pianos, organs)
Kimberly-Clark Corp.
A dynamic force with paper
Kimco Auto Products, Inc.
World's foremost rebuilders of auto-
motive parts
Kinnear Corp.
Saving ways in doorways since 1895) (roll-
ing doors)
Kitchen Kompact, Inc.
The best birch line
Klopman Mills, Inc.
A man you can lean on, that's Klopman
(fabrics)
Knape and Vogt Mfg. Co.
Ask for K-V. . .it's a known value! (hard-
ware)
Knapp and Tubbs, Inc.
America's oldest and largest showroom
distributor of fine decorative fur-
niture
Knapp-Monarch Co.
Everybody appreciates the finest (Radi-
Oven)

Knox Gelatine, Inc.
    Start with—stay with Knox
Kobrand Corp.
    Excellence doubly safeguarded (Beefeater
        gin)
    First name for the martini, Beefeater
        (Beefeater gin)
    The imported one (Beefeater gin)
Kohler and Campbell, Inc.
    Heirloom quality pianos since 1896
Kopp Glass, Inc.
    Unusual reliability and service. . .the usual
        at Kopp Glass
Koppers Co., Inc.
    Check with Koppers
Kraft Foods Div., Kraftco Corp.
    All fresh-fruit good! (jellies, preserves)
    The finest of natural cheeses—naturally
        from Kraft
    For good food and good food ideas
    The good kind to keep handy—because
        they stay soft (marshmallows)
    The kind you cook up fresh. . .and quick
        (home cooked dinners)
    Look for this famous name in the oval
        (Philadelphia Brand cream cheese)
    The quick kind you cook up fresh (home
        cooked dinners)
Kroehler Mfg. Co.
    A world of furniture made in a way that
        makes a world of difference
Kroydon Golf Corp.
    Hottest name in golf
Krueger Metal Products Co.
    Another fine creation by Krueger (furni-
        ture)
Krylon Dept., Borden Chemical Co.
    If you prize it. . .Krylon-ize it (spray paint)
Kwikset Div., Emhart Corp.
    America's largest selling residential lock-
        sets

L

LaBarge Mirrors, Inc.
    The look of quality
Laclede Steel Co.
    Producers of quality steel for industry
        and construction
Lake Central Airlines, Inc.
    We pamper passengers throughout mid-
        central U.S.A.

Lambert-Hudnut Mfg. Labs, Inc.
    The most elegant name in cosmetics
        (DuBarry)
James B. Lansing Sound, Inc.
    Discover what sound is all about (phono-
        graph high fidelity equipment)
    World renowned for perfection in sound
        (phonograph high fidelity equip-
        ment)
Lanvin-Charles of the Ritz, Inc.
    Promise her anything but give her Arpege
        (perfume)
Latchford Glass Co.
    A famous brand in glass
Latrobe Steel Co.
    The specialty steel company
Lead Industries Assn., Inc.
    Look ahead with lead
H. D. Lee Co., Inc.
    Guaranteed, the hardest working work-
        wear
    Official tailors to the West
Lee Machinery Corp.
    There should be a Lee in your future
Leeds and Northrup Co.
    Pioneers in precision (control equipment)
C. P. Leek and Sons, Inc.
    Since 1720, a family heritage of careful
        boat building
James Lees and Sons Co.
    Those heavenly carpets by Lees
Lehn and Fink Products Corp.
    Enchanting ladies choose Dorothy Gray
        (cosmetics)
    Really cares about people who care,
        Tussy (deodorant)
    Really cares about the sorcery of scent,
        Tussy
Lennox Industries, Inc.
    Don't be satisfied with less than Lennox
        (air conditioning, heating)
    It's nature's freshness—indoors (air condi-
        tioning, heating)
    Round the calendar comfort (air condi-
        tioning, heating)
William Lewis and Son
    Since 1874 stringed instrument house of
        the masters
Lewis-Howe Co.
    Taste as good as they make you feel
        (Tums)

Lewis-Shepard Co.
    World's largest exclusive manufacturer of
        electrical industrial trucks
Libby, McNeill and Libby
    The most experienced food processor in
        the world
Libby-Owens-Ford Co.
    The growing world of Libby-Owens-Ford
    The quality mark to look for (glass)
    This is the open world of LOF glass
    Where there's a window...there's a place
        for Thermopane
Liberty Mutual Insurance Co.
    Protection in depth
Life International
    Where telling the world means selling the
        world
Liggett and Myers, Inc.
    Tastes great. . .tastes mild, Chesterfield
        King (cigarettes)
    Tastes great. . .yet it smokes so mild
        (Chesterfield cigarettes)
Lightolier, Inc.
    America's first name in lighting
Lilli-Ann Corp.
    For the elegant petite (coats, suits)
Eli Lilly and Co.
    Prescription medicines around the world
LimiTorque Corp.
    When so much depends on a valve. . .so
        many depend on LimiTorque
The Lincoln National Life Insurance Co.
    Its name indicates its character
Lindsay Ripe Olive Co.
    The world's largest and finest
Lindy Pen Co., Inc.
    Originators of the world-famous ball pen
        utility (TM)
Link-Belt Co.
    Basic products and engineering for indus-
        try's basic work
Linton Mfg. Co.
    All ways look to Linton for leadership!
Lionel Toy Corp.
    Sane toys for healthy kids
Lipe-Rollway Corp.
    Delivers in the clutch, Lipe (motor truck
        parts)
    Pioneers in pneumatic bar feeding
Thos. J. Lipton, Inc.
    The brisk tea (Lipton)

Flavor so delicious only your figure
    knows they're low calorie
    (Wish Bone salad dressings)
Liquor Div., McKesson and Robbins, Inc.
    Fond of things Italiano? Try a sip of
        Galiano.
Long-Bell Lumber Co.
    A quality name in forest products
Longines-Wittnauer Watch Co.
    Leading maker of watches of the highest
        character for almost a century
    Since 1867 maker of watches of the high-
        est character
    The world's most honored watch (R)
Look
    The magazine of the American market
Lord Mfg. Co.
    The leader in vibration/shock/noise con-
        trol
Lorillard Corp.
    America's best tasting little cigar (Be-
        tween the Acts)
    The first new no-filter cigarette in years
        (York)
    For the best combination of filter and
        good taste Kent satisfies best (ciga-
        rettes)
    The one cigarette for everyone who
        smokes! (Kent)
    Satisfies best (Kent cigarettes)
    Smokes fresher—and tastes better than
        any other menthol cigarette,
        Newport
    Tastes better than any other menthol
        cigarette! (Newport)
The Louden Machinery Co.
    Since 1867. . .the first name in materials
        handling
Louisville and Nashville Railroad
    Rely on us
Louver Mfg. Co., Inc.
    World's largest manufacturer of ventilat-
        ing louvers
The Loveable Co.
    For the girl who knows value by heart
        (brassieres)
Lovejoy Flexible Coupling Co.
    First name in power transmission equip-
        ment
Lowerator Div., American Machine and
    Foundry Co.
    There is no equal (mass feeding equip-
        ment)

Ludwig Drum Co.
    Most famous name on drums
The Lufkin Rule Co.
    Measure up with the best
    White is right
    You're right with Lufkin
Lukens Steel Co.
    The specialist in plate steels
The Lunkheimer Co.
    The one great name in valves
Luzier, Inc.
    Personalized cosmetic services
Lyon-Healy Co.
    Harp-maker to the world since 1889
Lyon Van Lines, Inc.
    Let Lyon guard your goods (R)

M

M./B. Designs, Inc.
    Designs that dreams are made of (interior
        decoration)
MPA Magazines
    Your world of ideas and products
MPB, Inc.
    Missile quality ball bearings
E. F. MacDonald Co.
    Since 1922, leader in motivating people
Mack Trucks, Inc.
    "The Money Truck"
Mademoiselle
    For the smart young woman
Magee Carpet Co.
    Fashion loomed to last
Magnavox Co.
    The magnificent (television)
Magnolia Products, Inc.
    The seat of the in house (bathroom fix-
        tures)
Maidenform, Inc.
    Keep your eye on Maidenform (brassieres)
    This is the dream you can be—with
        Maidenform (brassieres)
Maine Dept. of Economic Development
    Industrious Maine, New England's big
        stake in the future
Majorica
    The world's most precious simulated
        pearls
P. R. Mallory and Co., Inc.
    It's good business to do business with
        Mallory (electronic instruments)

Malta Manufacturing Co.
    The line and design for creative window
        planning
Manatool Div., Perry-Fay Co.
    Progressive products for fluid control
        (metering valves)
Simon Manges and Son, Inc.
    We care about color (carpets)
Manhattan Industries, Inc.
    Internationally known mark of quality
        (shirts)
Mannesmann-Export Corp.
    Builds for the future, Mannesmann
Manpower, Inc.
    The very best in temporary help
Manufacturers Hanover Trust Co.
    . . .it's good to have a great bank behind
        you
Johns Manville Corp.
    One of the many quality home improve-
        ment products made by J.M.
Manzel Div., Houdaille Industries
    No one is in a better position to solve
        your lubrication problems
Marathon Div., American Can Co.
    For quality paper products you can't beat
        Marathon
    Softness is Northern (toilet paper)
    Two layers of softness. . .and one is purest
        white (Aurora toilet paper)
    Your paper problems are in good hands
        with Marathon
Marion Power Shovel Co.
    Progress begins with digging
Maritz, Inc.
    Motivating men to sell your product is
        our business
Markem Machine Co.
    Helping your product speak for itself
        (marking equipment)
Marlin Firearms Co.
    Symbol of accuracy since 1870
Marriott Motor Hotels, Inc.
    This is living. . .this is Marriott
Marsh and McLennan, Inc.
    Industry's leading insurance brokers
    On the job wherever a client's interest is
        at stake (insurance broker)
Martin Equipment Sales, American Laundry
    Machinery Industries
    . . .Certifies the most in dry cleaning (One
        Hour Martinizing)

The most in dry cleaning (One Hour
    Martinizing)
Martin Reel Co.
    Precision fishing reels since 1883
Marvella, Inc.
    Could it be the real thing? (pearls)
C. H. Masland and Sons
    The magic of Masland carpets
The Masland Duraleather Co.
    Where beauty is material
Masonite Corp.
    Shows the way! (building materials)
Massey-Ferguson, Inc.
    The big job matched line (agricultural
    machinery)
Master Lock Co.
    World's strongest padlocks
Olin Mathieson Chemical Corp.
    Don't say it can't be done. . .talk to Olin
    (cartons)
Matson Navigation Co.
    The vacation way to Hawaii
Matthews Co.
    Iron horse quality (agricultural equipment)
Maxwell House Div., General Foods Corp.
    Good to the last drop (coffee)
Maybelline Co.
    The most prized eye cosmetics in the
    world
Maytag Co.
    The dependable automatics (washing
    machines)
    The dependability people (washing
    machines)
McCall's
    First magazine for women
McCord Corp.
    Is go. . .go with it, McCord (automobile
    parts)
McCormick and Co., Inc.
    The house of flavor (spices, flavorings)
McCulloch Corp.
    Leadership through creative engineering
    (machinery)
McGraw-Edison Co.
    The complete line of electric cooking
    equipment (Toastmaster)
McGraw-Hill, Inc.
    Serving man's need for knowledge. . .in
    many ways (publishing)

McGraw-Hill Publications Div., McGraw-Hill,
    Inc.
    A good society is good business
    "Market-directed"
McGregor-Doniger, Inc.
    For the man on the move (clothing)
McIlhenny Co.
    There are imitations—be sure the brand is
    Tabasco (food sauce)
McNally Pittsburgh Mfg. Corp.
    Manufacturers of equipment to make coal
    a better fuel
McQuay, Inc.
    Make the seasons come to you (Crystal
    Tips ice machine)
Mecca Machinery Co.
    Masterworkers in machinery for printing
    and converting
A. L. Mechling Barge Lines, Inc.
    Personalized service that makes the big
    difference
Meehanite Metal Corp.
    Better castings through advanced foundry
    technology
Meilink Steel Safe Co.
    For a big difference in your profits. . .the
    line with the big difference
Meldan Co., Inc.
    . . .Keeping tradition alive (furniture)
Menley and James Labs
    It's your guarantee of quality (Con-tac
    cold remedy)
    Proprietary pharmaceuticals made to
    ethical standards (Con-tac cold
    remedy)
Merck, Sharp and Dohme Div., Merck and
Co., Inc.
    Where today's theory is tomorrow's
    remedy (drugs, pharmaceuticals)
Mercury Record Corp.
    Leadership through design (high fidelity
    sound equipment)
G. and C. Merriam Co.
    The leading name in dictionaries since
    1847 (Merriam-Webster)
    Since 1847 the trusted and authoritative
    name in dictionaries (Merriam-
    Webster)
    There's a world of difference in Webster
    dictionaries
    To be sure you're right. . .insist on
    Merriam-Webster

The trusted and authoritative name in
dictionaries (Merriam-Webster)
Mersman Tables
The costume jewelry of the home
Messinger Bearings, Inc.
Smoothing industry's pathway for nearly
half a century
Mesta Machine Co.
Better by design
Metal Hydrides, Inc.
Pioneers in hydride chemistry
Metalworking News
Thundering power in the eye of the
market
Metropolis Brewery of N. J., Inc.
America's original sparkling malt liquor
(Champale)
Metropolitan Furniture Adjusters
The company with the "know-how"
Metropolitan Life Insurance Co.
The fourth necessity
More choose Metropolitan. Millions more
than any other company.
There's no obligation. . .except to those
you love
Microprint, Inc.
Creator of advanced writing instruments
Middleby-Marshall Oven Co.
World's largest commercial oven manufac-
turer since 1888
Ralph A. Miele, Inc.
If it's chairs. . .it's Miele!
If Miele doesn't have it. . .no one has!
(chairs)
K. Mikimoto, Inc.
The originator of cultured pearls
Miles Laboratories, Inc.
Look for the label with the Big Red "1"
(One-A-Day vitamins)
Relief is just a swallow away (Alka-
Seltzer)
Speedy is its middle name (Alka-Seltzer)
Consult your doctor about your weight
problem (Sego)
Miller Brewing Co.
Brewed only in Milwaukee (Miller High
Life beer)
The champagne of bottle beer (Miller
High Life beer)
Polk Miller Products Co.
Better products for man's best friend
(Sergeant's)

Millprint, Inc.
Where the newest in packaging is happen-
ing today
Milwaukee Road
America's resourceful railroad
The railroad of "Creative Crews"
Minnesota Dept. of Business Development
Brainpower builds profits, Minnesota
Minnesota Mining and Mfg. Co.
For imagination in communication, look
to 3M business product centers
The tape that won't hurt coming off
(Micropore)
Minneapolis-Moline, Inc.
Engineered for longer life (tractors)
Minolta Corp.
Fine photography for 40 years
The name quality made famous (Zoom 8
camera)
Minox Corp.
The camera you never leave at home
A famous camera from camera-famous
West Germany
Minton, Inc.
The world's most beautiful china
Mira-Pak, Inc.
Pacemakers in flexible package-makers
Mirawal Co.
Quality products for quality living (build-
ing materials)
Mirro Aluminum Co.
The finest aluminum
The house of experience
Mishawaka Rubber Co., Inc.
Look for the red ball (shoes)
Mississippi
The hospitality state
Missouri Commerce and Industrial Develop-
ment Commission
Missouri in the center of your thinking
M. Mittman Co.
America's largest manufacturer of custom
day beds and sofa beds
Mobay Chemical Co.
First in urethane chemistry
Mobil Oil Corp.
For good advice. . .and good products. . .
depend on your Mobil dealer
There's a good future with Mobil
Modern Machine
Put your money where the market is
Modern Packaging
The complete authority of packaging

Molded Fiber Glass Companies, Inc.
Look to MFG for the shape of things to come

Monarch Life Insurance Co.
Lifelong security through programmed protection

Monet Jewelers
Master jeweler

Monogram Models, Inc.
The name for quality hobby kits

Monroe Auto Equipment Co.
World leader on highway and speedway

Monsanto Co.
Another example of how Monsanto moves on many fronts to serve you (chemicals)

Montag, Inc., Div. Westab, Inc.
Writing papers that create an impression

Montana Highway Commission
The big sky country

Monumental Life Insurance Co.
Protection in a new light

Moog Industries, Inc.
Moog means more under car business

Moore Business Forms, Inc.
"The right business form for every form of business"

Moore-McCormack Lines, Inc.
The "Champagne Touch"

Moorhead Machine and Boiler Co.
Assurance of quality, dependability since 1917

James Moroney, Inc.
Pennies more in cost...worlds apart in quality (J and B scotch)

Philip Morris, Inc.
Come to where the flavor is...come to Marlboro country (cigarettes)

Morris Machine Works
Master designers of modern centrifugal pumps

Morton Chemical Co. Div., Morton International, Inc.
Look for more from Morton

Morton Salt Co.
When it rains, it pours

Mosinee Paper Mills Co.
Value-engineered papers from the mills of Mosinee

Mosler Safe Co.
Quality is standard equipment

O. F. Mossberg and Sons, Inc.
For accuracy, Mossberg

Motor Service
The service shop authority

Motor Truck Div., International Harvester Co.
"Build a truck to do a job—change it only to do better"
No. 1 heavy-duty sales leader

Motorola, Inc.
New leader in the lively art of electronics

Mottahedeh and Sons
For connoisseurs by connoisseurs (interior design accessories)

Mr. John
"Designs for the world's best dressed"

G. H. Mumm and Co.
The word for champagne, Mumm's

Munsingwear, Inc.
It's worth the difference (underwear)

Murine Co., Inc.
Soothes. Cleanses. Refreshes. (eyedrops)

Murray Corp.
The line that moves (automobile parts)

Muskegon Piston Ring Co.
Since 1921. . .the engine builders source!

O. Mustad and Son
The fish hook people
For the discriminating sportsman (fishing tackle)

Mutual of New York
Men care for people, MONY

Mutual of Omaha Insurance Co.
The greatest name in health insurance

Mutual Products Co., Inc.
First name in paper punches

F. E. Myers and Bro., Inc.
The finest name in pumps, Myers

N

NAHB Journal of Homebuilding
The magazine for professional builders

NVF Co.
Products you can depend on. . .day in. . . day out (materials handling)

National Airlines, Inc.
Coast to coast to coast

National Association of Home Builders
The name of the game is living. Explore a new home today. (C)

National Automotive Parts Association
Assurance of quality

National Bakery Div., Package Machinery Co.
Favorite of the nation's bakers

National Blank Book Co.
　　The retailer's line
National Car Rental System, Inc.
　　The customer is always No. 1
National Cash Register Co.
　　First in carbonless papers
　　Multiple copies without carbons (N.C.R.
　　　　Paper)
National Castings Co.
　　Moving ahead fast. . .to keep you competi-
　　　　tive
National Commercial Disposers
　　Pioneers of disposers dedicated to quality
National Cotton Council
　　Cotton, you can feel how good it looks
　　100% cotton. The fiber you can trust.
National Distillers and Chemical Corp.
　　Famous. Smooth. Mellow. (Old Crow
　　　　Bourbon)
　　The greatest name in bourbon (Old Crow)
　　Head of the bourbon family (Old Grand-
　　　　Dad)
　　Smart, smooth, sensibly priced (Gilbey's
　　　　vodka)
National Gypsum Co.
　　First with better ways to build (Gold
　　　　Bond)
　　Material methods make the difference in
　　　　modern building, Gold Bond
　　One of many fine products that come
　　　　from 40 years of thinking new
　　　　(Gold Bond building materials)
National LP-Gas Market Development
Council
　　Of America's great sources of energy, only
　　　　National serves you in so many ways
National Lumber Mfrs. Assn.
　　It's built to sell when it's built of wood
National Mills Div., U.S. Industries
　　They fit (Round-The-Clock stockings)
National Oil Fuel Institute, Inc.
　　You can depend on it
National Petroleum News
　　For oil marketing
National Plastics Products Co.
　　Tops everything for lasting beauty
　　　　(Nevamar)
National Presto Industries, Inc.
　　The pressure cooker people
National Rain Bird Sales and Engineering
Corp.
　　The modern way to grow (sprinklers)

National Screw and Mfg. Co.
　　. . .Creating better ways to hold things
　　　　together
National Steel Corp.
　　Keep a cupboard full of cans
Nation's Business
　　What's happening. In business—to busi-
　　　　ness
Nationwide Life Insurance Co.
　　The name again. . .Nationwide Life
Nekoosa-Edwards Paper Co.
　　For every business need
　　For many converting purposes
　　For special industrial requirements
Nestle-LeMur Co.
　　Approved by professional hair colorists
　　　　(Nestle Color Tint)
New Departure-Hyatt Bearings Div., GMC
　　For modern industry
New Holland Div., Sperry Rand Corp.
　　First in grassland farming (agricultural
　　　　machinery)
　　Practical in design. Dependable in action.
　　　　(agricultural machinery)
　　Specialists in farmstead mechanization
　　　　(agricultural machinery)
New Idea Farm Equipment Co.
　　Where bold new ideas pay off for profit-
　　　　minded farmers
New Jersey Public Service Electric and Gas
Co.
　　Taxpaying servant of a great state
New Mexico Dept. of Development
　　Land of enchantment
New York Central System
　　Road to the future
New York Life Insurance Co.
　　Agent in your community is a good man
　　　　to know, The New York Life
　　Leader in business insurance
New York Shipbuilding Corp.
　　Where outstanding performance is stan-
　　　　dard
New York State Dept. of Commerce
　　Discover the new in New York State
New York Stock Exchange Members
　　Own your share of American business
　　Promoting high standards in the public
　　　　interest
Newell Mfg. Co.
　　First family in drapery hardware since
　　　　1903

Newman-Green, Inc.
Creative aerosol valve engineering
Newsweek
The newsweekly that separates fact from opinion
Niagra Therapy Mfg. Corp.
A trusted name. . .proved by medical research and the experience of millions (Niagra Cyclo Massage)
Nichols Aluminum Co.
The brightest name in aluminum
Nickel Plate Railroad
"The railroad that runs by the customer's clock"
Nimrod Ward Mfg. Co.
America's largest builder of camping trailers
America's largest selling camping trailer
Nippon Kokan
The most progressive name in steel
Nissan Motor Co., USA
The difference is value (Datsun automobiles)
Nocona Athletic Goods Co.
The name for quality athletic goods
Nopco Chemical Co.
A skilled hand in chemistry. . .at work for you
Norcold, Inc.
Refrigeration is our business. . .our only business
Norfolk and Western Railway
The nation's going-est railroad
Norge Div., Borg-Warner Corp.
Years from now you'll be glad it's Norge (domestic appliances)
C. A. Norgren Co.
First name in pneumatic protection
North American Aviation, Inc. (Now North American Rockwell Corp.)
Is at work in the fields of the future, North American Aviation
North American Philips Corp.
A bright new world of electric housewares (Norelco)
The close electric shave (Norelco)
The comfort shave (Norelco)
You can't get any closer (Norelco shaver)
North American Rockwell Corp.
And the future are made for you, North American Rockwell
The jet that justifies itself

North American Van Lines, Inc.
The gentlemen of the moving industry
North Carolina Department of Conservation
Where good government is a habit
Northern Electric Co.
World's oldest and largest manufacturer of electric blankets
Northern Natural Gas Co.
Ask the man from Northern Plains
Northern Pacific Railway
Route of the Vista-Dome North Coast limited
This is the way to run a railroad
Northland Ski Mfg. Co.
World's largest ski maker
World's most experienced ski maker
Northwest Airlines, Inc.
The fan-jet airline
The Northwestern Mutual Life Insurance Co.
"Because there is a difference"
Numatics, Inc.
The air valve people
Nunn-Bush Shoe Co.
Ankle-fashioned shoes
First in quality!
Nutone, Inc.
Known in millions of homes (high fidelity sound equipment)
The name known in millions of American homes (ranges, ovens)

O

Oakite Products, Inc.
If it's a question of cleaning/conditioning. . .ask Oakite
Office Products Div., International Business Machines Corp.
Machines should work. People should think.
Ohio Edison Power
This is the center of industrial America
Oil Center Tool Div., FMC Corp.
Where progress is a daily practice
Old Colony Envelope Co.
Where quality is traditional
Oldsmobile Div., General Motors Corp.
Escape from the ordinary
Look to Olds for the new
The rocket action car

Olga Co.
    Behind every Olga there really is an Olga
        (foundation garments)
Olsten Temporary Services
    Good people
Olympia Div., Inter-Continental Trading
Corp.
    Precision typewriters
Olympic Radio and Television Div., Lear
Siegler, Inc.
    From the space age laboratories of
        Olympic
Omaha Public Power District
    The land of elbow room and elbow grease
Omega Watch Co.
    For a lifetime of proud possession
Oneida, Ltd.
    Mark of excellence (silversmiths)
Ontario, Canada, Dept. of Tourism and
Information
    Friendly, familiar, foreign and near
Oregon Highway Dept.
    State of excitement
Otis Elevator Co.
    Instant elevatoring (T)
Owens-Corning Fiberglas Corp.
    Verified insulation performance
Owens-Illinois Glass Co.
    Takes many shapes to serve you, O-I
        Plastechnics (packaging)
Oxford Filing Supply Co.
    First name in filing
Oxford Paper Co.
    Lasting impressions begin with Oxford
        papers
Oxides Div., Cabot Corp.
    Where flame technology creates new
        products
Ozark Air Lines, Inc.
    The airline that measures the midwest in
        minutes

P

P-A-G Div., W. R. Grace and Co.
    The successful ones (agricultural hybrids)
P and D Mfg. Co.
    Ignition starts with P and D
P and O Lines
    Life at sea is like nothing on earth
    Run away to sea with P and O

PPG Industries, Inc.
    The fiberglass for finer fabrics
    Makes the glass that makes the difference,
        PPG
    When you start with metal. . .finish with
        Duracron!
Pacific Northern Airlines
    The Alaska flag line
Packaging Industries, Ltd., Inc.
    The world's largest manufacturer of blis-
        ter packaging machinery
Page Steel and Wire Div., American Chain
and Cable Co.
    The source for answers to wire problems
Paillard, Inc.
    Means Swissmanship, Hermes. . .a step
        beyond craftsmanship (typewriters)
Painter Carpet Mills, Inc., Div. Collins and
Aikman
    Artistry in carpets
Pakistan International Airlines
    Great people to fly with
    Great people to ship with
Palizzio, Inc.
    Any Palizzio is better than no Palizzio
        (shoes)
Pan American-Grace Airways, Inc.
    World's friendliest airline (Panagra)
Pan-American Life Insurance Co.
    "Dollar wise group insurance"
Pan American World Airways, Inc.
    First in Latin America
    First on the Atlantic
    First on the Pacific
    First 'round the world
    Makes the going great, Pan Am
    World's largest air cargo carrier
    World's most experienced airline
    You're better off with Pan Am
Panasonic
    Today's leader in tomorrow's look (radio
        receiving apparatus)
Parents Magazine
    On rearing children from crib to college
Parfums Corday, Inc.
    Anything can happen when you wear
        Fame
Parke, Davis and Co.
    Better medicines for a better world
Parker Pen Co.
    Maker of the world's most wanted
       pens

Parsons and Whittemore, Inc.
  World leaders in the development of pulp
    and paper mills for the use of local
    fibers
Pasco Packing Co.
  World's largest citrus plant
Pasmantier, Inc.
  Finest in china since 1735 (Richard
    Ginori)
Patcraft Mills, Inc.
  Carpets of distinction
  First in fashion (carpets)
Ben Pearson, Inc.
  The nation's big name in archery
Peck and Peck
  For that certain kind of woman (retail
    store)
Peerless Roll Leaf Co.
  Marks practically everything best, Peerless
Pellon Corp.
  Keeps the shape (synthetic fabric)
Pen Metal Co., Inc.
  A name to remember (building materials)
Pendleton Woolen Mills
  Always virgin wool
Penn Fishing Tackle Mfg. Co.
  The reels of champions
J. C. Penney and Co.
  Always first quality (retail store)
Pennsylvania Power and Light Co.
  The heart of the market
Pepsico, Inc.
  Come alive! (Pepsi-Cola)
  For those who think young (Pepsi-Cola)
  Taste that beats the others cold (Pepsi-
    Cola)
  You're in the Pepsi generation (Pepsi-
    Cola)
Permatex Co., Inc.
  Made for the professional! (R) (gasket
    sealant)
Personal Products Co.
  Because. . .(Modess)
Personal Products Div., Lever Bros. Co.
  Creams your skin while you wash, Dove
Petelco Div., Pyle-National Co.
  The "one stop" creative lighting source
Peterson, Howell and Heather
  Car plan management and leasing special-
    ists
N. Pfeffer
  For gifts of love (R) (jeweler)

Chas. Pfizer and Co., Inc.
  Science for the world's well-being (R)
    (drugs, pharmaceuticals)
Philadelphia Carpet Co.
  Quality since 1846
  Since 1846, the quality of elegance under-
    foot
Philco Corp.
  Famous for quality the world over (R)
    (television)
Phillips Petroleum Co.
  Go first class. . .go Phillips 66 (gasoline)
Phillips Research Laboratories
  Trust in Phillips is world-wide
Phillips-Van Heusen Corp.
  Younger by design (Van Heusen shirts)
Phillipson Rod Co.
  World's finest
Phin, Inc.
  Innovators in the design and manufacture
    of quality labeling equipment
Phoenix of Hartford Insurance Cos.
  Restituimus—"We restore". .since 1854
Photoswitch Div., Electronics Corp. of
America
  New ideas in automation control
Pickering and Co., Inc.
  For those who can hear the difference
    (phonograph high fidelity equip-
    ment)
  The world's largest and most experienced
    manufacturer of magnetic pickups
    (phonograph high fidelity equip-
    ment)
Pigments and Chemicals Div., National Lead
Co.
  More years to the gallon (Dutch Boy
    Paints)
Pilot Radio Corp.
  Unquestionably the world's finest stereo-
    phonic console
Piper Aircraft Corp.
  More people have bought Pipers than any
    other plane in the world
Pit and Quarry
  Editorial excellence in action
J. C. Pitman and Sons, Inc.
  World's first and largest manufacturer of
    deep fat frying equipment
Planters Peanuts Div., Standard Brands, Inc.
  The name for quality
  —Not only light but deliciously light
    (peanut oil)

Plastic Industries, Inc.
America's foremost leg specialists

Plastic Sheeting Div., Eastman Chemical Products, Inc.
Look to Eastman to look your best!

Plastics Div., Seiberling Rubber Co.
World's broadest line of thermoplastic sheet materials, Serlon

Platts Bros., Ltd.
The first name in textile machinery

Plymouth Div., Chrysler Corp.
Let yourself go. . .Plymouth
Look what Plymouth's up to now

Plymouth Golf Ball Co.
World's largest exclusive manufacturer of golf balls

Polaroid Corp.
Don't say sunglasses—say C'Bon! (TM)

Ponderosa Mouldings, Inc.
Chief of the mouldings

Pontiac Motor Div., General Motors Corp.
Wide-track

Pope and Talbot, Inc.
Products of wood technology for construction and industry

Potash Co. of America
The salt of the earth

Potlatch Forests, Inc.
Depend on Potlatch for everything in quality lumber
Symbol of quality (R)

Polyvinyl Chemicals, Inc.
Specialists in high polymers

Port Authority of the City of St. Paul
Make the capital choice

H. K. Porter Co., Inc.
Who changed it? (machinery)

The Wm. Powell Co.
Men who know valves know Powell
World leader of the valve industry since 1846

Powell Muffler Co.
Built stronger to last longer

Power
To energize your sales crew, put Power behind it

Powermatic, Inc.
Today's ideas. . .engineered for tomorrow (machinery)

John Robert Powers Products Co.
For women whose eyes are older than they are (makeup)

Precision Fastener Div., Standard Pressed Steel Co.
Costs less than trouble, UNBRAKO

Precision Valve Corp.
Leaders by design

Prince Gardner Co.
Distinctive designs in leather accessories

Procter and Gamble Co.
"Always an adventure in good eating" (Duncan Hines packaged foods)
Best cooks know foods fried in Crisco don't taste greasy!
Eliminates drops that spot, Cascade (detergent)
Give your dishwasher the best (Cascade detergent)
It floats (Ivory soap)
Moist as homemade (Duncan Hines cake mixes)
99 44/100% pure (R) (Ivory soap)
No wonder more women rely on Ivory Liquid to help keep their hands soft, young-looking!

Prodex Div., Koehring Co.
In design and performance, always a year ahead (machinery)

Product Engineering
The no. 1 buy in the design field

Progressive Farmer
The magazine that moves the men who move the merchandise

Prophet Co.
The good food service

Pro-Phy-Lac-Tic Brush Co.
The green cleans in-between. . .the white polishes bright

The Prudential Insurance Co. of America
The future belongs to those who prepare for it
Has the strength of Gibraltar, The Prudential
The strength of Gibraltar

Public Service of Indiana, Inc.
Industry's friendliest climate

The Pure Oil Co.
Be sure with Pure
Fire up with Firebird (gasoline)
Worth changing brands to get

Purex Corp., Ltd.
Pool products from a name you know, Purex (Guardex)
You'll find the woman's touch in every Purex product

149

Q

QANTAS
Australia's round-the-world jet airline
Quaker Oats Co.
Maker of America's number 1 cat food
(Puss 'n Boots)
Shot from guns (breakfast cereal)
Quaker State Oil Refining Corp.
Engine life preserver

R

RCA Corp.
His master's voice (phonograph records)
The most trusted name in electronics
The most trusted name in sound
The most trusted name in television
The world's most broadly based electronics company
R and K Originals, Inc.
America lives in R and K Originals
(women's apparel)
Rado Watch Co.
The peak of Swiss watchmaking perfection
Railway Age
One of America's great weeklies
Ramada Inns, Inc.
"Luxury for less" (R)
Rand McNally and Co.
Serving America's schools, homes, commerce and industry (publishing)
Rapala Div., Nordic Enterprises, Inc.
World's most wanted lure (fishing tackle)
Rath Packing Co.
Smoked with hickory (ham)
Rawlings Corp.
"The finest in the field" (R) (sporting goods)
Raybestos-Manhattan, Inc.
The complete brake lining service
Reliability in rubber, asbestos, sintered metal, specialized plastics
Rayette-Faberge, Inc.
For twenty-five years, first in professional hair care
Raymond Handling Equipment, Ltd.
Originator and world's largest builder of narrow aisle trucks
Ray-O-Vac Div., ESB, Inc.
Big name in batteries
Raytheon Co.
The most complete line of electronic ovens

Reader's Digest
People have faith in *Reader's Digest*
World's best seller
Reading Railroad
On-time-delivery is our #1 concern
Recordak Corp.
First and foremost in microfilming since 1928
Red Cedar Shingle and Handsplit Shake Bureau
The crowning touch of quality
Red Devil, Inc.
World's largest manufacturer of painters' and glaziers' tools—since 1872
Reda Pump Co.
The best pump. The best buy.
Reliance Electric and Engineering Co.
Builders of the tools of automation
Remington Office Systems Div., Sperry Rand Corp.
The automated answer to the paper explosion
Renfield Importers, Ltd.
The centaur. . .your symbol of quality
(Remy-Martin cognac)
Don't be vague. . .ask for Haig and Haig
(Scotch whiskey)
"An inch of Pinch, please" (Scotch whiskey)
Pop goes the Piper (Piper-Heidsieck champagne)
Pride of Cognac since 1724 (Remy-Martin)
Republic Molding Corp.
Always first with the best (Polly-Flex Housewares)
"Woman's best friend" (Polly-Flex Housewares)
Republic Steel Corp.
In stainless, too, you can take the pulse of progress at Republic
You can take the pulse of progress at Republic Steel
Resina Automatic Machinery Co., Inc.
Tops them all, 'Cap' Resina
Revco, Inc.
Leader in the manufacture of custom built-in refrigeration
Revere Copper and Brass, Inc.
First and finest in copper and brass. Fully integrated in aluminum.
Revere-Wollensack Div., Minnesota Mining and Mfg. Co.

150

What you want is a Wollensack (tape
recorder)
Revlon, Inc.
Cherished as one of the world's seven
great fragrances (Intimate)
From the world's most renowned cos-
metic research laboratories
Rex Chainbelt, Inc.
Industry's helping hand
Reynolds Aluminum Supply Co.
Service that never sleeps
Reynolds Metals Co.
Oven-tempered for flexible strength!
(Reynolds Wrap)
Spanning the spectrum of packaging
(Reynolds Aluminum)
Where new ideas bring you better packag-
ing
Where new ideas take shape in aluminum
R. J. Reynolds Tobacco Co.
The best tobacco makes the best smoke
(Camel cigarettes)
For a taste that's Springtime fresh (Salem
cigarettes)
A real cigarette (Camel)
I'd walk a mile for a Camel (cigarettes)
Softness freshens your taste, Salem (ciga-
rettes)
Tastes good. . .like a ciagarette should,
Winston
Rheem Mfg. Co.
World's largest manufacturer of steel
shipping containers
Rice Council
Easy, delicious. . .versatile, nutritious. . .
Caryl Richards, Inc.
Everyone knows if it's Caryl Richards, it
is just wonderful for your hair
Riegel Paper Corp.
The merchant-minded mill with variety
and reliability
Risqué Shoes Div., Brown Shoe Co.
Look Risqué from the ankles down
Rival Mfg. Co.
It's fun to own a gift by Rival (household
products)
Rival Pet Foods Div., Associated Products,
Inc.
When it comes to cooking for dogs—Rival
has no rival
Robbins and Myers, Inc.
The name that means quality (Trade Wind
ventilating hood)

Roberts Co.
Keeps you years ahead, Roberts (machin-
ery)
Value keeps you years ahead, Roberts
(machinery)
Roberts Div., Rheem Mfg. Co.
The pro line (tape recorders)
Weldon Roberts Rubber Co.
Robertshaw Controls Co.
The name that means temperature control
P.S. The last word in "automatic con-
trol" is still Robertshaw
A. H. Robins Co.
Making today's medicines with integrity. . .
seeking tomorrow's with persistence
Rock Bit Div., Timken Roller Bearing Co.
Your best bet for the best bits
Rock Island Lines
The railroad of planned progress. . . geared
to the nation's future
Roehlen Engraving Works
Where engraving is still an art
Rohr Corp
Dedicated to the pursuit of excellence
Rollway Bearing Co.
Think straight. . .think Rollway
Romweber Industries
Furniture of timeless beauty
Preferred for America's most distin-
guished homes (furniture)
Ronson Corp.
Automatically better (cigarette lighters)
The people who keep improving flame
(cigarette lighters)
Will Ross, Inc.
Products you can trust from people you
know (surgical dressings)
Roto-Rooter Corp.
And away go troubles down the drain
(machinery)
Roux Labs, Inc.
Professional cosmetics for lovelier hair
color
Royal Crown Cola Co.
America's most modern cola (Diet-Rite)
America's no. 1 low-calorie cola (Diet-
Rite)
Drink RC—for quick, fresh energy
Royal Typewriter Co., Inc., Div. Litton
Industries
Every year, more Royal typewriters are
bought in America than any other
brand

John Royle and Sons
   Pioneered the continuous extrusion proc-
      ess in 1880 (plastics machinery)
Rubbermaid, Inc.
   Means better made, Rubbermaid (house-
      hold products)
Rubee Furniture Mfg. Corp.
   It's the very finest because it's Rubee
Ruberoid Co.
   Fine flooring
Ruby Lighting Corp.
   America's largest manufacturer of lighting
      reproductions
Russwin-Emhart Corp.
   "Unlocking new concepts in architectural
      hardware since 1839" (keys)
Rust-Oleum Corp.
   Distinctive as your own fingerprint (anti-
      corrosive)
   Proved throughout industry for over 40
      years
   Quality runs deep, Rust-Oleum
   Stops rust! (R)

S

SCM Corp.
   The quick brown fox (Smith-Corona
      typewriters)
   Think ahead—think SCM (typewriters)
SKF Industries, Inc.
   When you've got to be right (bearings)
Sabena Belgian World Airlines
   Europe's most helpful airline
St. Joseph Lead Co.
   Die casting is the process. . .zinc, the metal
   Producers of zinc for American industry
The St. Paul Insurance Cos.
   Serving you around the world. . .around
      the clock
St. Regis Paper Co.
   The original polyethylene coated freezer
      wrap (Poly Wrap)
Samsonite Corp.
   Business case that knows its way around
      the world
   The luggage that knows its way around
      the world
   The luggage that sets the pace for luxury
   The more living you do, the more you
      need Samsonite (furniture)
San Antonio Municipal Information Bureau
   Vacationing in San Antonio is a family
      affair

San Francisco Convention and Visitors
Bureau
   You can't get the whole picture in just a
      day or two
Sandoz, Inc.
   Original research serving the physician
      (drugs, pharmaceuticals)
   Thinks ahead with textiles, Sandoz (dyes)
Sanford Truss, Inc.
   World's largest roof truss system
Santa Fe System Lines
   The railroad that's always on the move
      toward a better way
The Sardis Luggage Co.
   For people who travel. . .and expect to
      again and again (Starflite Luggage)
Savage Arms Div., Emhart Corp.
   World's most complete line of sporting
      arms and accessories
The Savings and Loan Foundation, Inc.
   Where you save does make a difference (R)
Scandia Packaging Machinery Co.
   Means craftsmanship, Scandia
H. J. Scheirich Co.
   The most beautiful kitchens of them all
Schenley Import Co.
   The aristocrat of liqueurs (Cherristock)
   The gold medal Kentucky bourbon since
      1872 (I. W. Harper)
   It's always a pleasure (I. W. Harper bourbon)
Schick Electric, Inc.
   The mark of quality (shavers)
Schieffelin and Co.
   From the largest cellars in the world
      (Moët champagne)
   Have the genius to chill it (Chartreuse)
   No scotch improves the flavour of water
      like Teacher's
   ...so glamorous you have to be told
      they're hypo-allergenic (Almay
      cosmetics)
   When you mix with CinZano you mix
      with the best (vermouth)
   The world's best climate makes the
      world's best rum (Puerto Rican
      Rums)
   "Yes, I know. . .Marie Brizard" (liqueurs)
Schilling Div., McCormick and Co., Inc.
   It's no secret. . .Schilling flavor makes all
      the difference in the world!
Jos. Schlitz Brewing Co.
   The beer that made Milwaukee famous
   Real gusto in a great light beer

152

Schlumberger, Ltd.
 Leads in automatic log computation
  (electronic data processing)
Oscar Schmidt International, Inc.
 Making music possible for everyone
  (Guitaro)
S. A. Schonbrunn and Co., Inc.
 The coffee served at the Waldorf-Astoria
  (Savarin)
 The coffee-er coffee (Savarin)
A. Schrader's Son
 First name in tire valves for original equip-
  ment and replacement
Schwab Safe Co., Inc.
 Our products are your protection
Peter J. Schweitzer Div., Kimberly-Clark
Corp.
 Whenever good impressions count, rely
  on carbonizing papers by Schweitzer
 World's largest manufacturer of fine car-
  bonizing papers
Scientific Anglers, Inc.
 Think system
 World's largest exclusive fly line manufac-
  turer
O. M. Scott and Co.
 Leaders in lawn research
 The grass people
 The lawn people
Scott Paper Co.
 Makes it better for you, Scott
Scott Testers, Inc.
 The sure test. . .Scott
Scovill Mfg. Co.
 Does a lot for you
Scripto, Inc.
 Engineering with imagination (fountain
  pens)
Seagram Distillers Co.
 Known by the company it keeps (Sea-
  gram's Canadian VO)
 Say Seagram's and be sure (7 Crown)
Sealy Mattress Co.
 Sleeping on a Sealy is like sleeping on a
  cloud
 Your morning is as good as your mattress
G. D. Searle and Co.
 Research in the service of medicine
Sears Roebuck and Co.
 You can't do better than Sears
Karl Seeger
 Known the world over as the world's best
  (luggage)

Seiko Time Corp.
 Modern masters of time
Selas Corp. of America
 Worldwide in heat and fluid processing
Selectron International Co.
 Feature rich (Aiwa Tape Recorders)
Selig Mfg. Co., Inc.
 In a word. . .it's Selig (furniture)
Martin Senour Co.
 Master of color finishes since 1858
  (paint)
 Master of color since 1858
Sentry Insurance Co.
 Looks out for you
 The small business that got big serving
  small business
Servisoft Div., Water Treatment Corp.
 The only nicer water comes from clouds
Serta Associates, Inc.
 Words to go to sleep by (Perfect Sleeper
  Mattress)
 You sleep on it. . .not in it!
The Seven-Up Co.
 The uncola
 Your thirst away, 7-Up
John Sexton Co.
 Quality foods
The Shaler Co.
 "The Profit Line" (automobile lubrica-
  tion equipment)
Sharon Steel Corp.
 America's foremost producer of custom
  steels
Munson G. Shaw Co. Div., National Distillers
and Chemical Corp.
 Imported from Spain, of course. True
  sherry is (Duff Gordon)
Shaw-Walker Co.
 Built like a skyscraper (R) (files, desks)
W. A. Sheaffer Pen Co.
 Your assurance of the best (TM)
The Sheffer Corp.
 The muscles of automation, Sheffer
  cylinders
Shell Oil Co.
 Sign of a better future for you
Shephard Niles Crane and Hoist Corp.
 Giving industry a lift since 1878
Sherwin-Williams Co.
 Coatings, colors, and chemicals for indus-
  try
 Cover the earth (paint)

Ship 'n Shore, Inc.
Lead the Ship 'n Shore life (blouses)
Showerfold Dor Corp.
Leader in bathroom fashion
Shulton, Inc.
What Scandinavian men have (Teak toilet goods)
Shure Brothers, Inc.
High fidelity phono cartridges. . .world standard wherever sound quality is paramount
Silent Gliss, Inc.
Manufacturers of quality drapery hardware since 1903
The silent drapery track (R)
Simmons Co.
World's largest mattress maker
Simmons Fastener Corp.
Quality fastening products for industry
Simplicity Pattern Co., Inc.
The pattern people
Simpson Timer Co.
Sell Simpson and be sure (building materials)
Sinclair Oil Corp.
A great name in oil
Singer Co.
Diversified—worldwide
What's new for tomorrow is at Singer today!
Skelly Oil Co.
For quality you can depend on. . .depend on Skelgas
Ski Industries America
Authentically ski (R)
Skil Corp.
Go with the pick of the pros (power tools)
Makes it easy, Skil (power tools)
Slazengers, Inc.
Covers a world of sports
Slick Airways
Freight by air
Slingerland Drum Co.
The foremost in drums
The Smead Mfg. Co.
Your one-source solution to every film problem
Elwin G. Smith and Co., Inc.
"Builds walls for keeps, Smitty"
H. P. Smith Paper Co.
Pioneers in polycoatings

Kenneth Smith
Hand made to fit you (golf clubs)
Lew Smith Beads
"Custom of course"
Smith-Douglass Div., Borden Chemical Co.
You can depend on the integrity and quality of Smith-Douglass (fertilizer)
Snap-On Tools Corp.
Choice of better mechanics
For all industry
Service-backed shop equipment
Sommers Brass Co., Inc.
Exacting standards only
Sonoco Products Co.
Quality papers for industry since 1889
Sony Corp. of America
The tapeway to stereo (R)
South Bend Tackle Co., Div. Gladding Corp.
Creating world-famed fishing tackle since 1893
South Dakota Dept. of Highways
Friendly land of infinite variety
The Southern Co.
Power for progress (public utility)
Southern Pacific Co.
Serving the golden empire
Southern Railway Co.
"Accent is on you, Southern's"
Innovations that squeeze the waste out of distribution
Look ahead, look South
Southern Railroad Co.
Serves the south, Southern
Southwest Sun Country Assn.
Now's the time to get away to it all!
Spanish National Tourist Office
The place to go
Spencer Chemical Div., Gulf Oil Corp.
Don't just fertilize. . .Spencerize
In plastics, it's Spencer. . .for action
Sperry Rand Corp.
The first computer (Univac)
Is saving a lot of people a lot of time, Univac (electronic data processing)
We're synergistic
Spicer Div., Dana Corp.
Specify Spicer (automobile parts)
Spode, Inc.
Don't wait to inherit Spode (tableware)
Sponsor
The magazine of broadcast advertising

Sports Illustrated
   Each week the facts add up to success
   Sports isn't just fun and games
Square D Co.
   Where quality is a tradition. . .and an obli-
      gation (electrical control equipment)
   Wherever electricity is distributed and
      controlled
Squibb Beech-Nut, Inc.
   A leader in dental research
   A name you can trust (drugs, pharmaceuti-
      cals)
   The priceless ingredient, Squibb quality
      (drugs, pharmaceuticals)
Stakmore Co., Inc.
   The chair that stands by itself
   The folding furniture with the permanent
      look (chairs)
Standard Brands, Inc.
   America's largest selling corn oil marga-
      rines (Fleishmann's)
   Beginning a second century of leadership
      (Chase and Sanborn coffee)
   Brighten up with Instant Tender Leaf Tea
   The brighter tasting tea! (Instant Tender
      Leaf)
   Everything's better with Blue Bonnet on
      it (margarine)
   The tender-textured gelatin (Royal)
Standard Motor Parts, Inc.
   World's foremost heavy-duty ignition line
      (Blue Streak)
Standard Oil Co. of California
   The chevron—the sign of excellence
Standard Oil Div., American Oil Co.
   As you travel ask us (R)
   Call the man who puts the farmer first—
      your Standard Oil Farm Man
   See what happens when you start using
      American ingenuity
   We take better care of your car
   You expect more from Standard and you
      get it
Standard Products Co.
   Where your sealing is unlimited (building
      products)
Standard Tool and Mfg. Co.
   Better products at a lower cost through
      better methods
Stange Co.
   Silent partners in famous foods (R) (color-
      ing, flavoring)

Stanlabs, Inc.
   Sharing the responsibilities of modern
      medicine
Stanley Home Products, Inc.
   Where the nicest people meet the nicest
      things
Stanley Tool Div., Stanley Works
   The tool box of the world
The Stanley Works
   Helps you do things right (hardware)
Starcraft Co.
   America's most popular boats
   Wide world of recreation, The Starcraft
      (boats, camping trailers)
Stardust Hotel and Golf Club
   Where your "resort dollar" buys more
Star-Kist Foods, Inc.
   The tender tuna with the delicate taste
Startex Mills, Inc.
   King of the kitchen (towels)
State of Louisiana Dept. of Commerce and
Industry
   Means profits for business
· State of Washington
   The surprising state
Stayton Canning Co.
   To serve something fancy start with
      something fancy (Flav-R-Pac)
Steel and Tube Div., Timken Roller Bearing
Co.
   The men who make it make the difference
Steelcase, Inc.
   Design/plus (office furniture)
StenoCord Dictation Systems
   World's easiest-to-use dictating machines
The Steril-Sil Co.
   Leadership through quality (utensil han-
      dling equipment)
Sterling Faucet Co.
   Where quality is produced in quantity
John B. Stetson Co.
   Born in America. Worn round the world.
      (hats)
J. P. Stevens and Co., Inc.
   Fine fabrics made in America since 1813
   Just everyday things for the home made
      beautiful by Stevens (linens)
The Stiffel Co.
   The royalty of lamps
Stitzel-Walker Distillery, Inc.
   Your key to hospitality (Old Fitzgerald)

Stokely-Van Camp, Inc.
America's first, finest, and favorite pork and beans
Color is nature's way of saying flavor. Stokely is your way of getting it. (vegetables)

Story and Clark Piano Co.
The world's most beautiful organs

Stow and Davis Furniture Co.
Distinguished furniture for distinguished offices

Strapping Div., Signode Corp.
Let's find better ways. . .we'll follow through

Stromberg-Carlson Corp.
"There is nothing finer than a Stromberg-Carlson" (radios)

Struthers Thermo-Flood Corp.
Leaders in thermal engineering design

Successful Farming
Our readers manage the country

Sugar Information, Inc.
Sugar's got what it takes

Sun Electric Corp.
A new high in auto test equipment. . .a new high for you!

Sun Oil Co.
Quality. . .the best economy of all

Sunbeam Corp.
Built with integrity, backed by service (household products)

Sunkist Growers, Inc.
If you could see inside oranges, you'd buy Sunkist every time
The way the best lemons sign their name

Sunray DX Oil Co.
America's most customer-minded oil company!

Sunset
"Dedicated to serving the families of the West and Hawaii. . .no one else"
The magazine of Western living

Sunsweet Growers, Inc.
Make Sunsweet your daily good health habit

Superior Industries, Inc.
Where big ideas turn into aluminum extrusions

Superscope, Inc.
You never heard it so good (Sony Superscope)

Supima Association of America
World's finest cottons

Supplex Co.
The original reinforced plastic hose

Swank, Inc.
Jewelry of tradition for the contemporary man

Swedish American Line
The white viking fleet

Swift and Co.
In industry world-wide (chemicals)
The two most trusted names in meat (Swift's Premium)
You can trust the man who sells this brand (Swift's Premium)

Swingline, Inc.
World's largest manufacturer of staplers for home and office

Swiss Air Transport Co., Ltd.
Swisscare. Worldwide.
Swiss-care world-wide on the privately owned airline of Switzerland

Sylvania Electric Products, Inc.
A flair for elegance (television)
Total communications from a single source through Sylvania

Symons Mfg. Co.
More savings with Symons (building materials)

Synthane Corp.
You furnish the print. . .we'll furnish the part (laminated plastics)

Synthetics Finishing Corp.
You can rely on America's oldest and most experienced custom finisher (interior decoration)

Syracuse China Corp.
The beginning of taste

Syroco Div., Dart Industries, Inc.
America's foremost manufacturer of decorative accessories since 1890

T

T.I.M.E. Freight, Inc.
Super service

T.V. Guide
America's biggest selling weekly magazine

Tampax, Inc.
Invented by a doctor—now used by millions of women
You feel so cool, so clean, so fresh. . .

Tappan Co.
You cook better automatically with a Tappan

You live better automatically with a
Tappan
Tarter, Webster and Johnson Div., American
Forest Products Corp.
For quality western lumber products,
look to T, W, and J
W. A. Taylor and Co.
The brandy of Napoleon (Courvoisier
cognac)
Jamaica's legendary liqueur (Tia Maria)
Taylor Instruments
Instruments mean accuracy first, Taylor
World-wide competence in control
Technicolor Corp.
Greatest name in color (movie film)
Tectrol Div., Whirlpool Corp.
Total environmental control (cold stor-
age)
Teletype Corp.
Machines that make data move
Where the data movement started and
startling moves are made
Tenneco, Inc.
Building business is our business
From natural gas and oil. . .heat, power
petrochemicals that mean ever
wider service to man
Tennessee Dept. of Conservation
America's most interesting state
Texaco, Inc.
Localized for you (Texaco Sky Chief
gasoline)
Lubrication is a major factor in cost
control
Trust your car to the man who wears the
star
Texas Eastern Transmission Corp.
Pipeliners of energy
Texas Gas Transmission Corp.
Serving the big river region
Texas Instruments, Inc.
Rely on T I
Texas National Bank of Commerce of
Houston
All the bank you'll ever need in Texas
Textile Div., The Kendall Co.
Wash easier, dry faster, absorb more, wear
longer (Curity Diapers)
Textile Machinery Div., Crompton and
Knowles
First in fabric forming equipment

Textiles Div., Monsanto Co.
The luxury of velvet with the worry left
out (Islon)
Nothing but nylon makes you feel so
female
Nothing but Spandex makes you look so
female
Textured Yarn Co., Inc.
Continuous filament textured nylon
(Tycora)
Thermador Electrical Mfg. Co. Div., Norris
Industries, Inc.
Seven leagues ahead (R) (ovens)
Therm-O-Disc, Inc.
Leadership through accomplishment
Thermo King Corp.
World leader in transport refrigeration
Thermogas, Inc.
America's fastest growing fuel
Thermoid Div., H. K. Porter Co., Inc.
Install confidence. . .install Thermoid
(automobile equipment)
Thilmany Pulp and Paper Co.
Functional papers
Thomasville Furniture Industries, Inc.
By design. . .furniture distinguished for
value since 1904
Thompson Medical Co., Inc.
The best friend your willpower ever had
(Slim-Mint gum)
The modern aid to appetite control (Slim-
Mint gum)
Timbertone Decorative Co., Inc.
First with the finest in wallcoverings. . .
always!
Time
The most important magazine to the
world's most important people
Talk to the right people in the right places
The weekly news magazine
Timken Roller Bearing Co.
Quality turns on Timken
Tinnerman Products, Inc.
Look for the Tinnerman "T", the mark
of total reliability (fastening de-
vices)
The mark of total reliability ("Speed
Nuts")
E. H. Titchener Co.
Working wonders with wire
Tokheim Corp.
Symbol of excellence (gasoline pumps)

Toledo Scale Co.
Prime source for weighing equipment and
technology
Torginol of America, Inc.
A generation of worldwide acceptance
(flooring)
Torrington Co.
"The Innovators"
Progress through precision
Toronto-Dominion Bank
Where people make the difference
Toshiba America, Inc.
The international one (home entertain-
ment equipment)
Towmotor Corp.
The one-man gang (R) (materials han-
dling)
Toy Tinkers Div., A. G. Spalding and Bros.,
Inc.
Quality toys with a purpose (Tinkertoy)
Toyota Motor Distributors, Inc.
"Built tough for you" (automobiles)
Get your hands on a Toyota. . .you'll neve
let go (automobiles)
Trailer Train Co.
Border to border. . .coast to coast!
Trane Co.
For any air conditioning
Trans World Airlines, Inc.
Nationwide, worldwide depend on. . .
The things we'll do to make you happy
Up up and away (S.M.)
Transamerican Freight Lines, Inc.
Vital link in America's supply line
The Travelers Insurance Cos.
For all kinds of insurance in a single plan,
call your Travelers man
You can get all types of insurance under
the Travelers umbrella
Ernest Treganowan
Distinctive floor coverings since 1917
Treo Co., Inc.
Shapemakers to the world's most beauti-
ful women
Triangle Package Machinery Co.
Superior performance through design sim-
plicity
True
The massive men's market in print
True Temper Corp.
Adds science to fisherman's luck (fishing
tackle)
The right tool for the right job

Trust Co. of Georgia
Where banking is a pleasure
Tryco Mfg. Co., Inc.
Dependability in the field. . .safety for the
operator (agricultural machinery)
Tungsten Ignition, Tungsten Contact Mfg.
Co.
Puts the "go" in ignition!
Tyler Corp.
Boost profits with the competitive edge
(agricultural chemicals, machinery)
Tyler Refrigeration Div., Clark Equipment
Co.
World leader in commercial refrigeration

U

U.S. News and World Report
News of consequence for people of conse-
quence
U.S. Van Lines, Inc.
Dedicated to people on the move
Moving up
UTA French Airlines
Sailing the South Pacific skies
Ultra Sonic Seal, Inc.
Originators and designers of ultrasonic
sealing equipment
Uncle Ben's, Inc.
Measure of quality (rice)
The rice people, Uncle Ben's
Union Barge Line Corp.
When distribution is the question UBL
has the answers
Union Carbide Corp.
The discovery company
"Power to spare" (Eveready Flashlight
batteries)
The Union Central Life Insurance Co.
Procrastination is the highest cost of life
insurance. It increases both your
premium and your risk.
Union Pacific Railroad
Be specific, route Union Pacific
Be specific. . .say "Union Pacific"
Gateway to and from the booming west
Gateway to and from your world markets
The wheels of transportation help turn
the wheels of industry
Trans Union Corp.
8 Companies running hard
Uniroyal, Inc.
The finest in expanded vinyl fabric
(Royal Naugahyde)

The finest in vinyl upholstery (Royal
    Naugahyde)
The modern mattress (Koylon)
World's largest manufacturer of industrial
    rubber products
United Air Lines, Inc.
    The extra care airline
    Fly the friendly skies of United
    Known for extra care
    The nation's largest airline
    Welcome aboard
United Audio Products, Inc.
    The finest. . .the record proves it since
        1900, Dual's (high fidelity sound
        equipment)
United California Bank
    The bankers who do a little more for you
United Mink Producers Assn.
    World's finest mink
United of Omaha
    Security is our business (insurance)
United States Borax and Chemical Corp.
    Go where you get choosing range
United States Gypsum Co.
    The greatest name in building (building
        materials)
    Pioneering in ideas for industry (metals)
United States Lines, Inc.
    Luxury and comfort with utmost safety
United States Savings Bonds
    Help yourself as you help your country
    Safe as America
United States Steel Corp.
    Where the big idea is innovation
United Van Lines, Inc.
    Moves the people that move the world,
        United
    Moving with care. . .everywhere (R)
Universal Geneve
    Le couturier de la monte (watches)
Universal Metal Products, Div. UMC indus-
tries, Inc.
    Leads the industry in quality and depend-
        ability (cabinets, vending machine
        parts)
Universal Oil Products Co.
    Better ideas from UOP
    Where research is planned with progress
        in mind (R)
The Universal Pad and Tablet Corp.
    "The finest pads have purple bindings"

Valvoline Oil Co. Div., Ashland Oil and
    Refining Co.
    World's first—world's finest
Van Raalte Co., Inc.
    Because you love nice things (lingerie)
Vanadium-Alloys Steel Co.
    Metallurgy is our business
Vanguard Recording Society, Inc.
    Recordings for the connoisseur
Vanity Fair Mills, Inc.
    All is vanity. . .all is Vaniry Fair (lingerie)
Vantage Products, Inc.
    The jeweler's quality watch
Varo Optical, Inc.
    Mastery of precision optics
Ventura Travelware, Inc.
    So high in fashion. . .so light in weight
Venture
    The traveler's world
Vernon Div., Metlox Mfg. Co.
    Fine dinnerware (Vernonware)
Verson Allsteel Press Co.
    Originators and pioneers of allsteel stamp-
        ing press operation
Vick Chemical Co.
    More dentists use Lavoris than any other
        mouthwash. Shouldn't you?
    The "Twin Formula" head cold tablet
        (Vicks Tri-Span)
    World's most widely used brand of cold's
        medication (Vicks Vapo-Rub)
Victor Computer Corp.
    Put errors out of business
Victor Golf Co.
    The brightest star in golf (Burke-Worth-
        ington)
Victor Manufacturing and Gasket Co.
    The only 100% coverage line for cars,
        trucks, tractors, stationary engines
Victor Sports, Inc.
    Often imitated, never duplicated (Davis
        tennis rackets)
Victory Metal Mfg. Co.
    The world's largest manufacturer of
        reach-in refrigerators and freezers
Victory Sports Net Div., The Fishnet and
Twine Co.
    "Weavers of the world's finest netting"
Vidmar, Inc.
    Store more. . .better. . .at less cost
Viking Glass Co.
    Treasured American glass

Viking of Minneapolis, Inc.
 Your assurance of quality in tape compo-
  nents
Viko Furniture Corp.
 Carefree furniture
Virginia Dept. of Conservation and Economic
Development
 Birthplace of the nation
 Mix fun and history in Virginia
Virginia Mirror Co.
 A heritage of quality, craftsmanship,
  service
Viyella-International, Inc.
 There are imitations, of course (fabric)
Vogel-Peterson Co.
 The coat rack people
Henry Vogt Machine Co.
 The finest ice making unit ever made
Von Duprin Div., Vonnegut Hardware Co.,
Inc.
 The safe way out
Vulcan-Hart Corp.
 The world's finest the world over (mass
  feeding equipment)

W

Wagner Electric Corp.
 The quality line (automobile parts)
 The superior brake fluid
Hiram Walker, Inc.
 "The best in the house" (R) in 87 lands
  (Canadian Club whiskey)
 The elegant 8 year old (Walker's Deluxe
  bourbon)
 The incomparable (Imperial whiskey)
 Knowledgeable people buy Imperial
  (whiskey)
 Nothing else quite measures up (Walker's
  Deluxe bourbon)
 Wherever you go, there it is! (Hiram
  Walker bourbon)
Hiram Walker-Gooderham Worts, Ltd.
 A rainbow of distinctive flavors (Hiram
  Walker's cordials)
Wallace Silversmiths Div., The Hamilton
 Watch Co.
 Grows more beautiful with use
Waltham Watch Co.
 One of the great watches of our time
Warner and Swasey Co.
 Precision machinery since 1880

Warner-Lambert Pharmaceutical Co.
 Another clinical-strength medication from
  Warner-Lambert
 The different antacid (Gelusil)
S. D. Warren Co., Div. Scott Paper Co.
 Papers for the printer who puts quality
  first
Waterman Hydraulics Corp.
 Specialists in fluid power control
Watkins Products, Inc.
 First in home service
Watson Mfg. Co., Inc.
 The company of specialists (filing equip-
  ment)
Watts Regulator Co.
 The name that protects your name
Wayne Pump Co.
 World's largest manufacturer of gasoline
  pumps and service station equip-
  ment
Weavewood, Inc.
 Beautiful on the table. Carefree in the
  kitchen. (Weavewood-Ware)
Weber Marking Systems, Inc.
 Mark it for market. . .the Weber way
The Weis Mfg. Co.
 Specialists in filing supplies and equip-
  ment since 1894
Wells Mfg. Co.
 Maximum capacity (CaPac automobile
  parts)
 Performance insurance (CaPac automobile
  parts)
Wembley Ties, Inc.
 The aristocrat of polyester neckwear
 The "color guide" (TM) tie
 Takes the guessing out of dressing (R)
The West Bend Co.
 New ideas for happier homemaking (small
  appliances)
West Point-Pepperell, Inc.
 The search ends at Wellington Sears
  (textiles)
 Twin names in quality towels (Martex and
  Fairfax)
Westab, Inc.
 World's largest manufacturer of school
  supplies and stationery
Westclox Div., General Time Corp.
 America's "wake-up" voice
 Progress in the world of time
Western Air Lines, Inc.
 The jet with the extra engine

The unbeatable way to jet home
Western Union International, Inc.
  All around the world
Western Union Telegraph Co.
  Obviously it must be Western Union
Westinghouse Electric Corp.
  You can be sure if it's Westinghouse
Westvaco Corp.
  Inspirations lead to new value in paper
      and packaging, Westvaco
David Wexler and Co.
  Made with the extra measure of care
      (Cordova guitars)
Wheel Horse Products, Inc.
  Famous for power mowers for over 50
      years (Toro)
  Reliables. . .the powerful performers, Reo
      (lawn, garden equipment)
  Sign of the leader in lawn/garden equip-
      ment
Whirlpool Corp.
  The very good washer (RCA Whirlpool)
White Furniture Co.
  The South's oldest makers of fine furni-
      ture
White Motor Co.
  World leader in heavy duty trucks
White Stag Mfg. Co.
  The skier's tailor since 1927
Whitecraft, Inc.
  . . .The name for fine rattan furniture
Whitehall Labs Div., American Home Prod-
ucts Corp.
  Largest selling pain reliever (Anacin)
Whitey Research Tool Co.
  For exacting service (machinery)
  Matchless valves for exacting service
Whitlock Associates, Inc.
  First in quality conveyors and driers for
      the plastics industry
Whitten Machine Works
  The best way to better yarns (R)
John Widdicomb Co.
  For more than a century makers of fine
      furniture in traditional and modern
      idiom
Julius Wile Sons and Co., Inc.
  The drier liqueur (DOM Benedictine and
      Brandy)
  La grande liqueur francaise (DOM Bene-
      dictine)
  Let this seal be your guide to quality

World-famous Spanish sherries (Williams
      and Humbert dry sack)
Wilkerson Corp.
  Protecting the new in your pneumatics
Williams Gun Sight Co.
  "On the range"
Wilson and Co., Inc.
  If this Gold Seal is on it—there's better
      meat in it
  Label protects your table, The Wilson
Wilson Sporting Goods Co.
  Play to win with Wilson
  A progressive past. A golden future.
Wirebound Box Manufacturers Assn.
  It gets there right in Wirebounds
Wisconsin Div. of Economic Development
  "We like it here"
Wisconsin Knife Works, Inc.
  Engineers to the woodworking industry
Wisconsin Motor Corp.
  World's largest builder of heavy-duty air-
      cooled engines
Wisconsin Vacation and Travel Service
  The land that was made for vacations
Wix Corp.
  The gold standard (automobile parts)
Wolf's Head Oil Refining Co., Inc.
  It pays to be particular about your oil
Wolverine World Wide, Inc.
  Breathin' brushed pigskin (R) (Hush Pup-
      pies shoes)
J. R. Wood and Sons, Inc.
  Dream carved rings (Art Carved)
Wood and Hogan
  America's most distinguished source for
      fine English furniture
Lee L. Woodard Sons, Inc.
  Style authority in wrought iron (furni-
      ture)
Woodco Corp.
  For the beautiful point of view (R) (win-
      dows)
Wool Carpets of America
  The answer is wool. . .it costs less in the
      long run
World Airways, Inc.
  World's largest charter airline
  The world's largest independent airline
House of Wrisley, Inc.
  For the private world of the bath
Wurlitzer Co.
  Means music to millions, Wurlitzer
  World's largest builder of organs and
      pianos

Wyeth Laboratories Div., American Home
   Products Corp.
   Service to medicine (R)

X

Xerox Corp.
   Now everybody can have Xerocopies

Y

Yale Express System, Inc.
   "Speed with economy"
York Corp.
   The quality name in air conditioning and
   refrigeration

Z

Zebco Div., Brunswick Corp.
   Where the action is! (fishing tackle)

Carl Zeiss, Inc.
   Birthplace and centre of modern optics
   Symbol of excellence in West German
   optics (Zeiss Ikon)
Zenith Radio Corp.
   Built better because it's handcrafted
   (television)
   The handcrafted T.V.
   The quality goes in before the name goes
   on (television)
Zippo Mfg. Co.
   The lighter that works
Zodiac Watch Co.
   Sign of the right time
Zurn Industries, Inc.
   A step ahead of tomorrow

Chronology of Slogan Lists Published in *Printers' Ink*

Prior to 1957, *Printers' Ink* had maintained an extensive collection of advertising slogans for more than 35 years through its Clearing House of Advertising Phrases. New additions were printed regularly from 1927. Although the service has been dormant for over a decade, the following listing of publication dates and page numbers in reverse chronological order can provide—should the searcher desire it—an invaluable historical source.

January 11, 1957, p. 62 (last time published)
February 24, 1956, p. 75
July 1, 1955, p. 54
October 23, 1953, p. 69 (Section II)
May 15, 1953, p. 51
July 18, 1952, p. 66
January 19, 1951, p. 50

June 17, 1949, p. 56
July 25, 1947, p. 125
January 10, 1947, p. 72
June 14, 1946, p. 80
April 13, 1945, p. 83
July 9, 1943, p. 73
June 26, 1942, p. 48
October 10, 1941, p. 57
December 13, 1940, p. 69
April 5, 1940, p. 73

October 20, 1939, p. 72
July 28, 1939, p. 65
January 19, 1939, p. 69
October 20, 1938, p. 39
December 30, 1937, p. 56
June 20, 1935, p. 78

July 26, 1934, p. 84
December 7, 1933, p. 76
September 14, 1933, p. 96
July 20, 1933, p. 82
May 25, 1933, p. 64
April 27, 1933, p. 81
February 9, 1933, p. 82
November 24, 1932, p. 82
September 15, 1932, p. 66
June 23, 1932, p. 86
May 12, 1932, p. 88
April 7, 1932, p. 98
February 18, 1932, p. 73
December 31, 1931, p. 76
November 26, 1931, p. 94
July 30, 1931, p. 92
August 20, 1931, p. 121

January 3, 1929, p. 36
July 21, 1927, p. 157
June 2, 1927, p. 147
February 17, 1927, p. 152 (contains list of
    dates back to 1919)

Caboni, Marc. *Comment Trouver un Slogan?* Bruxelles, Caboni, 1945.

Ferrer Rodriguez, Eulalio. *El Lenguaje de la Publicidad en Mexico.* Mexico, Ediciones EUFESA, 1966.

Freese, A. Dermott, comp. *The Slogan Builder's Guide.* Upland, Ind, Freese, 1936

Frey, Albert W. *Advertising.* N. Y., Ronald, 1947

Graham, Irvin. *Encyclopedia of Advertising.* N. Y., Fairchild, 1952.

Gray and Rogers, Inc. Comp. *Slogan Sampler.* Philadelphia, Gray and Rogers, 1966.

Hayakawa, Samuel Ichiye. *Language in Thought and Action.* 2nd ed. N. Y., Harcourt, Brace, 1964.

Ketchum, Alton. "How the Slogan Fits into Marketing." *Printers' Ink*, p. 30-31, Dec. 20, 1963.

Lambert, Isaac E. *The Public Accepts.* Albuquerque, University of New Mexico Press, 1941.

Lucas, Darrel Blaine and Steuart Henderson Britt. *Advertising Psychology and Research.* N. Y., McGraw-Hill, 1950.

"Newspaper Advertisements." *Harper's New Monthly Magazine* 16: 781-89 (Nov 1866)

Pei, Mario. *The Story of Language.* Philadelphia, Lippincott, 1949.

Robbins, Phyllis. *An Approach to Composition Through Psychology.* Cambridge, Mass., Harvard University Press, 1929.

Rowsome, Frank. *They Laughed When I Sat Down.* New York, McGraw-Hill, 1959.

"The Slogan Society." *Time.* p. 96-8 (Oct 16, 1964).

Spofforth, Walter. *Slogans:* The Slogan Makers Book. St. Paul, Minn., Inter City, 1928.

Stevenson, Burton. *The Home Book of Quotations.* 9th ed. N.Y., Dodd, Mead, 1964.

Sunners, William. *American Slogans.* N. Y., Praebar, 1949.

Whittier, Charles L. *Creative Advertising.* N. Y., Holt, 1955.

Wood, James Playsted. *The Story of Advertising.* N. Y., Ronald, 1958.